Human rights obligations in education:

The 4-A Scheme

Human rights obligations in education:

The 4-A Scheme

Katarina Tomasevski

Human rights obligations in education: The 4-A Scheme, *Katarina Tomasevski.*
Published by Wolf Legal Publishers, ISBN: 90 5850 135 3.

Publisher: Willem-Jan van der Wolf
Editing: José v.d. Sanden, Laurien Talsma, Daphne van Mierlo

Published by:

Wolf Legal Publishers (WLP)
P.O. Box 31051
6503 CB Nijmegen
The Netherlands
Tel: +31 24-3551904
Fax: +31 24-3554827
E-Mail: wlp@hetnet.nl
http://www.wlp.biz

Table of Contents

List of tables and figures:

List of Cases

Preface

This book aims to enable people to recognize human rights violations in education. There are many, everywhere, but most of them remain unrecorded. My focus are the human rights obligations of governments, individual and collective, which clarify what governments should and should not do. My aim is to encourage people to call human rights violations by their proper name. In countries where children at not at school, the government may be violating their right to education. If it has done all it can but cannot ensure that all children go to school, it cannot be held responsible. Those who are responsible are often found within this mythical *international community* or ours, but they cannot be held to account (as yet) because they have exempted themselves from the rule of law. Their mutually contradictory position in insisting that individual states respect the rule of law while they do not do likewise is difficult to defend if challenged. My intention is to lay the groundwork for such challenges by explaining who and how human rights law matters.

Moreover, we have become accustomed not to see major problems in education where children go to school. The parents may find the treatment of their children at school appalling and go to court where they can. Human rights require posing a deeply unpopular question whether education itself can violate human rights. The bitter lessons we should have learned from abuses of education to prepare genocide should have taught us to recognize human rights violations through education but, alas, there is an abyss between the *should* and the *is*. We have equipped ourselves with a vast armoury of human rights standards but they lie dormant, unknown, unused and thus useless. My experience has been that the vast majority of teachers and pupils, professors and students, have never heard of the human rights standards forged specifically to protect their rights. As long as they are poorly known, they are not applied.

People may feel that something is wrong, but remain unaware that a law which specifically outlaws such a wrong exists and should be enforced. An example was e-mailed me on 13 January 2005 by 'a person'. She described what upset her thus:

> Within this last year, I had a dramatic experience. One day, a student whose family was visiting from an African country came to show them our ministry. The family, father and mother, were so gracious and appreciative of our ministry, they asked to have their picture taken with me (just a secretary). Both parents had degrees. After a few months passed, I again saw the student. He reported that his family had returned home and, one day, the father and 300 other educated people in that town were collected and killed. When I asked the student why, he replied that it was because they were educated.

What upset me was that I could think of several countries where this might have taken place in 2004 but my search for public exposure of such human rights violations proved fruitless. Because killing people for being educated is intolerable, we have equipped ourselves with international human rights law.

After the turn of the millennium, an international responsibility to act if a government cannot or will not do so has attained a grudging acceptance. Our mythical *international community* will not act because it includes abusive governments as equal members. Moreover, international organizations are accountable to governments, not to people. Without a supranational authority to impose and enforce human rights, it is domestic pressure upon governments that forces them to deliver on their commitments, and it is peer pressure which sustains that commitment on the global level. Its absence allows human rights to be violated or ignored with impunity. Bringing the law to bear upon the abuses which it was designed to prevent requires people to expose and oppose them. Many people will do nothing, some will react like 'a person' did, instinctively denouncing a wrong but shying away from taking a further step. The principal lesson learned from the global human rights movement is that opposing human rights violations is the first step towards upholding the *human* in the human rights equation.

A toolbox has been forged during the past four decades to enable people to expose and oppose torture and a similar process is needed for education. Equating education with torture and arguing that may constitute a human rights violation clashes with the powerful global propaganda which presents education as inherently good. There just needs to be more of it and the quality should be better. A human rights lawyer like myself is a spoilsport and, often, a nuisance, for suggesting that both denial and provision of education can be a human rights violation. The underlying logic is simple. Because governmental power is easily abused to torture people, its power to make education compulsory can also be abused to brainwash children instead of educating them. Where a government tolerates corporal punishment, a child beaten for not doing her sums fast enough, or running fast enough, learns that might is right.

A simple message that education can be used well as well as abused badly opens the was for human rights. This book argues that human rights are safeguards against abuse of power. Power can be abused by denying education. Also, education can be abusive.

Human rights work becomes easier when we acknowledge that moral principle is something that puts one at variance with accepted practice, that daring to insist that society should embody its professed human rights principles is often labelled utopian, or worse. Everything becomes even easier when we define human rights as a process. Wherever there is abuse, there are always people who will expose it and some will try to right the wrong. Human rights protection was built on their courage to speak truth to power. It was institutionalized through nudging and shaming governments into substituting the rule of law for the law of the ruler. The Red Cross has defined the path to be travelled towards a situation "in which no one- neither those who give orders, nor those who carry them out, nor those who let the abuses happen – can say: 'I didn't know.'"[1]

---

[1] International Committee of the Red Cross – Special report: stemming the tide of violence. ICRC activities in relation to the international community's prevention strategies, ICRC, Geneva, 1998, p. 5.

2

That most educators and educatees (apologies for this strange term) do not know how human rights should apply in education was a sobering experience for me. That most knew *why* this should happen has boosted my enthusiasm.

The killings which upset my anonymous internet pal tend to be attributed to ethnic or religious fault-lines in society rather than to governments' policies, least of all to education. Global reporting on education alternates between the millions who are out of school and the learning accomplishments of those who are at school. Crucially important issues have been brushed aside. Dictators have been known to deny education, lest people would learn about rebellion against oppression. Denial of education creates ripple effects whereby all other human rights are in jeopardy. Illiterate people are precluded from political representtation and cannot redress their plight through political processes. Pakistan provided an illustrative example in 2003 by requiring all members of parliament to hold a university degree and 96% of the populating was thereby excluded from running for office. [2] Subsequent litigation questioned the type of university degree that would be acceptable rather than the premise: the government first denied education to the vast majority of its population and then precluded them from political representation so as not to bring to an end its abuse of power.

Education can be deadly when used to prepare genocide. Pre-military education brainwashes the young into accepting that *they* are the enemy and should be killed, and are then instructs how to kill. Some people, like myself, giggled our way through pre-military education, memorizing and repeating what we were taught and never believing a word, and trying to hit the moon during the compulsory target practice. We learned that *schooling* was one thing and *education* something different. A list of intolerable abuses of education would be very, very long if it was compiled. Why is such a list not compiled? Education International publishes triennial reports, a snapshot of progress and retrogression in 162 countries.[3] Human rights organizations tend to follow the cold-war boundaries and focus on torture, disappearances or death penalty. One likely reason is that their core staff are lawyers. If they had human rights during their legal education, it did not include education rights. Another is that most of these lawyers went to private schools and expensive universities, the plight of poor children denied public education is for them a problem of poverty or development rather than human rights.

Trying to nudge people to react to human rights violations in education has been my hobby the past eight years. 'A person' who e-mailed her concern about people killed for being educated searched for an interface between human rights and education and discovered my website (www.right-to-education.org). This interface is also the core theme of this book

2 *Pakistan-EU links risk stagnation*, European Voice, 17-21 March 2003.; Pakistan, *Far Eastern Economic Review*, 10 July 2003.
3 *EI Barometer of Human and Trade Union Rights in the Education Sector 2004*, Education International, Brussels, www.ei-ie.org.

The website was created to supplement my work as the Special Rapporteur on the right to education of the United Nations Commission on Human Rights. The Commission exists no longer but few people knew what that it was during its lifetime. Because it was composed of governments, and the majority of its members tended to sit therein to protect themselves (and governments in general), the Special Rapporteurs were external experts, appointed in their personal capacity to carry out human rights work without remuneration. The right to education was my mandate from 1998 to 2004.[4] This experience re-inforced what I had learned long ago, namely that human rights are too important to be left to governments.

The 4-A scheme was my response to the need to explain what governments should and should not do; what the right to education is and what amounts to its violation; how human rights should be protected in education; how education should be changed to enhance rather than undermine equal human rights.
An array of missions to different countries enabled me to learn what needs to happen to advance the right to education. People like myself, who enjoyed years of education, all the way to post-doctoral studies, have to acknowledge that it was a matter of luck, not right. To transform the luck of the few into the right of all is my mission statement.

The human rights rationale is that education leads to rebellion against tyranny and oppression as it should. (This is *education* as different from *schooling*.) This was written into the preamble of the Universal Declaration of Human Rights. The insurance policy of governments likely to be at the receiving end of a rebellion is to immunize people by denying them education. The absence of government-provided brainwashing can work to their advantage because they need not un-learn what schooling imposed upon them. The second line of governmental defence is to institute schooling which indoctrinates people to believe that no change is possible; that is instruction rather than education. Or, those who learn that things could be different might be killed so that they could not teach others, as 'a person' e-mailing me was shocked to learn.

This book draws on the advantage of my distance from education (I am a human rights lawyer) and my proximity to it. I have had to learn a great deal about education during the past eight years and have managed, to my deep joy, to pass peer reviews in education journals as if I were an 'insider'. Distance is necessary to ask impermissible questions and proximity is needed to know which questions to ask. I have often defined myself as a bridge-builder, translating the language of human rights into something that educators and educationists (and educatees) could understand, and translate the language of education to human rights lawyers.

---

4   My experiences as the Special Rapporteur have been described in Tomasevski, K. – Has the right to education a future within the United Nations? A behind-the-scenes account by the Special Rapporteur on the right to education 1998-2004, *Human Rights Law Review*, vol. 5, No. 3, Autumn 2005.

My asking in which language children are educated has often triggered silence; this is not globally monitored. Asking who has written the version of history which children are required to memorize as 'facts' was understood in Bosnia (where history textbooks had been produced and destroyed several times) but not elsewhere. Asking whether school children have a right to evaluate their teachers has often resulted in amazement at my impertinence. Instead of answers to such questions, there always were statistics aplenty. Because I went to school in Eastern Europe, I learned how to cope with reporting that all quantitative targets were met. Sharing my coping strategies endeared me to many and created as many enemies. I kept asking why central planning entered global education (through the MDGs, EFA, PRPSs, or FTI) after it had been discredited with the centrally planned economies.

Explaining what human rights is about became easier with practice. A cheerful World Bank economist (retired since but anonymous by his own wish) met me thus: "You are the first person I heard in my whole life who says that government should make education free. Where in the world does that idea come from?" It was not, as he suspected, some form of a neo-communist platform but rather a part of Western European input in the oldest international human rights treaties, forged more than eighty years ago to eliminate children labour. He liked my explanation (at least he said he did) but not its implications (because that would have altered World Bank's policy). Commonsensical explanations of the right to education are easy. School children understand the rationale whereby they enjoy free education so as to finance education of the next generation later, by working and pay tax. I tried this out on 11 year olds in Kampala and in Belfast and it worked well. I have been far less successful with the World Bank but I keep trying.

A strong incentive for this book were thriving misconceptions about the right to education. A European Union official described as a child-rights project funding an NGO which was paying school fees for primary school children. Only for girls, she hastened to clarify. I asked whether it was a good idea to subsidize school fees, which the government was charging in breach of its own law. Funding NGOs was good and girls' education was the top donors' priority. The law was another sector. I have made it into the pillar of this book because it makes all the difference. It certainly makes things difficult because the questions which human rights law imposes require difficult choices. Asking why donors do not react to human rights violations in education always creates a stir. One can see the logic in helping children go to school by channelling funds to education, and the damaged education resulting from halting the donors' funds for every reported violation. One can also see the illogic of helping children to learn to then be killed when they question government policy.

The human rights movement was built by people who had courage to break the silence which helps human rights abuses to thrive. Too little has been done as yet to expose and oppose abuses *of* education and *in* education. Rescuing the right to education from the blind alley into which it was forced during the Cold War requires seeing government in its double role, as a protector and a violator of human rights. Experience has taught us that it is always easier to mobilize people *against* than *for*. Thus, human rights activism initially targeted abuses of power by government, defining ever more precisely what governments should *not* do. In education, one should also define what governments *should* do. This is what this book is about.

Introduction

The rationale of the right to education is that it functions as a multiplier, enhancing all rights and freedoms when it is guaranteed while jeopardizing them all when it is violated. Ensuring education for all children has been governmental responsibility in many countries for a long time because it is informed by a sound rationale. Schooling a whole generation creates an educated labour force and an informed electorate. Depriving the young of education denies them – and their countries – a future. Even more important is education as institutionalized socialization of the young. Forging a nation-state was the key purpose of education when it became compulsory. It was made compulsory so as to teach new generations a common language and instil in them a sense of shared, collective identity. That education had been made compulsory before it became a right explains its key features.

Because the right to education, as an ostensibly universal concept, was grounded in the process of industrialization and nation-building, the model was – and remains – ill suited for rural populations. Rounding up children from scattered rural communities to transport them to a building called *school* is prohibitively expensive. Also, key purposes of education change. The official national language may not be known or used. If local languages are used instead, teachers have to be recruited and trained locally. But then, who decides on the profile of teachers? On what children and to be taught and how? On incentives for parents to free children from subsistence farming for full-time schooling? Such questions impose themselves and should be tackled. Of course, it is easier to ignore them but education suffers as do its supposed beneficiaries.

Government has to ensure that all children can go to school, otherwise education is compulsory only on paper. Then it has to nudge parents to send their children to school by making it attractive. Some will refuse if they see no purpose in doing so, some will object to schooling which the government has chosen for their children. Children have to accept the 8000 hours of sitting in a building called *school* as their duty. Asserting that education is their right implies that it is good for them. Many would disagree and are, therefore, not asked. In retrospect, quite a few can *prove* that education was not good for them because it qualified them for unemployment.

Endless questions stem from the interface between education and human rights. This book does not argue that we have ready-made answers to most of them but, rather, that these questions should inform education policy. I do not follow the evasive approach favoured by the United Nations. Bombastic statements such as "all human rights are universal, indivisible, interdependent and interrelated"[5] convey an artificial global consensus where there is none. Although I use international human rights law as the conceptual framework for this book, I treat is as work in progress. Formally, it constitutes binding obligations for

---

5   General Assembly – 2005 World Summit Outcome. High-level Plenary Meeting of the General Assembly at its fifty-ninth session, U.N. Doc. A/60/L.1, 20 September 2005, para. 13.

states. Really, governments representing their states can breach or ignore the law with impunity. The paradox is that international human rights law has been created by the states for themselves. Its beneficiaries have had no say in its formation and most have no access to justice when their rights are violated. Why, then, does this fragile intergovernmental construct matters? Why would educators and educationists want to know what human rights law says about education? Simply because there is nothing better. Human rights law represents the bare minimum to which governments have grudgingly agreed and which they will comply with only if forced to do so. However, it constitutes the border-line against sliding back into a denial that people have rights.

Human rights activism has developed around its initial mobilizing slogan, whereby exposing human rights violations is the first necessary step towards opposing them. This book describes typical human rights remedies, mounting cases against governments in response to human rights violations. Without access to remedy for their denial or violation, human rights are depleted of their core function, which is to provide safeguards against abuse of power. Exposing and opposing abuses of power is the purpose of human rights. Human rights law defines rights as claims addressed to governments. These specify what governments should and should not, and what they may do, how and why. Law is symmetrical and rights cannot exist without corresponding governmental obligations. Promised rights and freedoms are only as good as their monitoring (aimed at exposing abuses of power) and enforcement (opposing and redressing abuses of power). An endless variety of real-life issues ceaselessly force domestic courts and human rights commissions to clarify the nature and scope of the right to education and the corresponding governmental obligations. Pre-requisites for legal enforcement are knowledge that education is a right and access to institutions empowered to determine violations and enforce remedies. Such cases reveal shared understanding of human rights, the substantive contours of the right to education recognized worldwide. Beyond this common core, a great deal of disagreement persists.

Pleas addressed to educators and educationists, teachers and pupils, professors and students, education economists or statisticians, to inform themselves about human rights law falter at the scope of work this entails. Human rights lawyers tend to speak about the *international human rights system* but this is, in effect, a spaghetti bowl. Fragmented human rights safeguards require time, patience and a great deal of technical expertise to navigate that labyrinth. The associated literature, the "lawyer's law for fellow mandarins"[6], does not help but acts as a deterrent. A single court case, proudly cited by lawyers as making all the difference, tends to go over a hundred pages of densely written text, full of legal jargon. The bad side is that such a case may have vindicated a child's right to education after that child turned twenty and became a parent. The good side is that, although the case may have dealt with a single child, its importance is to prevent government from violating the right to education of other children, thousands or millions of them. This book aims to simplify the law as much as

---

6   Samaraweera, V. – Human rights and the ideology of the rule of law, *Law & Society Trust Review*, vol. 7, Issue No. 112, February 1997, p. 1.

this is possible and it uses only excerpts from many judicial cases. Defining human rights as safeguards against abuse of power and their attainment as a permanent process is its starting point.

Human rights work typically looks backward rather than forward and mobilization is triggered by gross abuses of governmental powers. Retroactive redress for violations has been the pillar of human rights work the past four decades, after human rights activism started in earnest in the 1960s. We celebrate older accomplishments and recall that the Universal Declaration of Human Rights (1948) is almost sixty years old. The link between free and compulsory education and the prohibition of child labour emerged in 1919, almost ninety years ago. These were promises. The commonly used term – international human rights *instruments* – says it all: these are tools whose value increases with usage, while they are worthless unless and until they are used.

The paradox of human rights is the double role of the state, as protector and violator. International human rights instruments are created by the states, represented by their governments. They define the intolerable, the universal minimum below which no government should be allowed to sink. The human rights which have been defined as universal entail corresponding governmental obligations. As elsewhere, human rights safeguards emerged in education to mould the role of the state. Decades of open and covert disagreement have not led to a global consensus. This books maps out where such consensus exists and where it is absent.

The long and complicated international human rights instruments did not, as is often suspected, result from the tendency of lawyers to make the law incomprehensible so as to create a market for their services. Rather, they stem from the disagreement amongst governments regarding their human rights obligations. Some governments, a minuscule minority now-a-days, insist on the human right to free-of-charge education and the corresponding government obligation to provide it as a free public service. This slant was popular during the Cold War and split human rights into two ideologically defined categories. The Soviet Union and her allies defined education as a free public service, provided but also controlled by the state. Freedom of choice was obliterated. Countering the ease with which a government can abuse education where it is its sole financier and provider, the West insisted on freedom *of* and *in* education. The victors of the Cold War amplified safeguards of freedom, including economic freedom, at the expense the right to free education. Without safeguards against economic exclusion, nominally guaranteed freedoms are emptied of real-life choices.

Both facets of education as a human right are explained in Chapter 1. Education is defined as a right while it is also compulsory. Compulsory education bestows upon governments a right to force the young to be taught whatever the government of the time decided they should be taught. A US/USSR 1977-1989 textbook study called its final report "*School Textbooks: Weapons for the Cold*

9

War."[7] Social scientists have defined education, alongside law enforcement, as a pillar of social control. Because school reaches the largest number of children and young people at their most impressionable age, education is perpetually contested. The right to education was defined as a civil and political right as well as economic, social and cultural right. Thus, governmental human rights obligations comprise ensuring at least some education for all children while respecting parental freedom of choice. Children are denied political rights and their parents and governments are supposed to decide what it in their best interest but often disagree. Most jurisprudence on the right to education is generated by such disagreements, and this book refers to a broad range of cases which highlight the questions that ought to be asked.

Education exhibits an interplay between dual processes of globalization and localization, especially at the cross-section between availability of education and access to it. The process of decentralization and/or localization facilitates adaptation of education *for* and *by* local communities but broadens and deepens inequalities by making the financing of education the sole responsibility of communities. The gap between haves and have-nots increases, institutionalizing educational deficit for the have-nots. Breaking this vicious circle requires governments, individually and collectively, to prioritize and equalize funding for education, from the local to the global level. Solidarity is, domestically, enforced through taxation, out of which public education is financed so as to equalize educational opportunities. Globally, we have failed to establish a system that guarantees a minimum universal entitlement throughout the world which was the purpose of making the right to education universal.

Chapter 2 brings in the conflict between international human rights law and international trade law, created during the first decade after the end of the Cold War. While denials of freedom in education are open to challenge, the very notion that education should be a free public service came under attack. J.K. Galbraith has described where we are today thus: "there is the private sector and there is the public sector. Once there were capitalism and socialism."[8] The focus on the state in human rights stems from its role in creating and enforcing law, affirming or denying individual and collective rights through the corresponding definitions of governmental obligations. Human rights safeguards were first developed in those areas where the state has given itself monopoly, such as policing and imprisonment. Safeguards against abuse of economic power remain underdeveloped. Obstacles are many. Paul Samuelson has identified one, having said: 'I don't care who writes the nation's laws if I can write its economics textbooks.'[9]

The decisive role of economists, those trained within or by the World Bank, results in broadening and deepening unequal access to education. Lyn Davies has asked: "How we ever let a bank decide educational policy will be a puzzle for

---

7   Pingel, F. – *UNESCO Guidebook on Textbook Research and Textbook Revision*, George Eckert Institute for International Textbook Research and UNESCO, Paris, 1999, p. 11.

8   Galbraith, J.K. – *The Economics of Innocent Fraud: Truth for Our Time*, Penguin/Allen Lane, London, 2004, p. 47.

9   Quoted from The puzzling failure of economics, *The Economist*, 23 August 1997.

educational anthropologists of the future." [10] Historians might solve this puzzle after diplomatic archives are opened in a couple of decades. In the meantime, many human rights questions cannot be tackled. Inequalities are hidden behind education statistics, which operate with averages and camouflage gender, racial, ethnic, linguistic or religious fault-lines. Chapter 2 describes diverse forms of exclusion from education, both where education is nominally a public service and where it has been transformed into a commodity for sale. The inevitable effect of exclusion is lack of formal educational accomplishments, easily converted into factual evidence of inferiority, and facilitating its perpetuation.

Statistical recognition of discrimination is necessary but absent. Formal recording of race, ethnicity or religion is banned in many countries. Hopes that making race or religion statistically irrelevant would also make them socially and politically irrelevant have not materialized, on the contrary. The absence of internationally comparable statistics on discrimination in education demonstrates the continuing prevalence of denial. Because racial or religious profile of education is neither formally recorded nor statistically monitored, it does not inform education strategies and discrimination continues unchallenged. Challenges falter because of the absence of statistical evidence.

Exclusion requires asking *why* people are poor, remain poor or become poor. Calling people vulnerable rather than tackling what makes them vulnerable does not help. Where poverty results from the denial of rights, as is often the case for girls and women, the remedy is to affirm and enforce all human rights as Chapter 2 shows. It uses the global failure to attain gender parity by the year 2005 to highlight why human rights matter.

Another illustration of the importance of human rights are attacks on schools because they epitomize an alien, imposed 'education'. Such attacks have demonstrated, in a frightening manner, why schooling may be rejected, even violently. [11] A design of education acceptable to everyone clashes with the practice of imposing uniform schooling upon everyone as Chapter 3 describes. This requires changing the very language we use. Our vocabulary embodies the hierarchy of rights-holders and the rights-less, with former colonizers freely moving around the world with self-granted rights as "expatriates" while the colonized are denied rights as "immigrants". Similarly, speakers of an international "language" provide expensive services for its mastery while those speaking a "vernacular" are denied even a right to call their language by its proper name. International ranks of language proficiency reward those whose "language of

---

[10]   Davies, L. – Comparative education in an increasingly globalised world, *Comparative Education Bulletin*, The Comparative Education Society of Hong Kong, No. 7 (2004), p. 6.

[11]   In its passive form, rejection of education has become known in West Africa as *déscolarisation*, the abandonment of formal education based on the former colonial language and designed for (now non-existent) public sector employment. (Lange, M.-F. – *L'école au Togo: Processus de scolarisation et institution de l'école en Afrique*, Karthala, Paris, 1998, pp. 237-295). In its violent form, as armed attacks on schools and teachers, rejection of education seen as an imposition of an alien ideology, language or religion by the government has been reported from numerous parts of the world, including Indonesia (Commission on Human Rights – Report of the Special Rapporteur on the right to education, Katarina Tomasevski: Mission to Indonesia, U.N. *Doc.* E/CN.4/2003/9/Add.1, paras. 38 and 49).

instruction is the same as the language spoken at home." [12] The ease with which one language of instruction, one syllabus and curriculum, and a single model for the training of teachers are put into practice conflicts with an education designed to accommodate and enhance diversity. The return to such an investment is preservation of our diversity but the ordinary yardstick of return of investment – financial gain – is absent.

It is impossible to learn to compete and to cooperate at the same time. As children compete against each other for better test results and higher grades, as do their schools and their countries, cooperation remains an abstract notion because children learn by example, not exhortation. The pressure of standardized testing transforms children into "cookie-cutter test takers," [13] omitting from the operative definition of education whatever is not tested. Competitiveness as a value which informs education creates educational failures, in contradiction of the basic requirement of human rights.

Abuses of education are frequent in its denial of diversity as Chapter 4 shows. The spirit and wording of international human rights law requires education to adapt to the best interests of each child. This has reversed the previous requirement upon children to adapt themselves to whatever schooling was made available to them. Adaptation necessitates affirming the right of each child to be regarded as different. A reality check shows that children tend to be reduced to few denominators that are statistically monitored and inform education policy. Although we know that no real person conforms to any statistical average, the sheer size of educational enterprise leads to planning on the basis of averages. Those at school are dressed in identical uniforms and ranked by identical tests which measure their learning performance. It is a sobering indictment of education that too many children and young people find education boring.

The ease with which children's mastery of mathematics can be tested, and test results internationally compared, leads to ranking countries, schools and children from the best to the worst. Uniform criteria for assessing learning accomplishments hide barriers to learning. Children do not start school as equals. Some come from expensive multilingual kindergartens, others have never had the luxury of holding a book in their hands. School can help alter these trajectories or institutionalize inequalities. Children of poor parents are victimized by their parents' need to ensure the survival of the family and their consequent lack of time for their children's education. At school, underperformance is treated as individual failure, ignoring barriers these children and young people face and exonerating the absence of governmental policies which should have eliminated them. Statistical monitoring of diverse abilities and disabilities of learners is impeded by the lack of agreement on their nature and

---

[12] Naumann, J. – Curriculum and languages: teaching in African languages and learning strategies, in: *Curriculum Development and Education for Living Together: Conceptual and Managerial Challenges in Africa, Final Report of the Seminar held in Nairobi, Kenya, 25-29 June 2001*, International Bureau of Education and Kenya National Commission for UNESCO, Geneva, 2003, p. 35.

[13] Suh-kyung Yoon – South Korea: Lessons in learning, *Far Eastern Economic Review*, 28 February 2002.

— well, isn't variety what you want.

there is even more disagreement on how education should respond to disability. Excellent performance in multiple-choice tests underpins the values which children and young people internalize through learning to conform and to compete. The message is that performance is valued, while effort is not. Worse, Europe's inability to articulate and defend the rights of school girls with headscarves, described in Chapter 4, demonstrates how long and uphill the road towards rights-based education is.

Chapter 5 describes conceptual bridges between the realms of education and human rights. The cross-cutting nature of the right to education derives from the decisive influence of education on *all* human rights. Education is indispensable for effective political participation and for enabling individuals to sustain themselves. It is the key to preserving – or obliterating – existing languages and religions. Richly endowed education may fail to rupture inter-generational transmission of xenophobia, while segregated education may foster disintegration of society or inter-community conflicts. Human rights inquiry spans both *hardware* and *software* so as to capture qualitative dimensions of education as well as the intersection of education and society. Gratifyingly, the global consensus on the minimal governmental obligations in education is reflected in the practice of states. What governments do is much more similar than what they say. Budgetary allocations for education reflect its importance and 88% of education is publicly funded in the OECD countries.[14] The postulated universality of the right to education necessitates asking why a similar pattern of expenditure is not advocated for developing countries. A series of indicators aimed at measuring governmental commitments and their performance is proposed to start answering such questions.

Chapter 6 brings together key changes which would ensue from integrating human rights in education. This is easy where human rights are defined as "what foreigners lack"[15] but difficult when abuses have to be identified and remedied in our own community. Bringing human rights home requires recognizing, exposing and opposing their violations. Engendering support for human rights law forms part of a political project after the juridical task of developing human rights law has been accomplished. Globally, there is no symmetry between human rights and corresponding governmental obligations. The postulated universality of the right to education has not generated a universal entitlement. This necessitates a collective commitment, which has yet to be engendered.

Educators and educationists know that education reform is a marathon, not a sprint. It entails diverting an aircraft carrier from its pre-programmed course. The time for translating planned alterations into educational practice is measured in years. The time for educational policies have an impact is measured in decades. And yet, electoral cycles demand to "show results now – in one

---

[14]   OECD – *Education at a Glance: OECD Indicators 2004*, Paris, 2004, p. 16.
[15]   Speech by Francesca Klug on the promotion of human rights, Human Rights in Education Conference, 26 September 2001, Department of Education and Northern Ireland Human Rights Commission, January 2002, p. 49.

month or half a year, not 15 years."[16] Change necessitates patience and persistence. Most importantly, it requires a consensus on what education is for.

[16] Mongolia: Faltering steppes, *The Economist*, 28 May 2005.

1

Availability

A common misinterpretation of education as a human right is to claim that people have an entitlement to all the education they may want, throughout their life, at government expense. Translating this into practice would bankrupt all governments because financing potentially boundless individual appetites for education is impossible. Nonetheless, one can find international declarations which claim that life-long learning is a human right. The United Nations excel at generating such promises. They are made by those who have neither the authority to create obligations for governments nor the means (nor often the will) to translate such promises into performance. There is no protection against abuse of human rights language. One can shame those seeking to fortify their privileges through the language of rights and point out the principle of equal rights for all rather than all rights for some and none for others.

This statement ought to be qualified because education may be available but only at a price. During the Cold War, the perception of government as the sole provider and financier of education permeated human rights discourse. Education was nationalized, in the sense of private education being taken over by government and more often than not banned. A similar process took place during the first decades of political independence in Africa. This created a distorted image of education. After the end of the Cold War, this distortion was replaced by another and much previously public education has been privatized.

Discerning what the right to education means in such swings of its global image is no easy task. Its starting point are definitions which have been accepted by governments and entail their corresponding obligations. These are found in the law which, on the international plane, comprises a series of human rights treaties that have been adopted through lengthy intergovernmental negotiations and, then, accepted as law by national parliaments.[17] Their wording may posit that "everybody has the right to education" but such general assertions are accompanied by clarifications. National constitutions and domestic laws define the meaning and scope of the right to education. This is – or is not – translated into practice through the corresponding budgetary allocations, rules for the deployment of public funds, and accountability for their use. The practice of states is the key source of international law and serves as a reality check. International human rights treaties tend to promise more than governments are willing and able to deliver and are not revised when the circumstances in which

---

[17] A description and analysis of these treaties can be found in Tomasevski, K. – *Manual on Rights-based Education: Global Human Rights Requirements Made Simple*, Collaborative Project between the UN Special Rapporteur on the right to education and UNESCO Asia and Pacific Regional Bureau for Education, UNESCO, Bangkok, 2004. This study is available on-line and details are provided at www.right-to-education.org.

widely.

Infact, they differ

reduced down to primary. useless.

they were adopted have changed beyond recognition. Moreover, the law does not guide global education strategies. Heavily indebted governments have to prioritize debt servicing even where it means that their obligations towards their own population remain unfulfilled.

Taken through this funnel, the right to education has gradually been reduced to the obligation to ensure primary education. Although defined as a right of all, children and adults alike, education as a governmental sector is age-based and primary education is prioritized. Definitions of education follow the development of the child, adolescent and young person, specifying what individuals should learn at each stage of their development. The right to education does not follow the child development logic, however, whereby the first years of the child's life are the most education-intensive and should be prioritized. The reason is specific to human rights. It derives from the experience that institutionalized schooling can amount to governmental abuse of power. One can easily imagine public opposition to infants being taken away from their family into some form of governmental educational institution and understand why early years of education are generally left to the family. Pre-primary education is accepted as a right in some countries but not its counterpart, that education is compulsory, which is globally accepted for primary education.

division bet. family & schools, religious schools

This division of responsibility between the family and the government regarding education should be taken one step further. This distinction has come to light in the Middle East through a puzzle: "some countries report a high youth literacy rate, yet their enrolment ratio is relatively low."[18] This dismantled an assumption that government is the only provider of education. While enrolment statistics tend to be confined to public (i.e. governmental) schools, religious schools reach large numbers of children and youth. Hence the gap between enrolment figures in public and/or governmental schools and literacy. High levels of literacy resulting from religious education demonstrate that alongside families, religious communities are a key provider of education. This remains unrecorded by governments and unknown within international educational bureaucracies.

Education outside governmental sector is often classified as *private*, which I discuss at the end of this Chapter because governmental obligations with respect to availability have to be explained first. This is best done by highlighting the core definition of the right to education for children. It requires education to be free of charge, an individual entitlement. The rationale is two-fold. One part relates to reaching all the children, which necessitates elimination of obstacles, especially financial. The other part relates to control over education. The prevalence of religious schools in the Middle East became a security concern in the aftermath of 9/11. Fears that the aims and contents of the teaching provided in religious schools may nudge boys and young men towards terrorism revealed that some of the respective governments did not know how many religious schools there were, let alone who teaches in them and what is taught. Pakistan is a good example. As its government relinquished its responsibility for providing

---

[18] *The Millennium Development Goals in Arab Countries*, UNDP, New York, December 2003, p. 8.

education, this amplified space for religious schools. General Musharraf explained in the aftermath of 9/11 that "the strength [of madrassas] is free board and lodging for hundreds and thousands of poor children, which Pakistan can't afford, certainly."[19] The cost of the government's claim that it cannot afford to educate children became visible in the post 9/11 obsession with religious schools breeding terrorists. The lack of knowledge about religious schools proved a major embarrassment. The Economist estimated that "Pakistan contains more than 586,000 students in nearly 4,000 madrassas. Some 16,600 of these students are foreigners." Later, estimates ranged between 7,000 and 20,000. For an unknown reason, the number has then been fixed at 12,000, out of which 7,000 are supposed to be encompassed by government-designed reforms[20] Hassan Abbas has claimed that there may be 30,000 madrassas, offering free education, food, housing and clothing, and thus attracting thousands of children and youth who are driven away from decrepit public education.[21] This example demonstrates why education was defined as a right and a corresponding governmental responsibility.

This example also illustrates why education should be free. Research in Latin America and the Caribbean has shown that investment in education is the key explanatory variable for children's ability to go to primary and secondary school. Where education is publicly funded and free at the point of use, access is universal. Where public funding is insufficient and has to be supplemented by private financial contributions, access is confined to those who can afford the cost. This introduces the criterion of affordability, which excludes all those who cannot pay the cost of available schools. The data have shown the poorest having an average of 3 years of education for the 11 years for the wealthiest, and the research team attributed 95% of the difference in school attendance to the level of public financing of education.[22]

These two facets of education, control over those who teach the children as well as access for as many children as possible – define education as a right and duty of each child. Because law is symmetrical, the right to education entails corresponding governmental obligations. Making education compulsory gives governments an opportunity to educate or to brainwash the children. This is often referred to as a right of the state. Its duties are also comprised in compulsory education as are those of parents. The underlying logic was aptly summarized in 1956 thus:

---

19 Gen. Pervaiz Musharraf: Absolutely secure, *Far Eastern Economic Review*, 20 December 2001.
20 Pakistan and America: My enemy's enemy, *The Economist*, 4 October 2003; Madrassa maths, *The Economist*, 21 May 2005; Pakistan's religious schools: The general at war, *The Economist*, 23 July 2005.
21 Abbas, H. – *Pakistan's Drift into Extremism: Allah, the Army and America's War on Terror*, M.E. Sharpe, New York, 2004.
22 CEPAL/UNESCO – Financiamiento y gestión de la educación en América Latina y el Caribe, versión preliminar, Trigésimo período de sesiones de la CEPAL, San Juan, Puerto Rico, 28 de junio al 2 de julio de 2004, Doc. LC/G.2249(SES.30/14), 11 de junio de 2004, p. 9.

Just as school legislation imposes upon the parent the duty of sending his children to school, States should accept the obligation of providing enough schools to educate all children.[23]

The global minimum

International human rights law defines the ends and means of education by specifying the rights and duties, freedoms and responsibilities of all key actors. The right to education involves (1) the government which has to ensure the enjoyment of the right to education, (2) the child as the privileged subject of the right to education and the bearer of the duty to comply with compulsory-education requirements, (3) the child's parents who are 'the first educators', and (4) professional educators, namely teachers.

A narrow definition of human rights as safeguards against abuse of power by the state is, for the child, necessarily complemented by duties of all adults and – especially – parental responsibilities. Parental obligations regarding their children are reinforced by the prohibitions abuse or exploitation. The government is responsible for securing the full realization of the rights of the child, including the enforcement of parental responsibilities towards their own children.

Children do not have legal standing to vindicate their rights before courts or human rights commissions in most countries. Legally, they are minors. Nor are they always in a position to effectively pursue complaints against denials and violations of their rights, including the right to education, even where they are formally allowed to do so. The child's right of access to justice does not exist in most countries. [24] A broad range of actors is involved in vindicating the rights of the child, ranging from parents and teachers to specialized institutions, such as children's ombudsmen. The recognition of the rights of the child necessitates the acceptance of obligations and responsibilities by all public authorities, parents and families, government agents and professionals dealing with children, as well as adults in general. Macro-economic and fiscal policies can undermine, indeed obliterate formal legal guarantees of children's rights. This is particularly important as children are not even in theory economically self-supporting, and depend on education to make them so. Depriving children of education mortgages the future of the country. Also, children lack the knowledge and experience necessary to articulate and defend their rights. They are still considered to be an object of protection rather than subject of rights in most

---

23   *Report on the Regional Conference on Free and Compulsory Education in Latin America*, UNESCO, Paris, 1956, p. 8.

24   The Committee on the Rights of the Child has repeatedly called for "an independent mechanism to register and address complaints from children concerning violations of their rights," recommending that this should be an independent child-friendly mechanism, accompanied by "an awareness-raising campaign to facilitate the effective use by children of such a mechanism." *Implementation Handbook for the Convention on the Rights of the Child*, UNICEF, Geneva and New York, Fully revised edition, June 2002, p. 171.

countries. Education was made compulsory for them so as to facilitate their learning and socialization while they remain free from adult responsibilities.

Figure 1
Subsidy and liberty in global human rights instruments

Universal Declaration: Education shall be free, at least in the elementary and fundamental stages. Elementary education shall be compulsory.	*Universal Declaration*: Parents have a prior right to choose the kind of education that shall be given to their children.
UNESCO Convention against Discrimination in Education: The States Parties to this Convention undertake to formulate, develop and apply a national policy which, ... will tend to promote equality of opportunity and of treatment ... and in particular: (a) To make primary education free and compulsory.	*UNESCO Convention against Discrimination in Education*: The States Parties to this Convention agree that: (b) It is essential to respect the liberty of parents, ... firstly to choose for their children institutions other than those maintained by the public authorities but conforming to ... minimum educational standards, and secondly, to ensure ... the religious and moral education of the children in conformity with their own convictions.
International Covenant on Economic, Social and Cultural Rights: Primary education shall be compulsory and available free for all.	*International Covenant on Economic, Social and Cultural Rights*: The States Parties to the present Covenant undertake to have respect for the liberty of parents ... to choose for their children schools, other than those established by the public authorities, which conform to such minimum educational standards as may be laid down or approved by the State and to ensure the religious and moral education of their children in conformity with their own convictions. No part of this article shall be construed so as to interfere with the liberty of individuals and bodies to establish and direct educational institutions, ...
Convention on the Rights of the Child: States Parties recognize the right of the child to education, and with a view to achieving this right progressively and on the basis of equal opportunity, they shall, in particular: (a) Make primary education compulsory and available free for all.	*Convention on the Rights of the Child*: No part of [articles 28 and 29] shall be construed so as to interfere with the liberty of individuals and bodies to establish and direct educational institutions ...
Convention on Migrant Workers Each child of a migrant worker shall have the basic right of access to education on the basis of equality of treatment with nationals of the State concerned. Access to public pre-school educational institutions or schools shall not be refused or limited by reason of the irregular situation with respect to stay or employment of either parent or by reason of the irregularity of the child's stay in the State of employment.	*Convention on Migrant Workers* States Parties ... Undertake to have respect for the liberty of parents, at least one of whom is a migrant worker, ... to ensure the religious and moral education of their children in conformity with their own convictions.

Full texts and information on these instruments are available at the website of the Office of the High Commissioner on Human Rights www.ohchr.org.

The close association between the poverty of families, communities and countries and the lack of education for their children necessitates elimination of obstacles to universalizing primary education. This is mandated by universal human rights standards whereby primary education should be free, all-encompassing and compulsory. Of course, the law cannot oblige governments to ensure education for all children if it is beyond their means. International human rights law therefore mandates progressive realization of the right to education. This necessitates provision of free primary education for all children as soon as this can be accomplished, and international cooperation is often necessary to facilitate this process.

International human rights law defines primary education as a public responsibility. For states, this is an obligation of result; governments have to ensure that all children are educated. Key provisions are excerpted in Figure 1 and reflect the global consensus which underpins them.

Two faces of availability: Subsidy and liberty

As Figure 1 shows, the obligation of the state to make education available constitutes one pillar of the individual right to education. When the government does the opposite and closes a school or a university, this constitutes an apparent human rights violation. A government will seldom have an acceptable justification for such an extreme measure and, in any case, it has the burden of proving that this was the case. The African Commission on Human and Peoples' Rights found that a two year long closure of universities and secondary schools in Zaire (as it was at the time) constituted a violation of the right to education.[25] As always, this was only one out of many symptoms of the government's policy of violating rather than respecting human rights. The European Court of Human Rights, in one of the many judgments relating to northern Cyprus, found that "the discontinuance" (that is, closure) of Greek-medium secondary schools amounted to a denial of the right to education.[26]

The closure of a school attended by aboriginal children in Australia (138 out of 142 learners were indigenous) was justified by budgetary savings necessitated by fiscal stringency. This line of argument was reinforced by declining enrolments in that school and low attendance. The Australian Human Rights and Equal Opportunity Commission found that the one important reason for closing the school was its image of 'an aboriginal enclave.' The closure of that school would trigger dispersal of the indigenous learners in the neighbouring schools. How they would have been absorbed and whether these 'Traeger Park children' would

---

[25] African Commission on Human and Peoples' Rights – *Free Legal Assistance Group, Lawyers Committee for Human Rights, Union Interafricaine des Droits de l'Homme, Les Témoins de Jehovah v. Zaire*, Communications 25/89, 47/90, 56/91 and 100/93 (joined), Decision of the Commission adopted at its 18th ordinary session at Prais (Cape Verde), *Ninth Annual Activity Report of the African Commission on Human and Peoples' Rights 1995/96, Assembly of Heads of State and Government, Thirty-second Ordinary Session, 7-10 July 1996, Yaounde, Cameroon.*

[26] *Cyprus v. Turkey*, judgment of the European Court of Human Rights of 10 May 2001, application no. 25781/94.

be additionally disadvantaged were the key questions that the Commission asked:

> [The] evidence [of teachers] emphasized the need to better equip young Aboriginal people for higher grades and their ultimate step into the wider community as young adults. Their fear that it is not sufficient merely to provide special classes or to rely on some broad based assertion that it is good for both white and aboriginal children to learn the details of the other's culture. There is, in their view, the fundamental need to develop the confidence and the self-esteem of each aboriginal children who either because of his or her racial background or disadvantaged economic or domestic environment or for some other reason, will have difficulty in relating to the new school. [27]

These examples show that it is relatively easy to prove a human rights violation when a government has closed an existing school. This obliterates a potentially available educational institution. Turning this argument around, where schools do not exist, is the government obliged to create them because otherwise education is simply not available?

Investment in education of all children was historically assigned to the state because it yields delayed economic returns and, moreover, only where education is combined with other assets. Human rights law prioritizes primary education, altering political choices that, on their own, work in other directions. A legal right to education is bestowed upon children because they lack political rights that would enable them to secure their education through political process. Also, primary education ought to be free for children because they cannot pay for themselves nor should they. This is reinforced by the corollary prohibition of child labour and the complementary rule linking school-leaving age with the minimum age for employment. The key correlate of childhood is freedom from adult responsibilities. This does not imply that education is free for their parents, community, society or the state. No human right is cost-free.

History has shown that compulsory education should be free so as to encompass all children. As long as families cannot afford the cost of education, compulsion cannot be enforced. In consequence, children will remain deprived of education and countries of educated and skilled populations. A governmental practice of making education compulsory while imposing charges, which preclude access for children who cannot afford the cost, is illustrated by a case in the People's Republic of China:

> Decision of the People's Government of Shalizhai Town on meeting out a penalty to ... for his violation of the compulsory education law
> Reason of the penalty: You are the custodian of pupil ..., and after a number of explanations and persuasions you still fail to send ... under your custody to school in violation of the Rules for Implementing the Compulsory Education Law of the People's Republic of China.

---

[27] Australia's Human Rights and Equal Opportunity Commission – *Aboriginal Students Support & Parents Awareness Committee Traeger Park School v. Minister of Education Northern Territory of Australia*, HREOCA 4, 26 February 1992.

Legal basis of the penalty: In accordance with the provision of Article 40 of the Compulsory Education Law, for parents and custodians of school-age children failing to send their children or children under their custody to school to receive compulsory education, in case they are urban residents, it is incumbent upon the district government or an agency designated by it to criticise them; in case they live in the countryside, it is incumbent upon the township government concerned to criticise them. After such criticisms, those parents or custodians still refusing to send their children or children under their custody to school may be imposed a fine or other sanction measures in the light of specific conditions so as to enforce the compulsory education law, resulting in sending their children or children under their custody to school.

Decision on the fine: Since you refuse to send a school-age child to school, you have violated the provisions of the Compulsory Education Law, you are imposed a fine of 1000 yuan. You are obliged to send the fine to the Office of Judicial Affairs of the Government on 28 April 1997. In case you fail to pay the fine in time, the Government will ask the People's Court to enforce it.

People's Government of Shalizhaiu Town
25 April 1997 [28]

The obvious question stemming from this court case is what happens if the parents are unable to pay neither the costs of compulsory education nor the fine. This question leads to the conflict between China's law and its practice. Compulsory education should be but is not free. The assumption that all children can go to school is based on the wording of law, which would then justify punishing parents if they deprived their children of education. Another question has to be added, namely the parental obligation is to send their children to a governmental school and to pay for it, while not giving them a choice. The recent legalization of private education has provided limited choice. But only for those who can afford to pay. The many layers of legal and practical difficulties in discerning the nature and scope of the right to education in China are illustrated in a part of the report which I issued after my mission to China as the Special Rapporteur on the right to education:

Although the term "the right to education" is used abundantly, China's Constitution and legislation define education as an individual duty adding a "right to receive education". Freedom to impart education is not recognized and demands for its affirmation have emerged: a mother has demanded to educate her child herself, and a child's book describing his abandonment of school so as to educate himself has become a best-seller. The legalization of private education has introduced parental freedom of choice, but only for those with purchasing power. Contrary to China's international human rights obligations, religious education remains prohibited in both public and private educational institutions.

The 1986 Compulsory Education Law stipulates that "the State shall subsidize the areas unable to introduce compulsory education because of financial difficulties." In the 1990s, 40 percent of children of compulsory school age in the poorest provinces could not attend school. The lowest levels of government, county and township, shoulder the biggest burden by providing 87% of public expenditure for education. The problem, as diagnosed by the World Bank, is "decentralized financing of basic education without adequate equalization transfers." These remain

---

[28]   Education for All: The Year 2000 Assessment – Final Country Report of China, available at www.unesco.org/education/efa/wef/countryreports/china/rapport_2_1.html (February 2000)

inadequate, "under-funded since their inception, rising in 1998 to only just under a meagre level of 2 percent of total transfers." The goals and methods for achieving education for all are thus at odds with each other, leading to adverse selectivity. Those the least able to finance education – the poorest – can afford the least schooling although they need free education the most.

The official statistics on school enrolment, all above 99 percent, conflict with reports of large numbers of children who cannot afford to go to school. The World Bank has confirmed that "the high out-of pocket costs of education [are consistently cited] as a primary reason for student drop-outs or non-enrolments." Private donations are sought for particularly talented but poor children. Caring individuals donate part of their salaries to pay fees that should not be charged in the first place. There are no statistics on the variety of fees that are charged, ranging from exam-paper fees to reading room permit charges, from desk fees to homework-correcting fees. In Beijing, the Education Committee has reportedly approved no less than 14 different fees. Although some are ostensibly voluntary, parents complain that all have to be paid. The Special Rapporteur is deeply concerned that school fees continue to be regulated rather than abolished. In March 2002, the then prime minister, Zhu Rongji, denounced local authorities for their failure to pay teachers' salaries and for imposing a range of charges, including in education, urging their abolition. However, the unified and/or standardized fees for compulsory education (*yi fei zhi*) were continued just after the Special Rapporteur's mission.

Parents have to send their children to school under the threat of legal enforcement, but they cannot choose education for their children. Furthermore, although the entire history of the right to education has confirmed that education cannot be made compulsory unless it is free, compulsory education has not been made free in China. The 1986 Compulsory Education Law stipulates that "the State shall not charge tuition for students receiving compulsory education", and the 1995 Education Law prohibits the charging of fees illegally, but the definition of fees that are illegal is unclear. Direct charges in the form of many different types of fees are notorious and huge, estimated at 200 billion yuan (US$ 24 billion) in the past decade. Local authorities have often resorted to the law on compulsory education to force parents to enrol their children, and fines have been imposed by courts for their failure to do so. A father in Lin Yi (Shan Dong province) committed a robbery in April 2001 because he was unable to pay school fees for his children. The 30 yuan he stole earned him three years in prison and left his children without the schooling which should have been free to begin with.[29]

This illustration of the impact on children and on their parents of a government's failure to ensure free education, which can then be made compulsory, indicates the imperfect state of international human rights law. There is no international access to justice for victims of the violation of the right to education unless states explicitly agree. There is no domestic access to justice unless individual states set it up.

---

[29] Commission on Human Rights – Report submitted by Katarina Tomasevski, Special Rapporteur on the right to education: Mission to People's Republic of China, 10-19 September 2003, U.N. Doc. E/CN.4/2004/45/Add.1.

Ensuring primary education: Legal and fiscal obligations

A key governmental obligation in education is that of result. It has to ensure free and compulsory education for all children. Since children are the privileged subjects of the right to education and education has been defined for them as compulsory, provision or financing of compulsory education features in the practice of the overwhelming majority of states. This, of course, does not undermine other government obligations in education which apply in parallel, such as to respect parental freedom of choosing education for their children or to safeguard human rights in education.

International human rights law is based on the experience that education cannot be universalized and made compulsory unless it is free. Direct, indirect and opportunity costs preclude access to education for many children. Thus, all international human rights instruments require compulsory education to be free. The underlying logic is that elimination of financial obstacles makes all-encompassing education impossible.

The purpose of human rights law is to transform allocations for education from discretionary into obligatory. This process entails acceptance of human rights correctives in decision-making, which is a political process at all levels, from local to global. Securing a match between governmental human rights obligation in education and fiscal allocations is a key objective of human rights law.
It bestows legal rights upon those actors who have the least access to decision-making: the children. Primary-school aged children who should be – but are not – in school are easily marginalized hence their legal right to free and compulsory education.

Education proverbially receives less funding than would be necessary to ensure quality education for all children. The main reason is that educational allocations are in most countries discretionary. This is the opposite to what the right to education requires. Ensuring conformity between the diversity of the intake and the corresponding inputs into the process of teaching and learning is an objective that remains an unrealized ideal for most children. Education proverbially received less funding than would be necessary to ensure quality education for all children. The main reason is that educational allocations are in most countries discretionary. Constitutionally guaranteed budgetary allocations, specified as, for example, 25% of the budget or 6% of GNP, translate the right to education into a genuinely guaranteed right.[30] A change in Indonesia in 2002 has been described as follows:

> One of the major developments registered in the reform of Indonesia's system of education is the adoption of the Fourth Amendment to the Constitution on 10 August 2002. The newly amended Constitution not only guarantees every

---

[30] In Brazil, for example, the 1988 Constitution specified that 18% of the federal budget and 25% of the budgets of state and municipal authorities have to be allocated for education. Committee on Economic, Social and Cultural Rights – Initial report of Brazil, U.N. Doc. E/1990/5/Add.53, 2001, para. 758.

Indonesian's right to education, but also the corresponding obligation of the state in this regard. Article 31 stipulates the government's obligation to ensure the fulfillment of the right of every citizen to basic education, as well as the financial responsibility which this fulfillment entails. In addition, the state must develop and implement a national education system, and earmark at least 20% of its own and local governments' budgets to meet the system's requirements. [31]

Such changes, if translated into practice, transform government commitment to education from rhetorical to fiscal, from discretionary into obligatory. This has yet to happen in Indonesia. The government's statement introducing the budget for 2005 acknowledged that its own constitutional and legal guarantees "have yet to be met". Merely 12% of the budget was allocated to education and the government stated that the obligatory allocations mandated by the 2003 law were being "gradually accommodated."[32] Guy de Jonquieres has commended that "investment is desperately needed in physical infrastructure, healthcare and basic education, all sadly neglected since Indonesia's 1997 financial crisis."[33]

As in Indonesia, budgetary allocations often force education authorities to distribute insufficient funds amongst a variety of nationally or locally defined priorities, while the funds are insufficient for meeting any of them. Therefore, the correspondence between children's entitlement to quality education and the government's obligations in the form of constitutionally guaranteed educational allocations is an important step in advancing the right to education. Lord Browne-Wilkinson has emphasized this point when he faulted an educational authority for not diverting money from other, discretionary uses, adding:

> To permit a local authority to avoid performing a statutory duty on the grounds that it prefers to spend money in other ways is to downgrade a statutory duty to a discretionary power.[34]

Although resource allocation is perceived as an inherently political decision, intrusions into decisions on resource allocation have been necessitated by the constitutional guarantees of the right to education. The first governmental obligation is to ensure that education is available. A group of senators in the Philippines challenged in 1991 the constitutionality of the budgetary allocation of P86 billion for debt servicing which compared to P27 billion for education. The Constitution of the Philippines obliges the government to assign the highest budgetary priority to education. The issue to be decided was, then, whether debt servicing, exceeding three times the budgetary allocation for education, was unconstitutional. The Court has found that education had constituted the

---

[31] Statement by the Indonesian delegation on the report of the Special Rapporteur on the right to education on her mission to Indonesia in July 2002 before the 59th session of the Commission on Human Rights, Geneva, 3 April 2003.

[32] State Address by the President of the Republic of Indonesia and Government Statement on the Bill on the State Budget for the 2005 Fiscal Year and Its Fiscal Note, Jakarta, 16 August 2004, text available at www.thejakartapost.com (August 2005).

[33] De Jonquieres, G. – Time for Indonesia's president to show his mettle, *Financial Times*, 2 August 2005.

[34] *R v. East Sussex Country Council ex parte T*, [1998] ELR 251, p. 259.

highest allocation while debt servicing was necessary to safeguard the creditworthiness of the country and the survival of its economy.[35]

English courts have examined the duty of local education authority to secure sufficient places at school for all children within the compulsory school age where children were deprived of primary education because of a shortage of teachers. They have held that the authority did whatever was in its powers to rectify the un-availability of education and was thus not in breach of its statutory duty.[36] They have also held that the obligation of the state to make education free requires the prohibition of charges for registering pupils, or their entry for examination, or for the transportation provided to pupils who live beyond walking distance.[37] Securing that education is accessible has also generated jurisprudence where transportation should be provided, free of charge, to facilitate compulsory school attendance of children who live beyond the walking distance to school. The House of Lords has held:

> In the case of pupils [living further away than walking distance], a local education authority would be acting unreasonably if it decided that free transport was unnecessary for the purpose of promoting their attendance at school, because if it were not provided the parents of these pupils would be under no legal obligation to secure their attendance. [38]

Also in Brazil, free and compulsory education as an individual public right has also been interpreted to include free transport if children cannot otherwise attend school.[39]

The meaning of free education was examined by the Constitutional Court of the Czech Republic upon a demand for free textbooks and teaching materials in primary and secondary school. The Court has clarified that 'free' means that in primary education the state bears the costs of establishing schools, their operation and maintenance, and may not demand tuition. It has added, however, that the state is not obliged to bear all costs:

> On 4 November 1994, the Court received from a group of Deputies of the Parliament of the Czech Republic a petition instituting a proceeding on the annulment of Government Regulation No. 15/1994 Sb. on the Provision Free of Charge of Textbooks, Teaching Texts, and Basic School Materials. The Group of Deputies asserts that it is in conflict with:
> - Article 33 of the Charter of Fundamental Rights and Basic Freedoms, which guarantees to all citizens the right to elementary and secondary education free of charge;
> - Article 28 of the Convention on the Rights of the Child pursuant to which the Czech Republic as a State Party bound itself to establish, free of charge, education

---

[35] Supreme Court of the Philippines – *Guingona, Jr. v. Carague*, G.R. No. 94571, 22 April 1991.
[36] *R. v. Inner London Education Authority, ex parte Ali*, [1990] C.O.D. 317, [1990] 2 Admin.L.R. 822, 828B.
[37] *R. v. Richmond upon Thames London Borough Council, ex parte McCarthy & Stone*, [1992] 2 A.C. 48.
[38] House of Lords – *Devon County Council v. George*, [1989] A.C. 573, 604B, per Lord Keith.
[39] Tribunal of the State Minas Gerais (TMG), Apelação Civel No. 000.197.843-6/2000.

for all children and to establish, free of charge, secondary general and specialist education and, in cases of need, to provide financial support as well. ...
The Government informed the Court ... of its position, to the effects that its Regulation No. 15/1994 was based upon authority given it by [the Education Act], pursuant to which the Government is to designate the extent to which textbooks, teaching texts, and basic school materials will be provided to students free of charge. ... Students, or their parents, are to pay for educational materials which are owned or used by the students, with the exception of materials which the state provides to students in the first year of elementary school ... The above-mentioned Regulation provides that textbooks for elementary school are also lent to students free of charge, but they do not become their property. In secondary school, the students purchase textbooks and they become their property. ... The Government is of the view that making textbooks and education materials available free of charge cannot be interpreted as a basic human right. ...
... The mentioned Regulation does not restrict the right to education free of charge nor does it affect it substantially. Education free of charge unquestionably means that the state shall bear the costs of establishing schools and school facilities, of their operation and maintenance, but above all it means that the state may not demand tuition, that is, the provision of primary and secondary education for payment. An exception is allowed for private and religious schools, which exist apart from the network of 'state' schools. ... According to the interpretation of [education free of charge] proposed by the petitioners, the state should see to the provision of everything directly related to the attendance at elementary and secondary schools, for example galoshes, school bags, pencil cases, writing equipment, physical education gear, etc. It is clear that education free of charge cannot consist in the state bearing all costs incurred by citizens when pursuing their right to education and the Government undoubtedly has authority to proceed in this way. ... The costs connected with putting the right to education into effect can be divided between the state and the citizen, or his legal representative. It is appropriate to keep in mind that it is in the citizen's own interest to obtain education (and this way also higher qualifications and better opportunities to make one's way in the labour market) and to make an effort himself to achieve it. The expenses connected with putting the right to education into effect are a long-term investment into the life of the citizen. The state bears the essential part of these costs, however, it is not obliged to bear all of them. ...
Therefore, ... the Court has rejected on the merits the group of Deputies' petition proposing the annulment of the Regulation.[40]

The meaning of *free* has gone much further that the Czech Constitutional Court has held, beyond direct and indirect costs of schooling, to also eliminate opportunity costs. The Supreme Court of India has accepted a "learn and earn" approach for non-hazardous employment of children below 14 years of age, mandating a reduction of their daily working hours to six with at least two hours of education at the expense of the employer. For hazardous work, the Court has recalled that child labour could not be eliminated without tackling the underlying poverty and suggested ensuring work for an adult member of the family *in lieu* of the child or, if this is impossible within the limits of the economic capacity of the country, the provision of a minimum income to the family in order to enable them to send the child to school payable as long as the child is attending school.[41]

---

40 Judgment of the Constitutional Court of the Czech Republic, Pl. US 25/94 of 13 June 1995.
41 Supreme Court of India – *Mehta v. State of Tamil Nadu*, Judgment of 10 December 1996, (1996)

In the United States, economic and social rights are not recognized and, furthermore, the Supreme Court has declared taxation as well as economic and social policy to lie beyond its purview. It has held that raising and disbursing tax constitutes a legislative function beyond the remit of courts. The core of the case was the financing of education at the district level out of property tax, which has created a great deal of difference between the levels of funding between rich and poor districts. The Court has refrained from questioning funding "depending on the relative wealth of the political subdivisions in which citizens live" to affirm "freedom to devote more money to the education of one's children." The argument continued in the opposite direction from where human rights would have led, with the Court favouring local autonomy at the expense of placing "the financial responsibility in the hands of the State."[42] However, the US Supreme Court has faulted denial of access to education "directed against children ... on the basis of a legal characteristic over which children have little control," highlight its cost: "It is difficult to understand precisely what the State hopes to achieve by promoting the creation and perpetuation of a subclass of illiterates within our boundaries, surely adding to the problems and costs of unemployment, welfare and crime. It is thus clear that whatever savings might be achieved by denying these children an education, they are wholly insubstantial in light of the costs involved to these children, the State and the Nation."[43]

The European Union has been a pioneer in setting the boundaries between the right to free and access to for-fee education. Having developed from the common market, it crosses the boundaries between public and commercial law in defining fundamental rights. Its definition of the right to education in the Charter of Fundamental Rights, included in the constitutional treaty, does not define education as an individual entitlement but rather lays down "the possibility" of receiving education. This "clarifies that free compulsory education has to be possible, not that all compulsory education has to be free."[44] The background is EU's need to refrain from interfering with the provision of free and compulsory education, which remains the sovereign prerogative of each member, while also furnishing the legal infrastructure for trade in education services. The European Court of Justice has differentiated between education as a paid service from education as an individual entitlement by the criterion of payment, specifying that fee-for-service "is absent in the case of courses provided under the national education system." [45] The practice within the European Union, where the right to free education has been preserved for children and young people in the compulsory education age, but post-compulsory education – both public and private – is subject to payment.

---

6 SCC 756; AIR 1997 SC 699; (1997) 2 BHRC 258.

[42] US Supreme Court – *San Antonio School District v. Rodriguez*, 411 U.S. 1 (1973), 21 March 1973.

[43] US Supreme Court – *Plyer v. Doe*, 457 U.S. 202, 15 June 1982.

[44] Winkler, R. – The right to education according to Article 14 of the Charter of Fundamental Rights of the European Union, *International Journal of Education Law and Practice*, Issue 1-2, December 2004, Special Conference Edition, p. 99.

[45] *Belgian State v. Humbel* [1988] ECR 5365, para. 15.

Freedom of (parental) choice

Governmental human rights obligations include ensuring that education is available as well as respecting parental freedom of choosing education of their children. In other words, the government ought to make education available for all school-age children, but it should allow the parents to opt out of public school. Compulsory education emanates from the power of the state to impose, regulate, compel and control education. The former European Commission on Human Rights spoke about "a right for the State to establish compulsory education."[46] As for all other powers of the state, human rights safeguards are necessary. Human rights safeguards in compulsory education have been articulated by the US Supreme Court thus:

> Students in such institutions are impressionable and their attendance is involuntary. The State exerts great authority and coercive power through mandatory attendance requirements, and because of the students' emulation of teachers as role models and the children's susceptibility to peer pressure. [47]

Parental freedom of choice concerning education of their children has been the counterweight to the imposition of uniform public education from the very emergence of international human rights standards. Human rights safeguards are orientated towards balancing the right of the state to compel children to be educated and the right of their parents to decide where and how. Indeed, compulsory education is a duty as well as a right of the child. That duty is justified as being in the child's best interest. The 1959 Declaration of the Rights of the Child laid down the entitlement of the child to receive education,[48] articulating the vision of the child as a passive recipient of education rather than the subject of the right to education.

As Figure 2 shows, respect for parental freedom to have their children educated in conformity with their religious, moral or philosophical convictions has been affirmed in all human rights treaties. Despite this global consensus, the obligation to make primary education all-encompassing is frequently, albeit erroneously, associated with state-provided schooling. Government can ensure education by funding diverse schools, but not operating any, as well as operating a country-wide network of public schools.

Respect for parental freedom to have their children educated in conformity with their religious, moral or philosophical convictions is affirmed in international human rights law and is legally enforceable in most countries. The rationale behind parental choice is not to legitimize their denial of their children's right to education. In a conflict between parental choice and the best interests of the child, the latter should prevail.[49] Rather, parental choice is guaranteed so as to

---

[46] *Family H. v. the United Kingdom*, Application No. 10233/83, *Decisions and Reports*, vol. 37, 1984, p. 105.
[47] US Supreme Court – *Edwards v. Aguillard*, 482 U.S. 578, 19 June 1987.
[48] United Nations General Assembly resolution 1386 (XIV) of 20 November 1959, Principle 7.
[49] As long as decision-making is divided between the parents and the state, each side may claim to

prevent state's monopoly over education, ensure freedom in education, and protect educational pluralism.

Figure 2: Universal guarantees of parental choice

Universal Declaration (1948):
Parents have a prior right to choose the kind of education that shall be given to their children.

UNESCO Convention against Discrimination in Education (1960):
The States Parties to this Convention agree that:
(b) It is essential to respect the liberty of parents, ... firstly to choose for their children institutions other than those maintained by the public authorities but conforming to ... minimum educational standards, and secondly, to ensure ... the religious and moral education of the children in conformity with their own convictions.

International Covenant on Economic, Social and Cultural Rights (1966):
The States Parties to the present Covenant undertake to have respect for the liberty of parents ... to choose for their children schools, other than those established by the public authorities, which conform to such minimum educational standards as may be laid down or approved by the State and to ensure the religious and moral education of their children in conformity with their own convictions.
No part of this article shall be construed so as to interfere with the liberty of individuals and bodies to establish and direct educational institutions, ...

International Covenant on Civil and Political Rights (1966):
The States Parties to the present Covenant undertake to have respect for the liberty of parents ... to ensure the religious and moral education of their children in conformity with their own convictions.

Convention on the Rights of the Child (1989):
No part of [articles 28 and 29] shall be construed so as to interfere with the liberty of individuals and bodies to establish and direct educational institutions ...

The practice of states reveals different approaches. Some define education as both a right and a duty, others only as a right, yet others regulate only the freedom of communities or families to educate their children without affirming children's entitlements vis-à-vis the state. Making education compulsory for all children within a determined age range – in fact not merely in law – depends on the availability of schools, elimination of all obstacles in access to them, or the perception of the quality and utility of education.

Western European heritage includes the right of the State to deprive a child of liberty for the purpose of educational supervision, embodied in the European Convention on Human Rights. This is part of the conceptualization of education as the duty of the child, enforced by placing a recalcitrant child in prison. The European Court of Human Rights, in interpreting that provision of the Convention, has found a human rights violation where a child was ostensibly deprived of liberty for the purpose of educational supervision while detained "in conditions of virtual isolation and without the assistance of staff with educational training" which, the Court held, could not further any educational purpose. [50]

---

represent the best interests of the child, but adults often disagree among themselves as to what the best interests of the child may be.
[50] European Court of Human Rights – *Bouamar v. Belgium*, Judgment of 29 February 1988, A-129.

The conditions were dreary: the child was detained nine times in less than one year, having spent 119 days in prison. The Court has, however, accepted that compulsory education could entail detention of a child in an institution over considerable period of time.[51]

The very notion of *compulsory* education entails the obligation of the state to secure access to school for all children. Education is legally compulsory in most countries of the world but there is a difference in its length from 4 to 13 years. [52] This large difference reflects the varying willingness and ability of governments to ensure that all children and young people complete a determined length of schooling.

Varying governmental approaches

Education provided or financed by the state is fairly recent in the history of education. The inherited mosaic of pre-state provision of education is reflected in the variety of the existing models. The current trend of privatization has reinstituted and further diversified this mosaic. Parallel existence of free (governmental and/or public) or fee-paying (private) schools is widely, but not universally recognized. A great deal of jurisprudence has focussed on public funding to facilitate the exercise of freedom to establish and operate schools. Governmental obligation to make primary education all-encompassing, free and compulsory may be implemented through subsidizing a diverse range of primary schools.[53]

The meaning of *private* varies a great deal. In its broadest sense, it encompasses all non-state-run schools, some of which may actually be partially or even fully funded by the state. The assumption behind the term *private* is that all such schools are profit-making while many are not. The term encompasses formal and non-formal education, religious and secular schools, minority and indige-nous schools, as well as schools for children with special needs. Some private schools provide education in a particular minority language or religion, accom-modate children with physical or learning disabilities, or are established as alternatives to state-provided education, but do not charge anything. Indeed,

---

51 European Court of Human Rights – *Nielsen v. Denmark*, Judgment of 28 November 1988, A-144.
52 The changing vocabulary of global education strategies, evidenced in shifts between "basic" and "primary" education, has not affected the practice of states as definitions of these terms are the prerogative of each state (or, in federal countries, the regional or other authority which regulates education). The practice of states reveals a tendency to prolong compulsory beyond primary education. An analysis of comparative education laws revealed in 1999 that compulsory was longer than primary education in 96 countries, with 40 countries having prolonged compulsory education to 10 years or more. Commission on Human Rights – Progress report of the Special Rapporteur on the right to education, Katarina Tomasevski, U.N. Doc. E/CN.4/2000/6, paras. 46-48.
53 The UNESCO Convention against Discrimination in Education demands in its Article 4 that states "ensure that the standards in education are equivalent in all public educational institutions of the same level", acknowledging that the standards in private institutions can and do vary a great deal.

there is a great deal of difference in the very classification of schools as public and/or state schools and private schools. Igor Kitaev has observed that "the same types of schools are called either 'public' or 'private' depending on who you talk to."[54]

The classification developed by UNESCO divides schools by the criterion of their management by the state or privately, and thus "government-aided schools are considered private if they are privately managed." [55] This is not supported in the practice of states nor in human rights jurisprudence. English courts have classified schools into state (i.e. public) and private by the criterion of their source of funding. If a school's funding comes out of public revenue, it is defined as a state school regardless of how it is managed. [56] The Supreme Court of India has followed the same approach, emphasizing that ensuring primary education for all children does not mean that the state should provide it through state schools, "it can also be done by permitting, recognizing and aiding voluntary non-governmental organizations, who are prepared to impart free education to children. This does not also mean that unaided private schools cannot continue. They can, indeed, as they have a role to play. They meet the demand of that segment of the population who may not wish to have their children educated in state-run schools." [57] The Human Rights Committee has found that a state "cannot be deemed to act in a discriminatory fashion if it does not provide the same level of subsidy for the two [public and private] types of establishment, when the private system is not subject to State supervision." In a similar case, the Committee has added that "the preferential treatment given to public sector education is reasonable and based on objective criteria." [58] Differently, the constitutional jurisprudence in Spain interprets Article 13 of the International Covenant on Economic, Social and Cultural Rights to require from the state even-handedness in funding public and private schools. The obligation of the state is to make education in both public and private schools free of charge as well as to grant scholarships to learners regardless of the school they have chosen. [59]

Within Europe, Ireland has an educational model based on parental choice and provision by the Church rather than the state. This has generated an interesting court case, *Crawley v. Ireland,* in which the obligations of the state to ensure that

---

54 Kitaev, I. – Privatization of education: An ongoing debate, *IIEP Newsletter*, vol. 19, No. 1, January-March 2001, p. 3.
55 UNESCO – *1998 World Education Report*, Paris, 1999, p. 118.
56 *National Union of Teachers v. Governing Body of St.Mary's Church of England Aided School*, [1995] ICR 317, EAT [1997] IRLR 242 (CA); *R. v.Haberdashers' Aske's Hatcham Trust, ex parte T* [1995] ELR 350; EA 1996, ss 482 (1) (b), (3); 483.
57 *Krishnan v. State of Andhra Pradesh*, 1993.
58 Human Rights Committee – *Carl Henrik Blom v. Sweden*, Communication No. 191/1985, Views adopted on 4 April 1988, *Selected Decisions of the Human Rights Committee under the Optional Protocol, Seventeenth to thirty-second sessions (October 1982 – April 1988)*, United Nations, New York, 1990, p. 219, para. 10.3; *G. and L. Lindgren and L. Holm et. al. v. Sweden*, Communications Nos. 298/1988 and 299/1988, Views of the Committee adopted on 9 November 1990, U.N. Doc. CCPR/C/40/D/298-299/1988 of 7 December 1990, para. 10.3.
59 Quoted from: Díaz Revorio, F.J. – *El derecho a la educación, Anuario Parlamento y Constitución*, vol. 2, 1998, pp. 267-308.

primary education is provided (rather than providing education itself) formed the core issue. The background was a dispute between a teachers' trade union and a local school management about the appointment of a school principal. Having failed to settle the dispute through negotiations, the teachers' union organized a strike, leaving schoolchildren without teaching. The parents tried to manage on their own, hiring retired, untrained and voluntary teachers, but they also started a court case against the government and the teachers' union. The government, represented by the minister of education, was held responsible for having failed to ensure the children's constitutional right to free education. After the minister organized school busses to take children to adjoining schools, which was an outcome of the beginning of the court case, the teachers' union issued a notice banning teachers in neighbouring schools from enrolling the children. That notice was subsequently withdrawn. The courts had to examine a host of questions about the meaning of the right to education and narrowly decided, 3:2, that the government should not provide education but provide for it, namely ensure that it is provided. Extracts from the judgment illustrate how governmental obligations have been interpreted:

> O'Higgins C.J.
> Article 42, section 4, of the Constitution lays down that "the State shall provide for free primary education". These words impose an obligation on the State which is of general application to all citizens. ... This Article was intended to avoid imposing a mandatory obligation on the State directly to provide free primary education. Such, if imposed, might have led to the provision of free primary education in exclusively State schools. Rather it was intended that the State should ensure by the arrangements it made that free primary education would be provided.
> The duty imposed on the State under Article 42 is a continuing one. If what has been provided proves ineffective or unworkable due to a change in circumstances, ... this does not relieve the State or the Minister from seeking alternative or other means or methods to provide what is guaranteed to children by the Constitution. ... If the requirements of a constitutional duty which is imposed on the State require particular action to be taken, the lack of appropriate statutory power or administrative machinery can be no excuse for not doing what is required. The fact is that the Minister not only declined to pay for the substitute teachers or to assist in any way in defraying the expenses to which the parents had been put, but at all times he maintained the attitude that he was not obliged to do anything.
> It is necessary to mention one other matter. The direction issued by [the teachers' union] resulted in teachers in neighbouring schools refusing to accept or teach children from Drimoleague. It was claimed that this was done in pursuance of a constitutional right. [S]uch teachers had no constitutional right to do what they did. However, if they had any such right so to refrain from teaching it was not a right which could be exercised for the purpose of frustrating, infringing or destroying the constitutional rights of others. Rights guaranteed by the Constitution must be exercised with regard to the rights of others. It is on this basis that such rights are given by the Constitution. Once it is sought to exercise such rights without regard to the rights of others and without regard to the harm done to others then what is taking place is an abuse and not the exercise of a right given by the Constitution.
> Kenny J.
> The distinction between providing free education and providing for it is brought out vividly in the Irish version ..., whose agreed literal translation is:-"The State

must make arrangements to have basic education available free." I think that the change from Article 10 of the Constitution of the Irish Free State -"All citizens have the right to free elementary education"- was intended to emphasize that the State's obligation was not to educate but to provide for it. Thus, the enormous power which the control of education gives was denied to the State: there was interposed between the State and the child the manager or the committee or board of management. [60]

Controversies regarding public funding to facilitate the exercise of freedom to establish and operate schools are endless because the practice of states varies with regard to subsidies for non-public schools. Much international jurisprudence has originated from demands upon states to finance alternatives to public schooling, the exercise of freedom to establish and operate schools guaranteed under international human rights law. Should such freedom remain available only to those who can pay all costs, or should government subsidize these costs in order to equalize its enjoyment?

The (former) European Commission on Human Rights has affirmed the right to establish private schools, subject to their regulation and supervision by the state to ensure that education conforms to the prescribed standards. [61] Furthermore, it held that States were not required to "subsidize private education of a particular type or level" [62] and the state had a right to subject such schools to regulation and supervision because it is responsible for ensuring that all education complies with prescribed standards. [63]

The Supreme Court of Canada, having examined a complaint against a denial of public funding to private religious schools, has affirmed that the purpose of public schools is provision of education for all members of the community. The exercise of parental freedom to educate their children in accordance with their religious beliefs in separate schools (or at home) prevents their children from taking advantage of public schools and creates costs for the parents.

The exercise of parental freedom does not lead to an entitlement to public funding, however. [64] Canada's constitutional arrangements have, however, entrenched unequal public subsidies for specific religious [65] and linguistic minorities.

---

[60] *Eilish Crawley, Kathleen McCarthy and Others, Infants, suing by their next friend, Patricia Croiwley, Plaintiffs, v. Ireland, The Minister for Education, The Attorney General and Others, Defendants* [1977 No. 1945 P.], 1 October 1979, *The Irish Reports*, 1980, pp. 102-131

[61] European Commission on Human Rights – Application No. 11533, *Jordebo Foundation of Christian Schools and Jordebo v. Sweden*, Decision of 6 March 1987, *Decisions & Reports*, vol. 51, 1987, p. 125.

[62] European Commission on Human Rights – *André Simpson v. United Kingdom*, Application No. 14688/89, Decision on admissibility of 4 December 1989, *Decisions and Reports*, vol. 64, p. 194; *Verein Gemeinsam Lernen v. Austria*, Application No. 23419/94, Decision of 6 September on the admissibility of the application, *Decisions & Reports*, vol. 82, 1994, p. 41.

[63] European Commission on Human Rights – Decisions concerning applications Nos. 6857/74 and 11533/85, *Decisions and Reports*, vol. 9, p. 27 and vol. 51, p. 125.

[64] Supreme Court of Canada – *Adler v. Ontario*, Judgment of 21 November 1996, [1996] 3 SCR 609, (1996) 140 DLR (4th) 385.

[65] The Supreme Court of Canada affirmed that educational rights "granted specifically to the Protestants in Quebec and the Roman Catholics in Ontario make it impossible to treat all Canadians equally. The country was founded upon the recognition of special or unequal educational rights for specific religious groups in Ontario and Quebec." *Reference re Bill 30, An*

Public funding of private education has acquired heightened importance with privatization and the introduction of school vouchers. These have altered the practice of public funding only for public schools and the allocation of children to particular schools by some objective criterion, such as distance. The introduction of school vouchers has meant a change in the definition of the obligations of the state – rather than having to ensure that all public schools comply with the requirements of quality, vouchers have enabled parents to shop around with the voucher in hand as payment. Through voucher schemes, governments have enabled parents to choose a school for their children, with the state's contribution to the child's education embodied in the voucher, usually amounts to the enrolment and/or tuition fee. The rationale has been that individual schools should be rewarded for attracting learners, while those unable to do so should be deprived of funding. At a higher level of abstraction, the rationale is to enhance competitiveness and/or broaden parental freedom of choice. An additional reason has been a wish to subject public schools to competition, seeing them as having monopolized education. This approach has generated a great deal of controversy by challenging the premise accepted in many countries, namely that the government is obliged to either provide all-encompassing public education or to subsidize a variety of non-public schools, in both cases ensuring that all schools comply with basic quality standards.

The voucher scheme introduced in 1993 in Puerto Rico was declared unconstitutional in the part which accorded to selected pupils a financial grant of $1,500 for transfer from public to private school.[66] The constitutional prohibition of diverting public funds to private schools reached back to the separation between the church and the state and was upheld, although the voucher scheme did not revolve around secular or religious schools. Rather, it aimed at financially stimulating transfer from public to private schools (thus also transferring tax revenue to private schools) with the aim of increasing choice, against the constitutional requirement for public funds to be used solely for public schools.

In a case which has addressed the financing of private schools, the Supreme Court of Colombia has clarified why education should continue to be defined as public service and thus not be governed by economic arguments alone:

> ... although the Constitution protects economic activities, private initiative and competition as well as recognizing the right of private entities to establish schools, these liberties cannot negate nor can they diminish the nature of education as public service and its social function; education is also and above all else a fundamental right.
> ... education – even if private – has to be provided in the conditions which guarantee equality of opportunity in access to education, and all forms of discrimination and 'elitism' are thus repugnant to its nature of public service with profound social contents; these, by virtue of excessive economic demands, automatically deny access to intellectually able persons solely because [of] their

---

Act to Amend the Education Act (Ont.), [1987] 1 S.C.R., p. 1199-1200.
[66] Supreme Court of Puerto Rico/Tribunal Supremo de Puerto Rico – *Asociación de Maestros v. José Arsenio Torres*, 30 de noviembre de 1994, 94 DTS 12:34.

levels of income. [67]

This overview of jurisprudence the right to education has highlighted the key purpose of public school: to provide education for all children, together. The preferential treatment of public over 'private' schooling in international human rights jurisprudence centres on the role of education in the socialization of children and the preference for inclusiveness over segregation, since "separate educational facilities are inherently unequal."[68] The exercise of parental freedom to educate their children in separate schools (or at home) prevents their children from taking advantage of public schools and creates costs for the parents. The exercise of parental freedom does not generally entail an entitlement to public funding, although there are differences even within Europe. Where a government permits alternative forms of schooling, it is obliged to set and enforce educational standards because the government is responsible for ensuring the right to education and protection of human rights in education. The duality of public/private education may replicate, and indeed aggravate, existing inequalities in society and these often coincide with racial, ethnic, religious, or linguistic fissures in society. This requires a thoughtful examination of different ways in which education is designed and defined. This is done in various ways but the strength of human rights law is its enforcement, and this is described next.

Enforcement of the right to education   *Justiciability?*

hv interpret of R2E

The insistence on the rule of law in human rights stems from the fact that governance is exercise of power and human rights are safeguards against abuse of power. The raison d'être of the right to education is to act as a corrective to the free market. Governments have human rights obligations *because* education should not be treated merely as a commodity.

The mobilizing power of a human face and human fate makes litigating human rights violations a powerful method of human rights education. The courage in challenging abuses of power is a powerful message. Different from educational statistics, which tend to be numbing rather than mobilizing, exposing and opposing human rights violations portrays their victims as individuals. It helps people understand the obstacles which poor people – especially children – face. It facilitates challenging and eliminating these obstacles through learning by doing.

No government can be legally obliged to do the impossible. The illogic of burdening any actor with obligations it cannot perform would collapse the rule of law. Accordingly, universal human rights are few and the corresponding

---

67 Supreme Court of Colombia – Request to determine that Article 203 (in part) of the Law No. 115 of 1994 is unconstitutional by Andres De Zubiria Samper, Judgment of 6 November 1997, C-560/97.

68 Commission on Human Rights – Progress report of the Special Rapporteur on the right to education, Katarina Tomasevski, U.N. Doc. E/CN.4/2000/6, paras. 36-37.

governmental obligations are set at the minimum which should be feasible in all corners of the world. Governmental obligations corresponding to economic and social rights are defined in terms of progressive realization. By definition, progressive realization has to do with differences in the stage of development and, especially, financial constraints. As put by Mark Malloch Brown, "you cannot legislate good health and jobs. You need an economy strong enough to provide them."[69] Nonetheless, the government can ensure that resources that could be invested in health or education do not disappear through corruption.

The most important feature of the legal enforcement of the right to education is that the governments concerned are already committed to the it under their constitutions and laws. The rule of law requires no more of them, but also no less, than to translate their commitments into reality. And yet, often they have to be forced to comply. This is crucial not only for human rights protection but also for upholding the rule of law. Otherwise, governments would be left free to transgress the law with impunity, which happens often when the victims of violations are poor children, whose right to education is most often violated with impunity.

Court cases are necessary because of the mixture of confusion and contention which hamper remedies for violations of the right to education globally. No right can exist without a remedy but this is not so in international human rights law. The international human rights treaties which were written during the heat of the Cold War, especially the International Covenant on Economic, Social and Cultural Rights, did not anticipate remedies.[70] Progress in this vast and heterogeneous category of economic, social and cultural rights cannot be easy because this very category was a cold-war construct. Although the Cold War is over, confusion continues as does implicit (or explicit) emptying economic, social and cultural rights of their substance. This is often expressed in positing that these rights are not justiciable which, were it true, would mean that they are not rights.

The work of national human rights institutions on the right to education has been particularly supportive of the right to education and human rights in education. They have different names (human rights or equal opportunities

---

69 UNDP – *Human Rights and Human Development: Human Development Report 2000*, United Nations Development Programme, Oxford University Press, 2000, p. iii.
70 The efforts within the United Nations to equate the status of economic, social and cultural rights with that of civil and political rights included intergovernmental negotiations about an optional protocol to the International Covenant on Economic, Social and Cultural Rights. Thus far, this process has been fruitless. The comments of States that are party to the International Covenant on Economic, Social and Cultural Rights on the Draft Optional Protocol (U.N. Docs. E/CN.4/1998/84, E/CN.4/1998/84/Add. 1, E/CN.4/1999/112, E/CN.4/1999/112/Add.1, and E/CN.4/2000/49) revealed the need to ascertain the existence of domestic legal remedies for economic, social and cultural rights before contemplating possible international remedies. Concerns of many States that commented on the Draft Optional Protocol highlighted the imprecision with which governmental obligations have been defined, the corresponding inexactness in definitions of individual rights, the necessity to dissociate governmental human rights obligations from general economic, social or cultural policy, and the systemic nature of problems concerning economic, social, and cultural rights which casts doubt on the utility of an individual complaint mechanism.

commission, *defensor del pueblo*, or ombudsman) and varying remits, which often include receiving and processing complaints of human rights violations. Because legal proceedings are routinely lengthy and undertaken only by trained lawyers, [71] ombudsman-type institutions have proved a useful complement. In its first annual report, the Uganda Human Rights Commission put it thus: "most complainants are simply vulnerable people, who say that court procedures are too complicated for them and that they do not have the money to engage private lawyers to pursue their cases."[72] Such institutions (where they function well) provide open access to all potential complainants, a cost-free procedure, and flexibility in the methods of work. However, they do not have powers to interpret law and, thus, complement rather than supplant the judiciary.

The judiciary interprets formal, and necessarily abstract, human rights guarantees in the specific circumstances. Courts do not act on their own motion but follow complaints of human rights violation or requests for judicial review where a claim has been made that harm to human rights is imminent or inevitable. The interplay between abstract legal norms and factual circumstances enables precise definitions of rights and violations. The government is a party to the case, and can present all factual and legal arguments, explain and justify its policy decisions or strategic choices. The courts have to provide reasons for their decisions which are, increasingly, reviewed internationally.

Relating to availability, jurisprudence follows the rule of inverse proportion: where education is the least available, its absence is not legally challenged. The most important reason is that the law cannot force a state to make education available if this is beyond its powers. Hence, human rights guarantees can be used as safeguards against misappropriation or misallocation.

An early, precedent-setting case against the Estate of Ferdinand E. Marcos succeeded in returning some of the misappropriated funds to the Philippines.[73] The Constitutional Court of Hungary has confirmed that social rights should be protected against austerity measures justified by economic crises. The means whereby government ensures the minimum standards guaranteed by the constitution are beyond the Court's remit but those affected ought to be provided with time and opportunity to seek alternatives.[74] Colombia's constitutional jurisprudence includes situations of unconstitutionality, where governmental policies and budgetary allocations impede the realization of guaranteed rights. The Constitutional Court ruled in February 2004 that formal constitutional guarantees related to economic and social rights of the internally displaced, including education, had not been translated into governmental policies and

---

[71] In the 1980s, when the enforcement of fundamental rights in India (known as public interest litigation) started in earnest, Justice Lodha in Rajasthan declared his happiness that "poor, ignorant, downtrodden suffers of injustice have been allowed to enter 'Temples of Justice' without formal dress, flowers, rituals or chanting of mantras." *Citizens of Bundi versus Municipal Board* AIR 1988 Raj 132-135.

[72] Uganda Human Rights Commission – *1997 Annual Report*, Kampala, July 1998, p. 13 .

[73] *New York Centre for Constitutional Rights Docket*, 1987.

[74] Zifzak, S. – Adjudicating social rights: Lessons from the Hungarian constitutional experience, *East European Human Rights Review*, vol. 4, 1998, No. 1, pp. 53-96.

supported by appropriate budgetary allocations. The plight of the internally displaced, after four decades of armed conflict and political violence, was known to all. Nevertheless, they were marginalized rather than prioritized. The Court was petitioned by 1150 internally displaced families, and diagnosed that the majority (70%) had not received assistance from the government. Its finding of unconstitutionality was accompanied by a judicial order to elaborate a detailed time-frame and secure the necessary resources within 12 months. The Court also listed specific rights of the displaced, including the right to a place at school for all internally displaced below 15 years of age. By having declared unconstitutionality, the Court has preserved its jurisdiction until the constitutionally protected rights of the displaced have been re-instituted and protected The Constitutional Court, in the words of Manuel José Cepeda, who delivered the judgment, faulted the government for its denial of the constitutionally guaranteed rights of the displaced. As a consequence, an unknown but a large number, probably over a million of the displaced were neither registered nor informed of the rights they had, budgetary allocations were diminished rather than increased with time. [75]

This paradigmatic case has highlighted the core purpose of enforcement: halting and reversing governmental practice of denying basic rights to a large, dispersed, impoverished and politically voiceless population. It has highlighted two important issues.

First, different from releasing an arbitrarily detained person, securing the right to education requires extensive and efficient institutional infrastructure which cannot be created overnight. Second, the task of the Court is to enforce constitutional obligations of the government. They include policy design and implementation, which remain government's prerogative as long as the constitutionally mandated minimum standards are met. Ensuring that they are met is the key purpose of human rights law.

---

[75] Corte Constitucional de Colombia – Sentencia T-025 de 6 de febrero de 2004, expedientes T-653010 y acumulados.

2

Accessibility

Education may be available, with access to it impeded for all those who cannot afford the cost. Therefore, this Chapter examines the state of education law today by adding the fifth A to the four which structure human rights law. Education continues as a human right but has also become a traded service. Hence, the obstacle of cost is not confined to the university but may jeopardize access to primary education, which should be every child's birthright. Also, legal obstacles may deny children's access to education. These are particularly widespread when children, or their parents, are not citizens.

Strategies may be designed with the slogan 'reaching the un-reached.' A crucial human rights question is the difference between the *un-reached* and the *excluded*. Out-of-school children tend to share features such as being female or migrants, or both. Gender discrimination is multi-faceted and girls are victimized also because of their race, ethnicity, religion or language. Domestic servants may start working at the age of four, at least 80% are girls, and 70% are come from categories victimized by discrimination, such as minorities or migrants.[76] Children with disabilities may be in practice excluded, whatever the law says, because schools and classrooms preclude their access. Children who are imprisoned may be excluded because the budgets of the institutions, which are in theory supposed to rehabilitate them, exclude education. Access to education for people deprived of their liberty is a legally recognized right if they are within compulsory school age. US courts have affirmed for children deprived of their liberty their constitutional entitlement to appropriate treatment which includes education [77] although education for inmates above 17 is a privilege.[78]

This shows that, as humanity, we have failed to make primary education available to all the world's children. That this should not remain so has been affirmed in the global Education for All (EFA) strategy as well as in President Bush's initiative 'No child left behind.'[79] Neither initiative is particularly well-known because EFA was supplanted by MDGs while 'No child left behind', the first initiative of President Bush after he had been elected for the first time, was supplanted by his war against terrorism. However, the choice of wording

---

[76] Sub-Commission on the Promotion and Protection of Human Rights – Child domestic workers in Benin, Costa Rica and India. Submission by Anti-Slavery International to the 25th session of the Working Group on Contemporary Forms of Slavery, Geneva, 14-23 June 2000.

[77] *Inmates of Boys' Training School v. Afflack*, 346 F. Supp. 1354 (D.R.I. 1972).

[78] *Bellamy v. McMickens*, US District Court for the Southern District of New York, 692 F.Supp. 205, Judgment of 15 July 1988.

[79] Commission on Human Rights – Report submitted by Katarina Tomasevski, Special Rapporteur on the right to education: Mission to the United States of America, 24 September – 10 October 2001, U.N. Doc. E/CN.4/2002/60/Add.1, paras. 20-22.

demonstrates an underlying consensus. In the realm of the law, Canada's Supreme Court has clarified that the constitutionally protected purpose of the public school system is to provide education to *all* members of the community. [80] This indicates a widespread consensus that we owe all children at least some education.

When the core global human rights standards mandating primary education to be free and compulsory were adopted, there was global consensus behind them. Enrolments rapidly expanded in the 1960s and the 1970s to halt due to economic crises and diminished public funding. [81] Decreased fiscal allocations for education led to diminished primary-school enrolments, [82] and also to a redefinition of the role of the state in education. Nevertheless, governments still finance 63% of the cost of education, while 35% is private funding and 2% comes from international aid. [83]

The global consensus whereby primary education should be both free and compulsory, which had guided education in the first decades after the Second World War, was jeopardized by consecutive economic crises in the past three decades. Although the two pillars of primary education – free and compulsory – are mentioned together in all international human rights treaties, they are reflected no longer in the practice of all states. Moreover, policies of international financial institutions tend to work in the opposite direction, [84] and these affect most countries in the world.

The first step towards eliminating exclusion from education is to make it visible. Keeping a problem invisible facilitates inaction. Exclusion is self-sustaining and it increases. Those with the least education tend to leave this heritage to the next generation. Girls who are married while they should be at school have children in their teens, who transmit that fate to the next generation.

---

[80] Canada's Supreme Court – *Adler v. Ontario*, [1996] 3 S.C.R., paras. 52 and 54.

[81] UNESCO – A summary statistical review of education in the world, 1960-1982, Doc. ED/BIE/CONFINTED 39/Rev. 1, July 1984.

[82] UNESCO data show that the percentage of children aged 6-11 enrolled in primary school declined between 1970 and 1985 from 95.1% to 90.0% in Belgium, from 90.6% to 85.8% in France, from 97.3% to 89.9% in Greece, from 93.2% to 88.7% in Ireland, from 87.9% to 78.2% in Italy, from 90.8% to 79.1% in the United Kingdom, and from 100.0% to 95.0% in the United States.

[83] UNESCO – *Bulletin of the UNESCO Education Sector*, Paris, No. 5, April-June 2003.

[84] The World Bank has questioned whether the state should provide education:" Although the state still has a central role in ensuring the provision of basic services – education, health, infrastructure – it is not obvious that the state must be the only provider, or a provider at all." (*World Development Report 1997*, p. 27) The Asian Development Bank has acknowledged that globalization impedes government obligations to ensure free primary education: "Globalization tends to direct governments away from equity-driven reforms for two main reasons. The first is that globalization increases the returns to high-level skills relative to lower-level skills, reducing the complementarities between equity- and competitiveness-driven reforms. The second is that in most developing countries and in many industrial countries, finance-driven reforms dominate education change in the new globalized economic environment, and such reforms tend to increase inequity in the delivery of education services." (*Key Indicators 2003*, Special chapter: Education for global participation, 2003, p. 43).

Categories of children that may be excluded from education vary between and within countries. Little comparative data is available in education statistics. The reporting process under human rights treaties, especially the Convention on the Rights of the Child, usefully covers this gap by highlighting those children that are particularly likely to be excluded.[85] The obstacles that ought to be overcome in combating exclusion from education vary, but all are exacerbated by poverty. The Convention on the Rights of the Child has provided the broadest global prohibition of discrimination, while the European Union has further extended the grounds of discrimination that ought to be prohibited.[86] This continuously evolving international legal framework facilitates analysis of similarities and differences between and within countries. Since there are no internationally comparable education statistics on the dynamics of discrimination on the grounds of race, language or minority status, creation of such data should be accorded priority. [87]

The Convention on the Rights of the Child has reiterated the obligation of all governments to ensure, individually and collectively, education for all children, especially to eliminate exclusion. Categories of children that may be excluded from education vary between and within countries.[88]
Little comparative data is available. Legalized and institutionalized denial of access to education has been globally outlawed. Outside the law, blurred terminology reigns. References are made to the vulnerable, marginalized and/or disadvantaged, and definitions of these terms vary. For example, the Philippine Commission on Human Rights has defined the disadvantaged as "women, children, youth, prisoners/detainees, urban poor, indigenous people, elderly, Muslims, persons with disabilities, internally displaced persons, informal labour, private labour, migrant workers, rural workers and public sector."[89] The EFA Dakar Framework has prioritized 'the poor and the most disadvantaged', and listed therein "working children, remote rural dwellers and nomads, and ethnic and linguistic minorities, children, young people and adults affected by

---

[85] An analysis of all government reports under the Convention on the Rights of Child has revealed that no less than 32 categories of children are excluded from education. Tomasevski, K. – *Education Denied: Costs and Remedies,* Zed Books, London, 2003, p. 126.

[86] The Convention on the Rights of the Child lists in its Article 2 twelve grounds of discrimination (race, colour, sex, language, religion, political or other opinion, national, ethnic or social origin, property, disability and birth), adding "other status" as human rights treaties always do in order to accommodate new or renewed grounds of discrimination. In its Article 21, the Charter of Fundamental Rights of the European Union has amplified the prohibited ground of discrimination to genetic features, membership of a national minority, age and sexual orientation.

[87] Commission on Human Rights – Report of the Special Rapporteur, Katarina Tomasevski, U.N. Doc. E/CN.4/2003/9, paras. 21-23.

[88] Cambodia has listed those excluded from education as: "orphans, abandoned children, children of poor parents, vagrants, domestic servants, juvenile delinquents between the ages of 7 and 17, disabled children, children who engage in prostitution, beggars and scavengers." (CRC/C/11/Add.16, 1998) In Thailand, "most of the children who had no access to schooling were living in remote rural areas, children of poor families, children living in slums, children living in areas that have a different language and culture, children of ethnic minorities such as hill-tribe children and island children. (CRC/C/11/Add.13, para. 342)

[89] Commission on Human Rights – *12 Years of Human Rights Advocacy: 1998 Annual Report,* Quezon City, p. 7.

conflict, HIV/AIDS, hunger and poor health; and those with special learning needs."[90]

There are two approaches to tackling educational exclusion. One defines the task as reaching the un-reached, enhancing the 'integrability' of the excluded. The vicious circle where poverty[91] causes the lack of education, which then precludes employment and perpetuates poverty. The other approach defines exclusion as a process whereby people are "pushed to the edge of society and prevented from participating."[92] Tackling exclusion requires halting and reversing exclusionary policies and practices, not only countering their effects. The focus moves from the excluded (called 'vulnerable' or 'disadvantaged' or 'marginalized') to the factors that lead to their exclusion. Denials of human rights are often among the key factors, especially for girls and women. Although these two approaches differ, both view education as the key to eliminating exclusion because most factors leading to exclusion can be mitigated by education. These two approaches have evolved into two different tracks. These are first described with regard to primary education, where there may be convergence in the near future. University education is discussed next because it demonstrates how far education policy has moved from the requirements of international human rights law.

Which yardstick: Equity or equality?

The term *equity* is used in education policy instead of *equality*. It seems to have been imported into education from Anglo-American English and also from economics. The term equity as it is used in education has been defined by the World Bank in terms of "disparities in the access to schooling across population groups as well as in the distribution of public spending among them."[93] The meaning of equity is uncertain and its translation into many languages impossible. An example is the Czech Republic because "the term equity has no real equivalent in the Czech language and was rejected as part of the communist egalitarian ideology."[94]

---

90   The Dakar Framework for Action – Education for All: Meeting Our Collective Commitments, Expanded Commentary, para. 19.
91   Definitions of poverty range between absolute figures which estimate the numbers of people who live on less than $1 per day to relative measures, defining as poor all those with a disposable income of less than half of the average of the country in which they live. Absolute figures are not helpful as they do not reveal how much people need for a standard of living deemed acceptable in the society in which they live.
92   Commission of the European Communities – Joint Report on Social Inclusion Summarizing the National Action Plans for Social Inclusion 2003-2005, December 2003, available at http://europa.eu.int/comm/emplyment_social/soc-prot/soc-incl.
93   The World Bank – *Education and Training in Madagascar: Towards a Policy Agenda for Economic Growth and Poverty Reduction. A Summary of Key Challenges*, Africa Region Human Development Working Peper Series, Washington D.C., September 2001, p. 3.
94   Cerych, L. – The educational reform process in the Czech Republic, in: Council of Europe – *Strategies for Educational Reform: From Concept to Realization, Symposium in Prague, 4-6 November 1999*, Council of Europe Publishing, Strasbourg, September 2000, p. 63.

In human rights, the term equity denotes lesser rights for girls and women. As explained by the Economic and Social Commission for Asia and the Pacific:

> The conflict surfaced at the Fourth World Conference on Women in Beijing where some Muslim delegations argued that Islam's model of equality recognized the importance of gender difference and that this was ignored in the setting of international standards on equality. They, therefore, demanded that the word "equality" be replaced by the word "equity".[95]

Radhika Coomaraswamy, then the UN Special Rapporteur on Violence against Women, warned against changing terminology from *equality* to *equity*. She pointed out that such a change was promoted by countries such as Sudan because equity was seen as a flexible replacement of equality, allowing departures from the principle of equality and diminishing women's rights.[96] This has been echoed by the CEDAW Committee, which has emphasized "that the terms 'equity' and 'equality' are not synonymous and interchangeable and that the Convention is aimed at the elimination of discrimination against women and ensuring equality."[97]

The concept of equality implies comparison and requires measurement. Non-discrimination necessitates redressing existing inequalities; they have to be identified, documented and quantified. The initial steps towards the operationalization of non-discrimination relating to economic, social and cultural rights were undertaken in the Limburg Principles, adopted by a group of academics and activists, by pointing out three clusters of measures: (1) elimination of *de jure* discrimination, (2) tackling *de facto* discrimination, which occurs "as a result of the unequal enjoyment of economic, social and cultural rights on account of a lack of resources or otherwise", and (3) adopting "special measures for the sole purpose of securing adequate advancement of certain groups and individuals requiring such protection as may be necessary in order to ensure to such groups and individuals equal enjoyment of economic, social and cultural rights".[98]

Non-discrimination is often understood only in its limited sense of formal guarantees of equal rights for all. In education, one may look no further than ascertaining that no category is legally denied access to education on the grounds of race, ethnicity, or sex. However, access to education largely reflects the inherited inequalities: girls will often have lower enrolment rate than boys, while members of minorities or migrants may in practice be excluded.

---

95   Economic and Social Commission for Asia and the Pacific – *Human Rights and Legal Status of Women in the Asian and Pacific region*, Studies on Women in Development No. 1, U.N. Doc. ST/SCAP/1730, United Nations, New York, 1997, p. 18.

96   Coomaraswamy, R. – Reinventing international law: Women's rights as human rights in the international community, The Edward A. Smith Visiting Lecturer, Human Rights Program, Harvard Law School, Cambridge, 1997, p. 22.

97   U.N. Doc. CEDAW/C/2002/EXC/CRP.3/Add.4/Rev.1, 23 August 2002, para. 21.

98   The Limburg Principles on the Implementation of the International Covenant on Economic, Social and Cultural Rights, U.N. Doc. E/CN.4/1987/17 of 8 January 1987, paras. 37-39.

Studies carried out to determine the impact of public policies on the existing inequalities confirm that neglect of discrimination reinforces it. However, education is not guided by international human rights law and there is no internationally comparable educational statistics by race, ethnicity or religion. Consequently, it is impossible to monitor progress and retrogression in access to education using internationally prohibited grounds of discrimination as the yardstick. With the exception of sex, discrimination remains unrecorded in international education statistics which creates a vicious circle: because discrimination is invisible, one can pretend that it not exist because it is officially unrecorded; because there is no quantitative data, anybody trying to prove that discrimination takes place is doomed to fail because there are no data. It is impossible to effectively oppose discrimination without exposing it first. In Indonesia, for example, formal recording of religion triggered controversy in the recent past.[99] In Europe, Greece and France do not acknowledge the existence of minorities, while quite a few governments refuse collection of data that would highlight discrimination of minorities invoking protection of privacy or confidentiality, or claiming that such data are 'sensitive'. [100] Education strategies and quantitative data underpinning them ought to include human rights safeguards to formally recognize diversity but protect all those who may be perceived as different from discrimination and victimization. This is an immense challenge because education strategies are, as yet, defined and decided upon separately. They are not informed by human rights law and use a different vocabulary. Moreover, they often undermine human rights law. This is shown by describing the global dissent regarding primary education during the past fifteen years and then highlighting the transformation of university education from an entitlement into a services that can only be purchased at a price. The effects of these developments are then brought back into the human rights framework by looking at their impact, which was exemplified in 2005 by the global failure to ensure gender parity in primary education.

Education strategy *versus* human rights law in primary school

An international community, informed by a shared vision of education, does not exist as yet. Rather, we have are parallel structures which do speak the same language. Educational vocabularies are diverse. It seems so obvious to ask, first, what it is that they say they are doing in education. Some speak about service delivery, others about education as a process of teaching and learning. The former use the language of efficiency and cost-sharing, the latter advocate the accommodation of children with special needs. Inevitably, one has to ask why this has become so confusing since the problem to be solved can clearly be seen by all involved. A short answer is that problems are defined in such a way as to

---

99 Commission on Human Rights – Report of the Special Rapporteur on the right to education on her mission to Indonesia, E/CN.4/2003/9/Add. 1, para. 27.

100 Open Society Institute – *Monitoring the EU Accession Process: Minority Protection, vol. II: Case Studies in Selected Member States*, Open Society Institute, Budapest, 2002, pp. 43-45.

support the preferred solutions.[101] Because there is no global commitment to finance the education of all the children, the term *right* to education is avoided because *access* to education does not entail corresponding governmental obligations. *Access* spans education purchased on the free market or financed through charity. More importantly, its lack cannot trigger an accusation of a human rights violation.

If we use human rights law as the yardstick, we are doing worse than we promised the world's children more than 80 years ago. Free and compulsory education was linked to the elimination of child labour in 1921 by the International Labour Organization (ILO). [102] The rationale was – and is – that the right to education unlocks other rights when guaranteed, while its denial precludes the enjoyment of all human rights and perpetuates poverty. Making education compulsory requires it to be free so that all children can go to school. International human rights law has affirmed, repeatedly, that education should be free and compulsory. Figure 3 includes excerpts from the international human rights treaties, global and regional, which display this unanimity. They all repeat the identical wording and one would, then, assume that this commitment which the governments have individually made to would inform their collective strategy. That this is not the case is seen in the right-hand column. The excerpts from global education strategies agreed at international conferences between 1990 and 2005 demonstrate that it took fifteen years for a newly forged vocabulary, which studiously avoided a mention of governmental human rights obligations, [103] to revert to an affirmation that primary education should be free and compulsory.

So, global strats. – such as Jomtien & Dakar avoid HR obligats – eg MDGs. 'til 2005

---

[101] Longer answers are provided in Tomasevski, K. – Globalizing what: Education as a human right or as a traded service, *Indiana Journal of Global Legal Studies*, vol. 12, No. 1, Winter 2005, pp. 1-78 [describing two parallel legal regimes, international human rights law and international law on trade in education services, and examines the effects of this legal duality in developing countries and countries in transition] and in Tomasevski, K. – *Human Rights Obligations in Education: The 4-A Scheme*, Wolf Legal Publishers, Nijmegen, 2005 [explaining governmental human rights obligations in education].

[102] ILO Convention No. 10 laid down in 1921 the prohibition of employment which prejudices children's school attendance, setting the age at 14. The ILO Convention 138 strengthened the correspondence between school-leaving age and the minimum age for employment raising it to 15.

[103] The split within the international community which created parallel and mutually opposed strategies for education is analysed in Tomasevski, K. – *Education Denied: Costs and Remedies*, Zed Books, London, 2003, pp. 93-106.

Figure 3
The fifteen year gap: Global education strategy *versus*
international human rights law

International human rights law	Global education strategy
Universal Declaration (1948): Education shall be free, at least in the elementary and fundamental stages. Elementary education shall be compulsory.	*Jomtien Conference on Education for All* (1990): Every person – child, youth and adult – shall be able to benefit from educational opportunities designed to meet their basic learning needs. Universal access to, and completion of, primary education (or whatever higher level of education is considered as "basic") by the year 2000.
UNESCO Convention against Discrimination in Education (1960): The States Parties to this Convention undertake to formulate, develop and apply a national policy which, ... will... in particular ... make primary education free and compulsory.	*Dakar World Education Forum* (2000): We re-affirm (...) that all children, young people and adults have the human right to benefit from an education that will meet their basic learning needs ... Ensuring that by 2015 all children ... have access to and complete free and compulsory primary education of good quality.
International Covenant on Economic, Social and Cultural Rights (1966): Primary education shall be compulsory and available free for all.	
Protocol of San Salvador to the American Convention on Human Rights (1988) The States Parties to this Protocol recognize that ... primary education should be compulsory and accessible to all without cost.	*United Nations Millennium Development Goals* (2000): Ensure that, by 2015, children everywhere, boys and girls alike, will be able to complete a full course of primary schooling.
Convention on the Rights of the Child (1989): States Parties ... shall, in particular... make primary education compulsory and available free for all.	*World Summit Outcome* (2005): We reaffirm our commitment to support developing country efforts to ensure that all children have access to and complete free and compulsory primary education of good quality.
Charter on the Rights and Welfare of the African Child (1990): States Parties to the present Charter ... shall in particular: provide free and compulsory basic education.	
(Revised) European Social Charter (1996): ... the Parties undertake, either directly or in co-operation with public and private organizations ... to provide to children and young persons a free primary and secondary education as well as to encourage regular attendance at schools.	

The process of forging a global education strategy can be summarized as follows. Education for All (EFA) emerged in 1990 through the Jomtien Conference, [104] which was convened against the diminishing coverage of primary education in

---

[104] *Final Report of the World Conference on Education for All: Meeting Basic Learning Needs, Jomtien, Thailand, 5-9 March 1990*, Inter-Agency Commission (UNDP, UNESCO, UNICEF, World Bank) for the World Conference on Education for All, New York, 1990.

the 1980s, especially in Africa, and the reduced governments' capacity to halt further retrogression. The 1990 Jomtien Declaration did not include a requirement for primary education to be free and compulsory. It stated that providing basic education for all was "the unique obligation" of national, regional and local authorities and immediately added that the authorities could not be expected to carry out that obligation alone, hence partnerships would be necessary with families, religious groups, local communities, non-governmental organizations as well as the private sector. Also, the documents generated at Jomtien Conference used terms such as "access to education" or "meeting learning needs" instead of the right to education. Because the Jomtien Declaration was adopted less than one year after the Convention on the Rights of the Child, two divergent approaches impeded a uniform, rights-based global education strategy. The Fourth Global Meeting of the International Consultative Forum on Education for All took place in Dakar on 26-28 April 2000 and adopted the Framework for Action.[105] It was based on the acknowledgment that the commitments made at Jomtien in 1990 had not been met. The World Bank's statement at the World Education Forum referred to free primary education as a long-term plan for the year 2015.[106] The education-related Millennium Development Goal (MDG) was formulated as follows: "Ensure that, by 2015, children everywhere, boys and girls alike, will be able to complete a full course of primary schooling."[107] The 2003/4 EFA Global Monitoring Report commended: "The MDG targets for education, however, are cautiously phrased – they omit the mention of 'free and compulsory' primary schooling."[108] The first review of MDGs, in September 2005, reverted to the formulation used in international human rights law, whereby primary education ought to be free.[109]

This lack of even a rhetorical unanimity, fifteen years long, demonstrates why the entry of human rights in education faces so many obstacles. The long battle to get the word *free* into global documents that address primary education highlights changes within our *international community* within the past two decades. These have influenced the practice of states, which is seen in their divergent interpretations of international human rights treaties which deal with university education.

---

105 The Dakar Framework for Action – Education for All: Meeting Our Collective Commitments, Text adopted by the World Education Forum, Dakar, Senegal, 26-28 April 2000, para. 3, available at http://www2.unesco.org/wef/en-conf/dakframeng.shtm.

106 The World Bank's president at the time, James Wolfenson, supported the "call that by the year 2015 free education be a right for all children up to age 15". Wolfenson, J.D. – A time for action: Placing education at the core of development, Presentation at the World Education Forum, Dakar, 27 April 2000, available at http://www2unecso.org/wef/en-news/coverage_speech_wolfen.shtm.

107 United Nations Millennium Declaration, General Assembly resolution 55/2 of 18 September 2000, para. 19, full text and further information available at www.un.org/millenniumgoals/.

108 *Gender and Education for All: The Leap to Equality: EFA Global Monitoring Report 2003/4*, UNESCO Publishing, Paris, 2003, p. 27.

109 General Assembly – 2005 World Summit Outcome, Doc. A/60/L.1, 20 September 2005, para. 44.

Purchasing power *versus* entitlement at the university

There is a human rights school which should be called fundamentalist because it insists on the text of a treaty that was negotiated decades ago and pursues its literal interpretation. The governments that negotiated it are long gone, the world has changed as has the role of the government in education, but the text should apply as if time stopped with its adoption. A good illustration is the International Covenant on Economic, Social and Cultural Rights, which anticipated that university education would become progressively free. The Committee on Economic, Social and Cultural Rights applies such a fundamentalist interpretation and argues that the Convention should be interpreted as written, despite the changed practice of states.[110] In the 1950s, when the Covenant was negotiated, this sounded like an excellent idea. The premise that education should be free was forcefully advocated by the Soviet Union and her allies. Free university education spanned ideological boundaries (it was accepted, until recently, throughout Western Europe and Latin America). The Covenant was not intended for legal enforcement, which made acceptance of its text easy but this also makes its violations pass with hardly any criticism.

An illustrative example is the United Kingdom. The introduction of tuition for university education in England defied the explicit requirement of the International Covenant on Economic, Social and Cultural Rights [Article 13(2)(c)], whereby access to higher education should be secured through progressive introduction of free education. The tuition fee was initially set at £1,025 for an academic year (25% of the average tuition costs). Moreover, it was introduced just one year after the previous government had announced that it 'had no plans to make students contribute to their fees.'[111] Subsequent controversies have revolved around the amount of tuition, while its charging is taken for granted. The fact that the government did the opposite to the explicit requirement of a human rights treaty to which the United Kingdom is a party, with impunity, demonstrates how little binding force the ICESCR has in practice. Its influence is likely to further diminish because of the shift from treating university education as a right to a profitable business. At the time when tuition fee was introduced, the estimated annual value of United Kingdom's export of education varied between £5 and 12 billion. Further increase was announced in the ambition for the United Kingdom to conquer 25% of the global market share in higher education.[112]

The boundary between free and for-fee education is set differently in domestic laws, sometimes not at all because this legal duality is new. In many countries, the end of compulsory education marks the exit from education as an individual entitlement under public law and the entry into education regulated by private

---

[110] Committee on Economic, Social and Cultural Rights – General comment No. 13: The right to education, U.N. Doc. HRI/GEN/1/Rev.6 (2003), paras. 17-20.
[111] Committee on Economic, Social and Cultural Rights – Third periodic report of United Kingdom of Great Britain and Northern Ireland, U.N. Doc. E/1994/104/Add. 11 of 17 June 1996, para. 231.
[112] Commission on Human Rights – Report submitted by Katarina Tomasevski, Special Rapporteur on the right to education: Mission to the United Kingdom of Great Britain and Northern Ireland (England), 18-22 October 1999, paras. 65-69.

law as a commercial transaction. In quite a few countries, that boundary is blurred. The reasons vary. In some countries, constitutions guarantee the freedom of parents and communities to provide and finance education, without a government commitment to make it free or compulsory. In many, there is a legal guarantee of free and compulsory education, but public primary education, which should be free, is only accessible against the payment of direct charges.

The practice of states parties to the International Covenant on Economic, Social and Cultural Rights, which includes an explicit requirement to make university education gradually free,[113] is slanted in the opposite direction. Even the views of many governments, the *opinion juris* necessary for determining whether governments interpreted their policy as legally required, tend to exhibit a commitment to for-fee rather than free university education. The range of governments' approaches to who has which rights regarding university education is illustrated by Argentina's guarantee of the right to higher education [114] and Australia's assertion of "the freedom to charge fees".[115]

The International Covenant on Economic, Social and Cultural Rights stipulated, in 1966, that post-compulsory education should gradually be made free.[116] Changes in the law during the past decades have reflected the practice of states, which has gone in the opposite direction.[117] Parties to the Covenant divide into five groups by the criterion of their policy on for-fee or free university education. These countries are more likely to be supportive of free university education because the Covenant explicitly states that this should be the case. However, this is far from the case. Governmental policy has been extracted from their reports and they are classified in groups on the for-fee to free diapason, for-fee being the furthest from the Covenant's requirement and free being the closest.

- The first group argues that **university education should be available only against payment.** This group includes countries such as Australia, Canada, Czech Republic, Israel, Ireland, Japan, Luxembourg, the Netherlands, New Zealand, Portugal, and Switzerland.[118] Japan reserved

---

[113] Article 13 (2) (c) says:" Higher education shall be made equally accessible to all, on the basis of capacity, by every appropriate means, and in particular by the progressive introduction of free education."

[114] U.N. Doc. E/1990/6/Add.16, 1997, para. 256.

[115] U.N. Doc. E/1994/104/Add.22, 1998, para. 306.

[116] Article 13 (2) of the ICESCR has repeated the usual formulation whereby primary education should be compulsory and free, adding that secondary education "shall be made generally available and accessible to all by every appropriate means, and in particular by the progressive introduction of free education" and also that "higher education shall be made equally accessible to all, on the basis of capacity, by every appropriate means, and in particular by the progressive introduction of free education."

[117] The UNESCO Convention against Discrimination in Education stipulates that primary education should be free and compulsory, the International Covenant on Economic, Social and Cultural Rights says that "primary education shall be compulsory and available free for all," while the Convention on the Rights of the Child defines as a governmental obligation to "make primary education compulsory and available free for all," urging governments to progressively achieve every child's right to education on the basis of equal opportunity."

[118] U.N. Doc. E/1994/104/Add.22, 1998, para. 307; E/1994/104/Add.17, 1997, para. 365; E/1990/5/Add.47, 2000, para. 606; E/1990/5/Add.39, 1997, para. 617; E/1990/6/Add.29, 2000, para.

51

the right not to be bound by the provision on the "progressive introduction of free education" in secondary and higher education, not affirming a right to education at that level but rather an "opportunity to receive education" through scholarships and reduced tuition for those who cannot avail themselves of that opportunity because of financial reasons.[119] Their justification is similar to that furnished by the government of United Kingdom, whereby "those who benefit from higher education should contribute towards its costs."[120] Also, many developing countries pertain to this group. In the Philippines, more than two-third of university education is provided at private institutions, which charge its full cost.[121] Others, like Guyana, Jamaica, and Nepal argue that they were forced to introduce "a cost recovery programme" while Mongolia describes it as a consequence of the transition from centrally planned to market economy.[122] The government of Jordan says that "the student assumes the full cost of university fees and textbooks, as well as all financial obligations" and the government of Sudan that "the student pays annual fees."[123]

- The second group defines the role of the state as **subsidizing some of the cost** of university education. Brazil's policy is to provide funding to students so as to "defray up to 70% of the fees charged by higher education institutions," while the Dominican Republic defines the purpose of such official assistance to make "the cost of higher education affordable."[124] In Estonia, payments are levied depending on assessments of the students' ability to pay and there is a scheme whereby some pay the full costs, others a part of it, and for a minority the full cost is subsidized. Similarly in Serbia, some students are financed out of government budget while others have to pay for themselves. [125] The government of South Korea "provides long-term tuition loans to students who have financial difficulties" while, similarly, in Tunisia "enrolment fees [are] chargeable to pupils whose parents are in a position to pay them".[126] The government of Russia has acknowledged that official student support constituted a small fraction of their expenses.[127]

- The third group acknowledges that **university education is not free in fact**, whatever the law may say. (It usually says that education should be

---

232; E/1990/6/Add.21, 1998, para. 226; E/1994/104/Add.24, 2001, para. 165; E/1990/6/Add.11, 1996, para. 325; E/1990/6/Add.33, 2001, para. 566; E/1994/104/Add.20, 1997, para. 327; E/1990/5/Add.33, 1996, para. 676.

119   U.N. Doc. E/1990/6/Add.21, 1998, paras. 226-227.
120   U.N. Doc. E/C.12/4/Add.8, 2001, para. 13.72.
121   U.N. Doc. E/1986/3/Add.17, 1994, para. 149
122   U.N. Doc. E/1990/5/Add.27, 1995, para. 108; E/1990/6/Add.28, 2001, para. 146; E/1990/5/Add.45, 1999, para. 46; E/1994/104/Add.21, 1998, para. 121.
123   U.N. Doc. E/1990/6/Add.17, 1997, para. 120 and E/1990/5/Add.41, 1998, para. 92.
124   U.N. Doc. E/1990/5/Add.53, 2001, para. 790; E/1990/6/Add.7, 1994, para. 93.
125   U.N. Docs. E/1990/5/Add.51, 2001, para. 714 and E/1990/6/Add.22, 1998, para. 156.
126   U.N. Docs. E/1990/6/Add.23, 1999, para. 357; E/1990/6/Add.14, 1996, para. 364
127   U.N. Doc. E/1994/104/Add.8, 1995, para. 295.

free.) It includes countries such as Armenia, Azerbaijan, Belgium, Benin, Bulgaria,[128] as well as countries whose governments acknowledge that some payments are levied upon students although this should not be the case, such as Guatemala and Panama.[129]

- The fourth group acknowledges that university education is not completely free of charge but the **government defrays some of the cost and provides students with financial assistance**, usually in the forms of loans. In countries such as Denmark, tuition fees are not charged as is the case in Finland, but other costs are charged to students, who are also entitled to student support, most of which usually has to be repaid. Similarly in France, tuition is not charged but enrolment fees have to be paid, while in Iceland tuition is also not charged to students but they pay registration fees.[130] The policy of defraying most directs costs of university education is usually conditioned on the students' successful performance as is the case in Cyprus.[131]

- The fifth group comprises **governments which keep university education free of charge**. The situation in the Nordic countries is similar, with Norway reporting that "the education itself is free of charge, and the students only pay a small fee which goes towards the activities carried out by the student welfare organizations", which is similar to Sweden.[132] In Latin America, government of Argentina "recognizes and guarantees the right to higher education", in Uruguay "all types of education, including university and higher education, are free of charge" as is the case in Venezuela.[133] In Mauritius "education at the tertiary level is free", in Morocco "every student who fulfils the academic entry requirements has the right of free access to higher education" and in Sri Lanka the commitment is to free primary, secondary and university education.[134] This group includes countries such as Algeria, whose wealth enables them to guarantee that "education is free of charge at all levels" and Libya, where this also includes "free board and lodging", and this was the case in Iraq in the 1990s.[135] The ideological commitment to free education is preserved in North Korea, whose government claims that "education has been completely free in every educational institution since 1959."[136] The

---

128 U.N. Docs. E/1990/5/Add.36, 1998, para. 272; E/1990/5/Add.30, 1996, para. 174; E/1990/6/Add.18, 1997; E/1990/5/Add.48, 2001, para. 330; E/1994/104/Add.16, 1996, para. 310.
129 U.N. Doc. E/1990/6/Add.34, 2002, para. 217 and E/1990/6/Add.24, 1999, para. 323.
130 U.N. Docs. E/C.12/4/Add.12, 2003, para. 407; E/C.12/4/Add.1, 1999, para. 442; E/1990/6/Add.27, 2000, para. 655; E/1994/104/Add.25, 2001, para. 194.
131 U.N. Doc. E/1994/104/Add.12, 1996, para. 356; E/1990/6/Add.10, 1996, para. 230; E/1990/6/Add.19, 1999, para. 321.
132 U.N. Docs. E/1994/104/Add.3, 1994, para. 429 and E/1994/104/Add.1, 2000, para. 255.
133 U.N. Doc. E/1990/6/Add.16, 1997, para. 256;
134 U.N. Docs. E/1990/5/Add.21, 1994, para. 340; E/1990/6/Add.20, 1998, para. 170; E/1990/5/Add.32, 1996, para. 316.
135 U.N. Docs. E/1990/5/Add.22, 1994, para. 230; E/1990/5/Add.26, 1995, para. 190; E/1990/7/Add.15, 1993, para. 20.
136 U.N. Doc. E/1990/6/Add.35, 2002, para. 87.

government of Senegal has a commitment free public education free, even as it acknowledges that it is not accessible to many at the primary level and to the majority at the university level: "from the pre-school level to university, public education is free of charge and received by all pupils and students subject to the availability of places." Similarly, the government of Slovakia has stated that "every citizen has the right to education free of charge at primary and secondary schools and, depending on individual abilities and possibilities of the society, at institutions of higher learning also."[137] The government of Syria has explained that "education is free of charge from the primary level to the end of the university level; the state does not charge any fees for education".[138]

Changes within Europe, epitomized in the Bologna process, have revealed different approaches to for-fee and free university education. The governments of Greece says that "higher education is public and is offered free of charge."[139] Similarly, the government of Germany used to argue that "institutions of higher education must be open to all social strata. This basic idea is incompatible with tuition fees or charges for higher education,"[140] but the Constitutional Court ruled against that policy. The background was that the policy against charging fees has been federal while the financial responsibility for universities pertains to individual states. The ability to charge was deemed necessary to improve the quality of universities.[141]

In Switzerland, the often quoted provision of the International Covenant on Economic, Social and Cultural Rights on the progressive introduction of free higher education was tested before courts and was failed as guidance for education policy. The increase in university registration fees following the financial crisis of universities in the early 1990s was brought before the Federal Tribunal as a breach of the Covenant. The Students' Union at Zurich University took as the case in point the increases in registration fees at Zurich University from 300 francs in academic year 1991/92 to 450 francs in 1993/94 and to 600 francs in 1994/94. The Federal Tribunal rejected the students' claim. It found the Covenant not to be directly applicable but, rather, addressed to the legislator and stated that "an individual may not assert a right to the progressive introduction of free further education." The Tribunal "considered that the legislator had the freedom to choose the means to attain the objective sought, namely to make higher education accessible to all. This objective may be achieved by other means than the progressive introduction of free education, and the term 'in particular' indicated only one of the possible means." [142]

---

137 U.N. Doc. E/1990/6/Add.25, 1999, para. 108.
138 U.N. Doc. E/1990/104/Add.23, para. 236.
139 U.N. Doc. E/1990/5/Add.56, 2002, para. 537.
140 U.N. Doc. E/C.12/4/Add.3, 2000, para. 225.
141 The German Constitutional Court overturns tuition ban, www.heise.de/english/newsticker/ 55581, 26 January 2005, and Germany divided over tuition fees ruling, www.dw-world.de/dw/article/0,1564,1470875,00.htlm, 27 January 2005.
142 U.N. Doc. E/1990/5/Add.33, 1996, paras. 676-677.

Another indictment on HE as an individual?

Further developments in university education may well obliterate the last vestiges of an individual entitlement. The rapid expansion of trade in education services has already transformed the university and the last countries that preserve free university education may have to succumb to the practice of the majority of states. Both common sense and available data tell us that this change will deprive the poor of access to university but what this will mean for girls and women is an open question. Tackling it necessitates, first, an excursion into the uses and abuses of education regarding its effect on equality and inequality and, then, a look at the approaches to gender parity in education which were developed globally in order to attain this goal by 2005. The failure to do so is an apt reminder that the import of human rights may have made a difference.

School reflects its surroundings and tends to reinforce prejudicial portrayals of victims of exclusion and discrimination. Education is embedded in the existing values but also helps create new values and attitudes. Hence, human rights law mandates its deliberate employment to eliminate discrimination. Children learn through observation and imitation, and start perpetuating discriminatory practices much before they learn the word *discrimination*. By the time their curriculum includes this abstract term, *discrimination*, they are likely to have internalized the underlying prejudice. Prejudice is formed in late childhood and adolescence and sustained from one generation to another through social usage. When it favours individual and group self-interest, it is easy to rationalize. Discriminatory practices are outlawed through legal prohibitions and sanctions, but their underlying rationale usually remains unexplored. It is customary to label this underlying rationale as irrational and believe that its cause is ignorance, which can then be eliminated through education. However, the very rationale for exclusion from education is often to preserve privilege. As early as 1957, the first United Nations study into discrimination in education highlighted as its underlying rationale the fear of losing privilege, [143] whose corollary was the denial of the right to education to potential competitors. By the 1990s, the denial of education to potential competitors became part of international trade law, which made it perfectly legal.

The fifth A: Enter affordability

The 1990s were a time of crisis-driven changes in education, which has continued into the new millennium. Governments – not only in developing countries – are struggling with budget deficits and decreasing revenue, public education is a frequent victim. A great deal of effort has been expended to seek other-than-governmental funding for education. Ideological justifications followed suit and the key global actor in education became the World Bank, leading Lyn Davies to ask:" How we ever let a bank decide educational policy will

---

[143] Ammon, C.D. – *Study of Discrimination in Education*, United Nations, New York, No. 1957.XIV.3, August 1957, p. 10.

be a puzzle for educational anthropologists of the future." [144] Objectives of education reform may be worded in terms of lifelong learning and knowledge-based economy, but reforms are driven by fiscal stringency, privatization, and liberalization of trade in education services. Increasing economic competitive-ness, which education is expected to foster, clashes with the values of co-operation and solidarity which underpin human rights. Conflicting demands upon education follow suit. Fostering income-earning skills and competitiveness clashes with protecting equal rights of all.

Proponents of globalization object if education is provided by governments "and so closed to foreign companies". [145] In that vision, education should be traded just like any other service, sold and purchased against a price. Financing by a government would be defined as an illegal state subsidy because it distorts competition. Human rights advocates resort to international human rights treaties whereby most, if not all education, should be provided or at least financed by government. The practice of states is situated in-between these two extremes.

It would be difficult to imagine a complete abolition of public education after it has been part of the global landscape almost two centuries. What the world would look like without any free public education can, unfortunately, be seen in quite a few African countries. The public reaction to an announcement that all education has to be paid, at full price, is easy to predict: a government announcing the end of free education would be unlikely to stay in power if it is accountable to its population. Such a dramatic shift in the policy of any government has not taken place and is not likely to. Education is re-moulded through small, incremental changes which are often opposed when their impact is felt, but this is usually too late. Such changes are seen in the vocabulary, which has obliterated the right to education and replaced it by access to education, the parallel processes of teaching and learning have become "service delivery", and we are no longer people with rights and duties, freedoms and responsibilities, but consumers of public services. [146] Education research has followed suit and "consumers of education" [147] have replaced bearers of human rights.

International human rights law defines education as a human right, interna-tional trade law as a service.[148] This reflects the two conflicting legal regimes for education we have today. International human rights law mandates state intervention, requiring it to ensure – at least – free and compulsory education for

---

[144] Davies, L. – Comparative education in an increasingly globalised world, *Comparative Education Bulletin*, The Comparative Education Society of Hong Kong, No. 7 (2004), p. 6.

[145] Legrain, P. – *Open World: The Truth about Globalization*, Abacus, London, 2002, p. 110-111.

[146] Le Grand, J. – *Motivation, Agency and Public Policy: Of Knights and Knaves, Pawns and Queens*, Oxford University Press, 2003.

[147] Crossley, M. and Watson, K. – *Comparative and International Research in Education: Globalization, Context and Difference*, Routledge Falmer, London/New York, 2003, p. 2.

[148] A detailed analysis of conflicts between international human rights law and international law on trade in services is contained in Tomasevski, K. – Globalizing what: Education as a human right or as a traded service?, *Indiana Journal of Global Legal Studies*, vol. 12, No. 1, Winter 2005, pp. 1-78.

all children. International law on trade in services legitimizes sale and purchase of education, excluding those who are unable to purchase education. Progressive liberalization of trade in education services supplants the requirement of human rights law for the progressive realization of the right to education.

The effects of progressive liberalization of trade in education will be reflected in education after a decade or two because all similar shifts take time to become reflected in educational outputs and impacts. Those in university education are seen already in the flow of students to the wealthiest countries and universities, and the consequent loss of both good universities and graduates in the poor countries.

Globalization of professional and academic qualifications has re-actualized the phenomenon of brain drain: developing-country students tend to stay where they studied. The OECD has reported on the high and increasing number of immigrants with tertiary education as well as programmes to enable foreign graduates to work in their country of study.[149] The return on university education, where the tuition alone could be an annual $30,000, cannot be met by an annual salary of half that sum in the country of origin. In theory, study abroad can be an important channel for the acquisition of knowledge by developing countries.[150] In practice, poor countries are further impoverished by the exodus of those who studied abroad. The lack of good university education at home further fuels their exodus.

Education as an internationally traded service generates immense profits for exporters.[151] Predictably, they have set the tone of negotiations under the GATS, urging other WTO members towards liberalization. Table 4 ranks countries with the largest numbers of foreign students by their number. The largest numbers are studying in the United States and the United Kingdom. It also adds the percentage of foreign students in the total number, which demonstrates that Australia and Switzerland rank first by the proportion of foreign students (18% both). A number of countries where one out of each ten students is foreign points to the efforts to attract foreign students.

---

149 OECD – *Trends in International Migration: Annul Report. 2004 Edition*, Paris, 2005, pp. 132-134.
150 The World Bank – *Knowledge for Development. 1998/99 World Development Report*, Oxford University Press, 1999, p. 146.
151 Global market shares in higher education for 2002 have been reported as 58% for the USA, 24% for the United Kingdom, 10% for Australia, 7% for Canada, and 2% for New Zealand. Böhm, A. et al. – *Vision 2020. Forecasting International Student Mobility: A UK Perspective*, British Council, London, 2004, p. 29.

Table 4
Foreign students in tertiary education,
academic year 2002/2003

Country	Number	% of total
USA	582,996	4
United Kingdom	227,273	10
Germany	240,619	10
France	221,567	10
Australia	179,619	18
Japan	74,892	2
Russia	68,602	1
Spain	53,639	3
Belgium	41,856	11
Canada	40,033	3
Italy	36,137	2
Switzerland	32,847	18
Austria	31,101	14
Sweden	28,664	7
Malaysia	27,731	4
Netherlands	20,531	4
Ukraine	18,170	1
Denmark	18,120	9
New Zealand	17,732	10
Cuba	17,215	7
Jordan	15,816	8
South Africa	15,494	2
Kyrgyzstan	13,440	7
Turkey	12,729	1
Hungary	11,226	3
Lebanon	12,210	8
Portugal	15,692	4
Norway	11,060	5
Saudi Arabia	11,046	2
Czech Republic	10,338	4

Note: Only countries with more than 10,000 foreign students have been listed, and they are listed in descending number of foreign students. Some figures are identical as those for the academic year 2001-2002 (such as for the USA or Japan) and it is possible that the UIS included the data for the previous year if no recent data were available.
Source: Global Education Digest 2004: Comparing Education Statistics Across the World, UNESCO Institute for Statistics, Montreal, 2004, available at www.uis.unesco.org.

In the United States, more than $11 billion was generated in 2000-2001 by foreign students in the USA alone, without an estimated commercial value of the export of US education services to more than a hundred countries. [152] In

---

[152] Commission on Human Rights – Report submitted by Katarina Tomasevski, Special Rapporteur on the right to education: Mission to the United States of America, E/CN.4/2002/60/Add.1, para. 38.

comparison, US aid for education is minuscule, estimated at an annual US$1,45 billion.[153] Moreover, the boundary between international trade in education and aid for education became blurred. In the 1990s, Australia allocated 70% of its aid to education to scholarships for foreign university students studying in Australia, while French aid for education benefited some 100,000 foreign students in France and 8,000 French teachers working in French-speaking Africa.[154]

Table 5
Brain-gain in wealthy countries: Proportion of university-educated foreigners

HOME GRADS

University-educated people born in other OECD countries	University-educated people born outside the OECD	University-educated people born in the country of residence
United States 49.9%	Canada 38.0%	Canada 31.5%
New Zealand 44.6%	South Korea 32.2%	New Zealand 27.2%
South Korea 44.2%	New Zealand 31.0%	United States 26.9%
Canada 40.6%	United States 24.8%	South Korea 26.7%
Sweden 40.1%	Sweden 24.2%	Sweden 22.8%
Switzerland 36.5%	Switzerland 23.7%	Germany 19.5%
France 36.4%	Hungary 19.8%	Switzerland 18.1%
Germany 30.4%	France 18.1%	France 16.9%
Hungary 29.6%	Germany 15.5%	Hungary 10.7%

The country you don't = 100% !! eg France = 71.4%

Source: OECD – Trends in International Migration: Annual Report. 2004 Edition, Paris, 2005, Table II.4: Persons with tertiary education by place of birth, selected OECD countries, p. 127.

how?

Table 5 highlights one facet of the increasing abyss between knowledge-based and education-deficit regions and countries. Rotimi Sankore has singled out the portrayal of African immigrants in the USA, based on the results of the 2000 census, which highlights their excellent educational accomplishments:

Africans have the highest level of education of any foreign-born residents;
Africans are 48% more likely than Asian immigrants to be university graduates;
Africans hold Ph.D. degrees at double the rate of European immigrants;
Africans are better educated than US natives;
Africans hold managerial and professional positions that parallel the levels of European and Asian-born residents. [155]

The abyss between that image and the state of education for Africans in Africa speaks volumes. When education systems have been "pressured into responding

[153] *Education for All Fast Track: The No-Progress Report,* Global Campaign for Education Briefing Paper, www.campaignforeducation.org., 11 September 2003.
[154] IWGE – *Education Aid Policies and Practices. Meeting of the International Working Group on Education (IWGE), Nice, France, 16 – 18 November 1994,* p. 18 and 25.
[155] Sankore, R. – Africa: Killing us softly, *New African,* November 2005, p. 12.

to the logic of free trade,"[156] other 'sectors' will follow. Primary education can be liberalized by governments of countries where it is not universally available and is, accordingly, not compulsory. The GATS allows exempting services provided "in the exercise of governmental authority,"[157] which encompasses compulsory education in the domestic legislation of most countries.[158] The legal situation is complicated and has not yet been addressed within the GATS. International human rights law mandates parental freedom of choice for the education of their children, thus disallowing state monopoly over education. Indeed, public and private education co-exist in most countries, as international human rights law mandates. Free parental choice can be exercised where free public education is guaranteed for all, and the option of private schooling broadens that choice. Where public education is not available or it only exists as "poor education for the poor", that choice is not free. Moreover, where public education should be free but is only accessible against payments, there is no choice at all.

Liberalization of trade in education services without human rights correctives undermines the right to education, which requires ensuring at least compulsory education to be free of charge, available and accessible to all. Even that may not be sufficient to eliminate the existing exclusion, as the continued discrimination against girls demonstrates. Indicatively, the sex of foreign university students is not recorded while gender parity was made *the* priority in global education strategies. This is, perhaps, the best illustration of the driving forces behind the failure of our international community to put into practice the first time-bound target which it committed itself to achieve.

Betrayed promise of gender parity in education

Education can be a means to attain gender equality but also to transmit gender inequality to the next generation. The right to education, and human rights in and through education add a qualitative dimension to the existing global focus on quantitative targets. At the turn of the millennium, global strategies converged around the goal of eliminating gender disparities in basic education

---

[156] Robertson, S.L. et al. – GATS and the education service industry: The politics of scale and global reterritorrialization, *Comparative Education Review*, vol. 46, No. 4, November 2002, p. 495.

[157] Article 1(3) of the GATS says that the term "services" includes any service in any sector except services supplied in the exercise of governmental authority, and then defines "a service supplied in the exercise of governmental authority" to include any service which is supplied neither on a commercial basis, nor in competition with one or more service suppliers.

[158] An affirmation that education constitutes a right in many countries has been furnished by the WTO secretariat: "Given its importance for human and social development, countries throughout the world tend to consider instruction up to a certain level – commonly primary and secondary education – as a basic entitlement. It is normally provided free of charge by public authorities and, in most countries, participation is mandatory. In addition, some degree of private participation in the supply, which varies among countries, exists as well. However, the underlying institutional arrangements may be very diverse, making the separation of public and private domains not always clear." (World Trade Organization, Council for Trade in Services – Education services: Background note by the Secretariat, WTO Doc. S/C/W/49, 23 September 1998, para. 12)

by the year 2005.[159] This target was not attained. Table 6 provides a quantified image of this failure. It lists those countries which were singled out for their gender disparity in primary school. Small or uneven progress shows that the target of gender parity was not attained. Moreover, the situation is usually the worst in those countries where no data has been collected as yet because data gathering tends to be the first step towards change. Table 6 also shows that *[but]* education statistics in primary education is outdated, usually by 3 or 4 years. *[not]* Differently, the data for foreign university students is collected and *[Sender]* disseminated, which points to the existing priorities. *[i.e. money to be made.]*

The British Secretary of State for International Development announced at the beginning of 2005 that at the meeting to assess MDGs "there will be no escaping the fact that we have collectively failed.[160] Such collective failures cannot be remedied because the promises made have carefully avoided affirming the equal rights of girls and reinforcing the corresponding governmental obligations.

Treating education as a human rights rather than a self-contained sector is sorely missing, and could have made all the difference in advancing towards the elimination of gender disparity in education. School girls often have to battle to go to school, as could be seen in the hunger strike of secondary school pupils in Kenya. Regina Kirop, one of the girls on hunger strike to protect excessive school fees at St Mary Mon Secondary School, had fainted during the eight day of hunger strike and was taken to hospital in Eldoret. Another broken promise was in the background: the government promised them scholarships for secondary education after they had refused to submit to female genital mutilation.[161] At the same time in France, newspapers carried photographs of secondary school girls (lycéens) resisting the police armed with shields and helmets, protecting their protest against an educational reform that they considered contrary to their vision of what education should be.[162]

---

[159] The Education for All (EFA) strategy includes a commitment to eliminate gender disparities in primary and secondary education by 2005 and achieve gender equality in education by 2015. (The Dakar Framework for Action – Education for All: Meeting Our Collective Commitments, Text adopted by the World Education Forum, Dakar, Senegal, 26-28 April 2000, para. 3, available at http://www2.unesco.org/wef/en-conf/dakframeng.shtm.) This commitment has been reinforced through its adoption as one of the Millennium Development Goals. (An overview of all globally agreed targets regarding gender equality has been done by UNIFEM in *Progress of the World's Women 2002: Gender Equality and the Millennium Development Goals*, New York, 2003, pp. 4-5)

[160] Department for International Development – *Girls' Education: Towards a Better Future for All*, DFID, London, January 2005, p. iii.

[161] Now girl on hunger strike faints as row on fees rages, *Daily Nation*, Nairobi, 21 April 2005.

[162] Laronche, M. – M. Fillon est accuse de laisser "pourrir" le movement lycéen, *Le Monde*, 9 avril 2005.

+ = better (improvement)
- = worse
O = no diff

only 24 (5.

Table 6
Gender gap in primary school enrolments

Less than 10% starting difference in the enrolment favouring boys				More than 10% starting difference in the enrolment favouring boys			
	1998	2000			1998	2000	
Algeria	-4%	-1%	+	Burkina Faso	-12%	-15%	
Angola*	-8%	-3%	-	Central African R.	-21%	-19%	+
Brazil	-4%	-7%	-	Chad	-26%	-23%	+
Burundi	-7%	-9%		Côte d'Ivoire	-16%	-17%	-
Comoros	-8%	-8%	O	Djibouti	-10%	-8%	+
Egypt	-6%	-5%	+	Ethiopia	-11%	-12%	-
Eritrea	-5%	-6%	-	Guinea-Bissau	-18%	-18%	O
Gambia	-8%	-5%	+	Iraq	-11%	-14%	-
Guatemala	-5%	-4%	+	Morocco	-12%	-7%	+
Guinea	-7%	-11%	-	Niger	-12%	-12%	O
Indonesia	-4%	-1%	+	Papua N. Guinea	-13%	-8%	+
Iran*	-3%	-1%	+	Senegal	-10%	-6%	+
Laos	-6%	-6%	O	Togo	-21%	-18%	+
Lebanon	-2%	-1%	+	Yemen	-33%	-35%	-
Mauritania	-4%	-4%	O				
Mozambique	-8%	-8%	O				
Oman	-2%	0%	+				
Philippines	-2%	+1%	+				
Saudi Arabia	-4%	-7%	-				
Sudan	-8%	-9%	-				
Syria	-7%	-5%	+				
Thailand	-2%	-3%	-				
Tunisia	-3%	-1%	+				
Zambia*	-2%	0%	+				

if need to see enrolmt rates too.

Note: A reduction of the gender gap can be attained if the enrolment of boys is decreased and these countries are marked with an asterisk. In Angola, the boys' enrolment diminished from 61% in 1998 to 39% in 2000, more than was the parallel decrease in the enrolment of girls. Similarly in Iran, the school enrolment of boys decreased from 81% in 1998 to 74% in 2000, and in Zambia it decreased from 74% in 1998 to 66% in 2000.

Source: The percentages have been calculated from the data collected by the UNESCO Institute for Education within monitoring of Education for All (www.unesco.org/education/efa or www.uis.unesco.org).
Only those countries for which the data were available for 1998 and 2000 have been included in the table. Not all the figures are based on precise measurements, many are estimates.

What can happen to school girls without human rights protection was also illustrated in 2003 through the case of Tatu Shabani, who was sentenced to six months in prison for not attending school. [163] Tatu had been a pupil of Mkuyuni primary school in Morogoro, in Tanzania, expelled after she had become pregnant. Pregnancy was a disciplinary offence leading to her expulsion, whereupon she could go to school no longer. Tatu was in a catch-22 situation, formally in breach of the law on compulsory school attendance but unable to

---

[163] Criminal case No. 322 of 2003 at the primary court in Morogoro Region, Tanzania.

comply. How Tatu's case will figure in education statistics is not known but, legally, she became a delinquent by the mere fact of having become pregnant as a primary school pupil. Pregnancy ended both her education and her childhood.

These different cases highlight the rationale for a human rights approach to education so as to capture obstacles beyond – not only within – education. There is an endless stream of policies and statements on what could be done for girls' education. Human rights spell out what *should* be done, using as the yardstick global minimum standards which most states in the world have accepted. Thus, it complements and strengthens development priorities. The key features of human rights law are outlined in Figure 7, through a comparison with the MDGs as the best known global blueprint for development.

Differences highlighted in Figure 7 do not undermine the shared core of global development strategies and international human rights law. Indeed, the focus on poverty reduction makes the right to education a powerful tool for make a change in the lives of girls and women. Poverty has been universally affirmed as a key obstacle to the enjoyment of human rights and it has a visible gender profile. The main reason is that poverty results from violations of human rights, including the right to education, which disproportionately affect girls and women. Various grounds of discrimination combine, trapping girls into a vicious downward circle of denied rights. Denial of the right to education leads to the exclusion from the labour market and marginalization into the informal sector or unpaid work, which perpetuates and increases women's poverty. This circular relationship requires human rights mainstreaming.

The focus of global strategies on the means of education, whereby all girls should start and finish primary school, can be usefully complemented by specifying the ends of their education. Also, since education is a lever to provide girls with choices in life, primary school may be too little. Worse, it can obliterate choice if the girls are taught that their destiny is to be submissive wives and mothers. In the words of Sheikh Abdul-Aziz al-Aqil, "the Muslim woman is a precious jewel whom only her rightful owner can possess, for he has paid dearly for that." [164] He is the breadwinner and her education is an optional extra because it is not meant to make her economically independent, as described for Algeria:

---

[164] Hirst, D. – Educated for a life of enforced indolence, *Guardian Weekly*, 19-25 August 1999.

Figure 7: Differences between human rights law and MDGs

Who?	Obligations of the state International human rights obligations form part of the law of the land. They pertain to the state and are not affected by changes of government.	Political commitments of a government Changes of government through electoral or non-democratic means routinely alter political commitments.
What?	Human rights are grounded in the rule of law Guaranteed rights can be claimed by the population as well as by other states since they form a part of international law. *but no remedy either!*	No remedy for the lack of performance Where monitoring reveals that targets have not been attained, there is no access to justice for those who would have benefited because MDGs do not create entitlements.
When?	Obligations are immediate Minimum global standards are binding upon governments. If beyond their capacity, they can seek international aid.	Long-term goals The year 2015 takes away the immediacy characterizing human rights.
How?	Legal responsibility Human rights bestow upon individuals the right to hold government legally responsible for violations, both domestically and internationally.	Monitoring *data* Accurate and up-to-date do not exist where they are most needed, while attainment benchmarks anticipate continued deprivation and rights deficit.
How much?	All rights for all girls and women Full and equal enjoyment of all human rights and the elimination of all forms of discrimination against women have not yet been attained anywhere, therefore continuous obligations of all governments.	Specified quantitative targets Benchmarks have been defined as "feasible in even the poorest countries", [165] leaving out too many quantitative (e.g. prevalence of child marriage) and all qualitative benchmarks (e.g. aims and contents of education).

Women's work does not have the same function as that of men, whose purpose is to ensure the survival of the family. For women, work is a means of saving. Traditionally, any remuneration that women obtain through work is for their personal use. In Algerian society it is a disgrace for a husband or father to depend upon the earnings of women. A man who can provide enough for his clan or family to live on must, as a sign of wealth, flaunt the fact that neither his wife nor his daughters have the need to work.[166]

International human rights law lays down a three-fold set of criteria, whereby girls should have an equal right to education, equal rights in education, and their equal rights should be promoted through education. The steps in meeting these requirements consist of, first, overcoming their exclusion from education. The global priority for girls' education has made large indents in their exclusion

---

[165] U.N. Doc. A/59/282 (2004), para. 77.
[166] Boulahbel-Villac, Y. – *The integration of Algerian women in France: a compromise between tradition and modernity, International Migration Policies and the Status of Female Migrants: Proceedings of the United Nations Expert Group Meeting on International Migration Policies and the Status of Female Migrants, San Miniato, Italy, 28-31 March 1990*, United Nations, New York, Sales No. E.95.XIII.10, 1995, p. 125.

promising to bring it to an end. The segregation of girls into separate schools is often the subsequent step. Separate educational institutions for girls and boys are envisaged in international human rights treatics.[167] The third step typically comprises assimilation of girls into schools designed for boys, to then move towards adapting education to girls.

Separate schools for girls and boys were an international norm as late as 1960. At the time, the UNESCO Convention on Discrimination in Education legitimised separation on the grounds of sex, religion and language. The rapporteur for that Convention, Pierre Juvigny, explained that "the separation of schools for pupils of the two sexes was still too widespread in practice for the Convention to be able to affirm that, at the international level, it amounted to a proscribed form of discrimination."[168] Although in the famous words of the US Supreme Court separate is always unequal, segregation in education persists for various reasons. Its human rights impact is not assessed, however. The European Commission on Human Rights has not held that the existence of single-sex schools constituted a form of discrimination.[169] The US Supreme Court has found single-sex higher educational institutions to be unconstitutional because they limited professional opportunities for the excluded sex.[170]

Promoting equality of opportunity through affirmative action for women has generated much controversy and a large number of court cases. In the United States, race has been the principal focus. The thrust of the jurisprudence towards legitimizing affirmative action in the 1960s has been reversed already in the 1970s to take a further slant against affirmative action in the 1990s. The US Supreme Court faulted quotas based on race and ethnicity as unconstitutional in 1978, [171] and subsequent jurisprudence outlawed the use of lower admission criteria for non-white applicants.

Preferential treatment for immigrants had been upheld by the Equal Opportunity Commission of the Netherlands,[172] in the form of training courses opened only to immigrants to facilitate their entry into the labour market. Discriminatory denial of access to women was found by the Dutch courts to have been practices by an association of hotelier-catering schools. They had determined a 50-50 ratio of students with the justification that such a ratio was

---

167 The UNESCO Convention against Discrimination in Education discourages separate educational systems or institutions, but permits them "for pupils of the two sexes, for religious or linguistic reasons, and private education is also permitted if its object is not to secure the exclusion of any group." The Convention on the Elimination of All Forms of Discrimination against Women has envisaged coeducation as a means towards the elimination of gender stereotypes, but has explicitly endorsed separate educational institutions, mandating that girls should have "access to the same curricula, the same examinations, teaching staff with qualifications of the same standard and school premises and equipment of the same quality."

168 Juvigny, P. – The Fight against Discrimination: Towards Equality in Education, UNESCO, Paris, 1963, p. 18.

169 European Commission on Human Rights – Applications No. 10228/82 and 10229/82, Decisions of 6 March 1984, Decisions & Reports, vol. 37, 1984, p. 96.

170 US Supreme Court – US v. Virginia, Judgment of 26 June 1996, and Missisipi University for Women v. Hogan, 458 U.S. 718, Judgment of 1 July 1982.

171 US Supreme Court – California v. Bakke, 438 U.S. 265, Judgment of 28 June 1978.

172 Equal Opportunity Commission of the Netherlands – Ruling 1997-121 of 28 November 1997.

required by the labour market. Since the number of female was much bigger than the number of male applicants, a complaint was lodged because many more women were rejected. The Dutch courts have found for the complainants, basing their judgment on the legal prohibition of discrimination and emphasizing that demands of the labour market could not override the law.[173]

Integrating girls in mainstream schools without altering the curricula and textbooks perpetuates the stereotypes that impede gender equality. School textbooks tend to portray women at home while men are making history. A survey of women in primary school textbooks has revealed that in Peru, for example, women are mentioned ten times less than men.[174] In Croatia, a study of secondary school textbooks has shown sons to span 42% of the material on family life and daughters only 17%.[175] A study of school textbooks in Tanzania has revealed that girls doing domestic chores were the favourite topic for explaining to children English and Kiswahili grammar.[176] This type of analysis is the first step towards change, which is taking place rapidly, in many countries and in all regions of the world. There are, however, obstacles.

The change of terminology from sex to gender challenges the historically constructed inferior role for women in public and private life, in politics and in the family, within and out of school, in the labour market and in the military. The purpose of human rights is to challenge and change this discriminatory heritage.

Research into the effects of education on poverty reduction has demonstrated the importance of secondary rather than merely primary education. Also, without secondary and university education, primary education is doomed to extinction because there will be no teachers. For girls, this is not only associated with the shortage of female teachers in many countries. Similar research findings show that secondary education helps to eliminate child marriage and/or early childbearing. Education statistically decreases fertility levels when it is at least seven years long.[177]

The length of schooling is, of course, only one component, the content of education is crucially important. A statement by the government of Laos, whereby "women's duties include bringing up children, as well as other

---

[173] Hof's-Gravenhage – Judgment of 27 October 1992, NJ 1993/680.

[174] Valdes, T. and Gomariz, E. – *Latin American Women: Compared Figures*, Instituto de la Mujer and FLASCO (Facultad Latinoamericana de Sciencias Sociales), Santiago de Chile, 1995, p. 105.

[175] Summarized results of the research projects entitled Portrayal of Women in Croatian Textbooks, carried out by a team led by Branislava Baranovic of the Institute for Social Research, are available on the website of women's human rights group B.a.B.e. (Be active, Be emancipated) at httn://members.tripod.com/~CRWOWOMEN/augustoo.htm.

[176] Mbilinyi, D.A. – Women and gender relations in school textbooks, in: Mbilinyi, D.A. and Omari, C. (eds.) – *Gender Relations and Women's Images in the Media*, Dar es Salaam University Press, Dar es Salaam, 1996, p. 93-94.

[177] *Women's Education and Fertility Behaviour. Recent Evidence from the Demographic and Health Surveys*, U.N. Doc. ST/ESA/SER.R/137, United Nations, New York, 1995; Singh, S. and Samara, R. – Early marriage among women in developing countries, *International Family Planning Perspectives*, vol. 22, No. 4, December 1996, p. 153.

[handwritten margin notes, top: "double discrimination? Dangers, of conflict? reinforcement of repressive cultural values."]

household duties"[178] depicts continued resistance to changing gender roles. Governments should take the lead because parental investment in their daughter's education may be negatively influenced by custom. In Bangladesh, "marriage of a female child often entails a considerable financial burden on the parents, and it is often perceived that investments made in the education of the girl child may not benefit her own family but the family of her husband and in-laws."[179]

Education is not financially self-sustaining, especially basic schooling for the poor. Hence, it was made governmental responsibility. What girls can later do with their education determines whether such education will become financially sustainable. Also, it influences private choices made by the parents and the girls themselves. If women cannot be employed or self-employed, own land, open a bank account, get a bank loan, if they are denied freedom to marry or not to marry, if they are deprived of political representation, education alone will have little effect on their lives. All other human rights – or the lack thereof – profoundly affect education. *[handwritten: a the other way round]* *[handwritten margin: ole with discuss in what's the pt of educat.]*

The right to education has been demonstrated to act as a corrective to the free market, with a growing acceptance of the necessity for government intervention. The importance of free public education for girls has been summarized by the government of Lebanon thus:

> It is worth pointing out that there is a connection between the preponderance of females over males in free education, as females outnumber males in State education in particular (and most of them are from low-income families). By contrast, there is a higher ratio of males to females in private fee-paying education (and the proportion of those from middle- and high-income families is appreciably higher than is the case in State education). This suggests that males take preference over females when the family has to pay fees to educate their children. The high cost of education and the diminishing role of the State school may therefore result in the practice of discrimination against females, as well as breaches of the principle of equal educational opportunities for both sexes. [180]

[handwritten: Cd. little use if live in repressive society. Other freedoms & rights have to be addressed.]

---

[178] U.N. Doc. CRC/C/8/Add.32 (1996), para. 74.
[179] U.N. Doc. CRC/C/3/Add.38, 1995, para. 52.
[180] U.N. Doc. CRC/C/70/Add.8, 2000, para. 209.

3

Acceptability

Within education, acceptability is denied only in terms of quality while human rights law imposes wide-ranging requirements. The need to integrate human rights in education is the most visible in this area as well as the least feasible because this process would dismantle the 'education industry'.
The yardstick of acceptability would necessitate ascertaining what is – and is not – acceptable to people (including small people whom we call children) and changing the contents and methods of teaching and learning accordingly.

The use of the child's mother tongue and/or language used at home during the introductory stage of public education would alter the recruitment and training of teachers as well as the design of learning materials. Democratizing decisions on what to teach and how would (almost certainly) eliminate the economies of scale which underpin the prevailing uniformity. Comparative studies have revealed "a high degree of homogeneity and consistency" in the contents of education. [181] More than half of the total instructional time in the first years of primary school is devoted to the three Rs reading, 'riting, and 'rithmetic). Educational systems then diverge in adding another language (as in Sub-Saharan Africa and Western Europe) or devoting a great deal of instructional time to religion (as in Middle East and North Africa). [182] Despite permanent calls for reforming education and endless initiatives, these features change so little in time and space as to appear immutable. Moreover, they are not seen as subject to change because the design of education is very, very rarely subject to public debate, least of all open to challenge.

Integration of human rights in education has triggered challenge and change. This has taken place occasionally, in the few corners of the world where people have been bestowed with a right to question the language of instruction, or the contents of history textbooks, or the use of corporal punishment.

Numerous court cases have been fought about acceptability of education, probing into its ends and means, orientation and contents, human rights safeguards for teaching and learning. Although such cases are brought up by an individual, they often raise systemic or policy issues. Much jurisprudence has been created under the European Convention on the Human Rights, since it was chronologically the first human rights treaty to establish supra-national legal

---

[181]   Benavot, A. and Kames, D. – *The Curricular Content of Primary Education in Developing Countries*, The World Bank, Washington, D.C., 1989, p. 48.
[182]   IBE – Instructional time and teaching subjects during the first four years of primary education, *Educational Innovation and Information*, No. 96, September 1998, International Bureau of Education, Geneva, 1998.

enforcement. International human rights law was interpreted to require "the State actively to respect parental convictions within the public schools" [183] in addition to its obligation to respect parental liberty to establish and operate alternative schools. International human rights bodies have confirmed that the law "prohibits any indoctrination of pupils".[184] Human rights challenges have gone particularly far in redressing denials of freedom of and in education. [185] Where a government made education secular, parents typically mounted legal challenges demanding religious education for their children. Conversely, where religious education was provided in public schools, parents demanded "freedom from religion". There is a rule of inverse correlation in this subject-matter and those education systems which conform to the definition of indoctrination do not permit challenge. Those that strive to be acceptable and permit challenge have the largest number of cases. The absence of litigation should not be mistaken for the absence of problems. Rather, problems remain unchallenged – and thus unsolved – as long as the affected individuals are deprived of the right to challenge education which they find unacceptable.

Censorship of school textbooks has been subjected to litigation rarely. A prominent *Ienaga* case in Japan (1965-1997), about descriptions of Japanese war atrocities during the Second World War in school textbooks, was discussed elsewhere.[186] The powers of state and locally elected school boards to determine education policy and curricula of public schools have been affirmed by US courts,[187] including decisions on the selection of school textbooks as well as the selection of books in school libraries. [188] In Canada, a 1997 decision to ban from kindergarten and primary school books used as teachers' reference depicting children with same-sex parents was nullified by the court because it had been made on religious grounds regardless of the requirement that schools be secular.[189] McDonalds took to court a Dutch publisher of schoolbooks because of the inclusion of a previously published newspaper article into a textbook for learning Dutch because that article depicted food offered in McDonalds restaurants as unhealthy and referred to the company's abusive practices in South America. The Dutch courts have found against McDonalds, deeming that the inclusion of the text had purely didactical purposes and noting that

---

[183] European Commission on Human Rights – *Kjeldsen, Busk Madsen and Pedersen v. Denmark*, Report of the Commission of 21 March 1975, and the judgment of the European Court of Human Rights, vol. 21, series B, p. 44 and 46.

[184] European Commission on Human Rights – *Graeme v. United Kingdom*, Decision of 5 February 1990, *Decisions & Reports*, vol. 64, 1990, p. 158.

[185] Different from human rights guarantees for religion, which affirm freedom of religion but not freedom in religion, those relating to education affirm both freedom of education (requiring states to allow non-state schools) and freedom in education (requiring states to recognize rights of learners in education, including their rights to question and challenge school curriculum, textbooks, methods of instruction, rules for school discipline or their administration and enforcement).

[186] Tomasevski, K. – *Education Denied: Costs and Remedies*, Zed Books, London, 2003, pp. 181-182.

[187] *Board of Education v. Pico*, 457 U.S. 853, 1982.

[188] *Smith v. Board of School Commissioners of Mobile County*, 827 F. 2d 684 (11th Cir.) 1987; *Mozert v. Hawkins County Board of Education*, 827 F. 2d 1058 (6th Cit.) 1987.

[189] Supreme Court of British Columbia – *James Chamberlain et. al v. The Board of trustees of School District No. 36 (Surrey)*, A972046, judgment of 16 December 1998.

McDonalds did not reacted when the newspaper article had originally been published. [190]

Such questions demonstrate how intriguing an apparently 'technical' choice of a particular text can be, let alone major decisions about a version of history which the young are required to learn. Although endless decisions shape education defining its content and context, they are rarely discussed as an exercise of power.

Government as educator, violator, regulator

Human rights law imposes upon education the requirement not to violate human rights. This collides with a widespread image of education as something inherently good. Endless campaigns demand more education, not a single one has been launched, as yet, *against* education where it violates human rights. A government whose policy is to violate human rights will do so in education. This policy one can see today in a handful of countries, such as Burma (Myanmar) or North Korea. In Burma, one can capture the gist of what the young are taught because the law lists children's duties. It stipulates that "every child shall abide by the following: (i) upholding and abiding by the law; (ii) obeying the advice and instructions of parents or guardians; (iii) pursuing education peacefully in conformity with the guidance of teachers; (iv) abiding by school discipline, work discipline and community discipline; (v) cherishing and preserving the race, language, religion, culture, customs and traditions."[191] The government of North Korea is the only one in the world which claims that the right to education is fully enjoyed by everybody: "By the progressive education system and the popular policy of education, every citizen fully enjoys the right to education. The right to education and its realization is guaranteed by the Constitution and the legislation on education. Education has been completely free in every educational institution since March 1959 by the Cabinet Decision on abolishing tuition fees. In the DPRK, there is nobody who has not received primary education thanks to the universal compulsory primary education system that has been enforced since 1956."[192] There is no independent verification of that assertion, however. The United Nations Commission on Human Rights adopts annual resolutions on "systematic, widespread and grave violations of human rights" in Korea, which have emphasized restricted access to the country as well as restricted access to information.[193] How many countries could be added where the government as educator fails to respect human rights is a question that can be answered only when assessments of education by human rights criteria become a part of both education and human rights work.

---

[190] Hof Leeuwarden, Judgment of 28 June 1989, NJ 1991/18, upheld by Hoge Raad, Judgment of 15 June 1990, No. 14181, NJ 1991/432.

[191] Initial report under the Convention on the Rights of the Child, 1995, CRC/C/8/Add. 9, paras. 27 and 118.

[192] U.N. Doc. E/1990/6/Add.35, 2002, paras. 84 and 87-88.

[193] Commission on Human Rights – Situation of human rights in the Democratic People's Republic of Korea, resolution 2005/11, adopted on 14 April 2005 with a vote 13-9-14.

Furthermore, governments that today profess adherence to human rights violated them *through* education not even a generation ago. In Canada, education was designed to deny human rights, especially to the indigenous. Gregory Dickinson has described

> the government's scandalous use, until the 1970s, of residential schools run under the auspices of churches and religious orders, whose mandate of assimilation was carried out by removing young children from their communities and families to be placed in institutions where they were punished for using their native languages and practicing their religions, and frequently sexually and physically abused by their teachers. [194]

There have been few challenges of human rights violations *through* education thus far. They target the government as a violator of human rights and are immensely difficult to tackle by international actors which work in education through that very government. They face a dilemma. Refusing to acquiesce to a governmental policy that violates human rights is likely to lead to their inability to continue working in that country. The price of staying on and facilitating development of education is their silence about on-going abuses. Upsetting a government that violates human rights is much more risky than turning one's back on the individuals whose rights have been violated. The price of speaking out is leaving the country and abandoning any improvement in its education they were striving to achieve. (And, almost always, the loss of a part of the budget.) Because this dilemma requires weighing values in conflict and paying the price whichever is chosen over another, it is avoided whenever possible.

Less difficult and less controversial facets of the interface between education and human rights revolve around the role of the government as a protector rather than a violator. This has become particularly pertinent with increased privatization of education, where the government is seen as a merely a regulator. The Supreme Court of India was faced in 1992 with a situation prevalent in many countries, mushrooming of private schools and universities unregulated by the state in the name of protecting freedom. Numerous 'schools' were established, keen to collect money from parents but, often, neither willing nor able to provide an education worthy of the name. The Court has found that education was too important to be left to an unregulated free market. It has added that the government should not remain passive and explained its obligations thus:

> This Court judicially noted mushroom growth of ill-equipped and understaffed unrecognized educational institutions in Andra Pradesh, Bihar, Tamil Nadu and Maharashtra and other States too are no exceptions. Obviously the field of education is found to be fertile, perennial and profitable business venture with least capital outlay. This case is one such case from the State of Maharashtra.
> It would appear that individuals or societies, without complying with the statutory requirements, establish educational or training institutions ill equipped to impart education and have students admitted, in some instances despite warnings by the

---

[194] Dickinson, G.M. – The right to education in Canada, *International Journal for Education Law and Policy*, vol. 1, 2004, Issue 1-2, Special Conference Edition, p. 82.

State Government and in some instances without knowledge of the State Government concerned, but with connivance at lower levels.
The ill-equipped and ill-housed institutions and sub-standard staff therein are counter-productive and detrimental to inculcating spirit of inquiry and excellence in the students. The disregard of statutory compliance would amount to letting loose of innocent and unwary children. [195]

Human rights law has thus affirmed the power and the corollary responsibility of the state to ensure that educational institutions conform to minimum standards (safety, water, sanitation, or qualifications of teachers). This entails defining the quality standards, bestowing permits or licenses upon individual educational institutions, and permanent monitoring so as to ensure that the required standards are applied in practice. A constitutional challenge of this power of the state in the Philippines has involved restrictions upon the parental right to educate their children according to their own values and a diminution of rights and liberties of school owners and teachers. The applicants have argued that parental freedom and freedom of establishing and running educational institutions should be protected against interference by the state. This line of argument has been rejected by the Supreme Court, which has upheld the constitutionally affirmed power of the state to control education so as to safeguard human rights of all involved as well as the public interest which education should promote. The Court has added that any intervention by the state ought to be accompanied by access to justice so as to enable challenging any alleged abuse of this power of the state.[196] A proper balance between the state's right to control and freedom of individuals and communities to shape education so as to make it acceptable by their own yardstick is by definition difficult to attain.

The right to education is defined, as is customary in human rights, in terms of the relationship between the individual and the state. In private education, the state is merely the regulator. In public education, access to school is legally enforceable in many countries but impoverishment of public education has highlighted the problem of quality. Access to schools of intolerably poor quality complies with quantitative targets and the statistics look good. It does nothing for the process of teaching and learning; the graduates may finish their 'education' illiterate and innumerate. Hence, *quality education* is a constant reminder that such quality is often lacking, that unacceptably poor education can be found in wealthy not only in poor countries. There is no human-rights blueprint for the quality of education because human rights lawyers, obviously, do not have professional competences beyond the law. Rather, human rights law enables challenging education of poor quality. Such cases enable the victims of neglect to hold the government responsible, using its guarantee that education should satisfy the minimal quality standards as the yardstick. This requires applying abstract legal principles to specific circumstances and, in many parts of the world, the law is created this way, through court cases. Each of them presents

---

[195] Supreme Court of India – *State of Maharashtra v. Vikas Sahebrao Roundale and Others*, judgment of 11 August 1992, paras. 2-3 and 12, 4 *Supreme Court Cases* 435.
[196] Supreme Court of the Philippines – *Philippine Association of Colleges v. Secretary of Education*, G.R. No. L-5279, 31 October 1955.

a real-life story which is used as window through which to view what happens in education in real life.

Poor public education in rich countries: The New York case

The United States of America [197] is an illustrative example of the complexity of human rights law. A great deal of on-going litigation aims to force individual states to ensure a minimum quality of education for all. Nominally, everybody has equal rights but there is no right to education in the US Constitution. The formal position of the US federal government that education is not a human right originates, in part, from the fact that it is not the federal government but governments of individual states that are responsible for education. Although human rights language is not much used against individual states, its counterpart – their obligations – is used a great deal.

Education is an enforceable right almost throughout the USA but this may amount to no more than forcing children to attend school, which does not imply that they learn. In the United States, 'the right to acquire useful knowledge' and/or an 'identifiable quantum of education' and 'basic minimum skills' was affirmed by the Supreme Court.[198] The right to education had initially been affirmed by the Supreme Court in *Brown v. Board of Education,* one of the most often quoted court cases in the history of education. The Court stated that "education, where the state had undertaken to provide it, is a right".[199] The politics of electing the Supreme Court judges results in its output altered when judges of particular ideological and political slant are supplanted by a different one. Thus, the very Supreme Court that had held education to be a right later decided that education is not a right [200] but rather a privilege.[201] Nevertheless, in 48 out of 50 states of the USA provision of public education is mandated by the states' constitutions and is recognized as a crucial function of the state. [202]

---

[197] A description and analysis of the key features of the right to education in the USA is contained in the report on my mission, carried out just two weeks after 9/11. Commission on Human Rights – Report submitted by Katarina Tomasevski, Special Rapporteur on the right to education: Mission to the United States of America, 24 September – 10 October 2001, U.N. Doc. E/CN.4/2002/60/add.1.

[198] US Supreme Court – *Meyer v. Nebraska,* 262 U.S. 390, 4 June 1923; *San Antonio Independent School District v. Rodriguez,* 411 U.S. 1, 21 March 1973.

[199] US Supreme Court – *Brown v. Board of Education,* 347 U.S. 483, 17 May 1954.

[200] US Supreme Court – *San Antonio Independent School District v. Rodriguez,* 411 U.S. 1, 21 March 1973.

[201] US Supreme Court – *Missouri ex rel. Gaines v. Canada,* 305 U.S. 337, 12 December 1938.

[202] US Supreme Court has acknowledged two dimensions of education. Firstly, for the political one, the Court has affirmed 'the public schools as a most vital civil institution for the presentation of a democratic system of government' ((*Abington School District v. Schempp,* 374 U.S. 203, 17 June 1963), as the primary vehicle for transmitting societal values (*Ambach v. Norwick,* 441 U.S. 68, 17 April 1979), as well as affirming that education is necessary 'to prepare citizens to participate effectively and intelligently' in the political system (*Wisconsin v. Yoder,* 406 U.S. 205, 15 May 1972). Secondly, education has been singled out as providing the basic tools 'by which individuals might lead economically productive lives' and denial of education is an unreasonable obstacle to advancement on the basis of individual merit (*Plyler v. Doe,* 457 U.S. 202, 15 June

Moreover, in 45 out of 50 states legal challenges of public financing have been mounted with the aim of enforcing an education of acceptable quality.[203]

A judgment of the Supreme Court of New York, which vindicated the entitlement to education of acceptable quality for poor, especially non-white children, demonstrates both advantages and disadvantages of the legal enforcement of the right to education. The most important advantage is the power of the courts to challenge governmental policies that deny children's right to education worthy of the name. This criterion has been termed 'adequacy' in the United States.[204]

The case was initiated in May 1993 and the final judgment was adopted in June 2003. The final ruling obliged the State of New York to ascertain the "actual cost of providing a sound basic education" and to reform public financing of education so that all school age children would have access to schools adequately resourced to provide such 'sound' education. The State of New York did not comply and the judicial follow-up continued in 2004 and compliance has not been ensured in 2005.[205] Extracts from the judgment follow:

> Plaintiffs, comprised of students, parents and organizations concerned with education issues, challenge New York State's funding of New York City's public schools. After pre-trial motion practice, appeals, and discovery, two claims were tried before this court from October 12, 1999 to May 15, 2000.
>
> In the first of these two claims, plaintiffs assert that the State has failed to assure that New York City's public schools receive adequate funding to afford their students the 'sound basic education' guaranteed by the Education Article of the New York State Constitution.
>
> In their second claim, plaintiffs assert that the State's funding mechanisms have an adverse and disparate impact upon the City's minority public school students – who comprise 73% of the State's minority students and approximately 84% of the City's public school enrollment -- in violation of specific implementing regulations of Title VI of the Civil Rights Act of 1964.
>
> The court holds that the education provided New York City students is so deficient that it falls below the constitutional floor set by the Education Article of the New York State Constitution. The court also finds that the State's actions are a substantial cause of this constitutional violation.
>
> *A. Summary of the Structure of New York City's Public Schools*
> New York City's public school system is the largest school district in the United States, comprised of approximately 1100 schools serving a student population of 1.1 million. In the 1999-2000 school year New York City's public schools employed over 135,000 people, including approximately 78,000 teachers, 19,000

1982); education 'prepares individuals to be self-reliant and self-sufficient participants in society' (*Wisconsin v. Yoder*, 406 U.S. 205, 15 May 1972).

[203] Rebell, M.A. and Wardenski, J.J. – *Of Course Money Matters: Why the Arguments to the Contrary Never Added Up*, Campaign for Fiscal Equity, New York, January 2004, p. 10, available at www.cfequity.org.

[204] Schrag, P. – *Final Test: The Battle for Adequacy in America's Schools*, The New Press, New York, 2003.

[205] A full chronology and documentation is available on the website of the Campaign for Fiscal Equity (www.cfequity.org) which filed the lawsuit.

teachers' aides, and 13,000 other administrators and pedagogical employees.

The students served by the New York City public schools come from varied backgrounds. Approximately 37% of students are Latino; 35% are African-American; 15.5% are White; 11.5% are Asian; and less than 1% are American Indian or Alaskan Native. Close to 180 languages and dialects are spoken by students as their native tongue. BOE classifies approximately 16% of City public school students as Limited English Proficient (LEP), a designation given to students who score below the 40th percentile on a language assessment test. The large number of English Language Learners (ELLs) in New York City is not surprising given that almost one in eleven students is a recent immigrant.

A defining characteristic of the New York City public school system is its high concentration of students from poor and low income families. In the 1998-99 school year, approximately 442,000 children – out of a total student attendance that year of 1,093,071 – came from families receiving Aid to Families with Dependent Children. In the 1997-98 school 73% of students from kindergarten through 6th grade were eligible to participate in the free lunch program, compared with 5% in the rest of the State. A large number of New York City public school students have special needs that require them to attend full-time or part- time special education programs. As of December 1, 1997, the most recent figure submitted in evidence, more than 135,000 students were enrolled in such programs.

The intersection of factors such as students' poverty, immigration status, and limited English language proficiency means that New York City has a high proportion of students at risk for academic failure.

B. Measuring a Sound Basic Education By Inputs and Outputs

In its 1995 decision the Court of Appeals directed this court to evaluate whether New York City public school students are receiving a sound basic education by examining both inputs, the resources available in public schools, and outputs, measures of student achievement, primarily test results and graduation rates. The inputs listed by the Court of Appeals fall into three large categories:

1. minimally adequate teaching of reasonably up-to-date basic curricula such as reading, writing, mathematics, science, and social studies, by sufficient personnel adequately trained to teach those subject areas;

2. minimally adequate physical facilities and classrooms which provide enough light, space, heat, and air to permit children to learn; and

3. minimally adequate instrumentalities of learning such as desks, chairs, pencils, and reasonably current textbooks.

A substantial number of BOE's approximately 1100 facilities require major infrastructural repair to items such as roofs and facades. Many more facilities are plagued by overcrowding, poor wiring, pock-marked plaster and peeling paint, inadequate (or non-existent) climate control, and other deficiencies that speak of a history of neglect.

2. The Causal Link Between Inadequate School Facilities and Student Outcomes

Plaintiffs presented numerous SED and BOE witnesses who testified that the physical plant of a school can have a marked effect upon learning. In the case of absent or obsolete science labs the connection is obvious. Students cannot learn a subject without the requisite tools to do so. Similarly, computer science classes, and the use of computers to support other subjects, cannot happen in schools that have antiquated wiring. The evidence is conclusive that the numerous City school buildings with these deficiencies impede learning.

Plaintiffs also offered probative evidence that the totality of conditions in crumbling facilities can have a pernicious effect on student achievement. As

former SED Commissioner Thomas Sobol testified:
If you ask the children to attend school in conditions where plaster is crumbling, the roof is leaking and classes are being held in unlikely places because of overcrowded conditions, that says something to the child about how you diminish the value of the activity and of the child's participation in it and perhaps of the child himself. If, on the other hand, you send a child to a school in well-appointed or [adequate facilities] that sends the opposite message. That says this counts. You count. Do well.
The court finds that this evidence is credible as it is based on the experience and intuition of knowledgeable educators. However, this evidence does not attempt to gauge the magnitude of the effect of school facility condition upon student performance.

G. Overcrowding and Class Size
Overcrowding has numerous negative consequences for students. Specialized spaces in school, such as gymnasiums, science labs, libraries and art rooms must be taken over for full-time classroom space thereby depriving students of the programs intended for those rooms. Marginal spaces in a school building, including undersized offices, hallways, and storage space, have been converted to classrooms.
Many school administrators have had to resort to the use of trailers and other temporary structures. Such structures outside the main school building isolate teachers and students from the rest of the school and often occupy much-needed playground space. The students taught in the temporary structures still must use the main school building's cafeteria and gymnasium. Temporary structures are often difficult to heat and they frequently lack sufficient power for computers. ...

I. Outputs: Graduation/Dropout Rates and Test Scores
The most telling measures of student performance are the percentage of students who actually graduate and the bundle of knowledge and skills that they possess on the day that they graduate. Accordingly, the court examines below evidence concerning: 1) how many students graduate on time, 2) how many drop out, 3) the nature of the degrees graduates receive, and 4) the performance of those who pursue higher education at the campuses of the City University of New York.

V. CAUSATION
There is a causal link between funding and educational opportunity. Many of the subsidiary findings of fact that form the foundation for this finding have been recited above. To summarize, the court has already found, inter alia, that:
Effective teachers and school administrators can boost student performance. New York City's school administrators and teaching force, particularly in its neediest districts, are inadequate.
Smaller class sizes can have a marked positive effect on student performance, particularly in early grades. At present New York City's school buildings are too overcrowded to effectively address this problem.
New York City's school buildings are in many cases so dilapidated or antiquated as to impede learning. Conversely, better school facilities can boost student achievement by providing students with the resources they need, such as up-to-date science labs, adequate climate control, and sufficient electrical capacity for computers and other instructional aids.

VII. REMEDY AND ORDER

New York State has over the course of many years consistently violated the Education Article of the State Constitution by failing to provide the opportunity for a sound basic education to New York City public school students. In addition, the State's public school financing system has also had an unjustified disparate impact on minority students in violation of federal law.

This court has held that a sound basic education mandated by the Education Article consists of the foundational skills that students need to become productive citizens capable of civic engagement and sustaining competitive employment. In order to ensure that public schools offer a sound basic education the State must take steps to ensure at least the following resources, which, as described in the body of this opinion, are for the most part currently not given to New York City's public school students:

1. Sufficient numbers of qualified teachers, principals and other personnel.

2. Appropriate class sizes.

3. Adequate and accessible school buildings with sufficient space to ensure appropriate class size and implementation of a sound curriculum.

4. Sufficient and up to date books, supplies, libraries, educational technology and laboratories.

5. Suitable curricula, including an expanded platform of programs to help at-risk students by giving them 'more time on task.'

6. Adequate resources for students with extraordinary needs.

7. A safe orderly environment.

In the course of reforming the school finance system, a threshold task that must be performed by defendants is ascertaining, to the extent possible, the actual costs of providing a sound basic education in districts around the State. Once this is done, reforms to the current system of financing school funding should address the shortcomings of the current system, by, inter alia:

1. Ensuring that every school district has the resources necessary for providing the opportunity for a sound basic education.

2. Taking into account variations in local costs.

3. Providing sustained and stable funding in order to promote long-term planning by schools and school districts.

4. Providing as much transparency as possible so that the public may understand how the State distributes School aid.

5. Ensuring a system of accountability to measure whether the reforms implemented by the legislature actually provide the opportunity for a sound basic education and remedy the disparate impact of the current finance system.

Finally, the court directs defendants to examine the effects of racial isolation on many of the City's school children. There is significant social science research that indicates that this isolation has a negative effect on student achievement. There is also some nascent research that indicates that steps to increase racial and socio-economic integration may be more cost effective in raising student achievement than simply increasing funds allocated to high percentage minority schools.

The court hereby declares that defendants' method for funding education in the State of New York violates plaintiffs' rights under The Education Article of the New York State Constitution; and

The court further declares that defendants' method for funding education in the State of New York violates plaintiffs' rights under regulations passed by the U.S. Department of Education pursuant to Title VI of the Civil Rights Act of 1964; and

The court orders that the defendants shall put in place reforms of school financing and governance designed to redress the constitutional and regulatory violations set forth in this opinion. Defendants shall have until September 15, 2001 to implement these reforms. The parties shall appear before the court on June 15, 2001 to describe the progress of these reforms. The court will retain jurisdiction over this matter for as long as necessary to ensure that the constitutional and statutory/regulatory violations set forth herein have been corrected. [206]

This case has demonstrated the need for persistence having taken a full decade. Those who were at school when the case had started finished school long ago. Thousands of pages of expert testimony and endless hearings were needed to determine what minimal quality criteria should be in place. Additional efforts have been necessary to force the authorities to comply with the court's orders. This process epitomizes the need for human rights protection and difficulties in securing it. It is always recalcitrant governments that ought to be forced to put into practice what they have promised in their constitutions.

Human rights safeguards for teaching

Although it is teachers who translate educational curricula into a language which children and young people can understand, there is little mention of teachers – even less of their rights – in global education strategies. Although education depends on the commitment and competence of teachers, inquiries into their fate often reveal that neither their labour rights nor their trade union freedoms are protected, despite fundamental international labour standards being legally enforceable in many countries as well as internationally.

In the words of Canada's Supreme Court, "teachers are the medium of the educational message;" the younger their learners, the more vulnerable they are to teachers' abuse of trust and influence.[207] Restrictions upon teachers are the greatest at the primary school level because young children are susceptible to proselytizing and/or indoctrination. They constitute a 'captive audience', as the US courts have often said. Academic freedom is fully recognized only at the university, "a community of scholars and students enjoying substantial internal autonomy".[208] In the words of the Supreme Court of the Philippines, academic freedom protects people and institutions to "inquire, discover, publish and teach the truth as they see it in the field of their competence."[209]

There has been no hesitation on the part of courts to affirm that teachers ought to be qualified to teach, including a perfect command of the language in which they will teach.[210] Such requirements upon teachers should be accompanied by an affirmation of *their* rights. Governments themselves often reports that this is

---

206 *Campaign for Fiscal Equity v. State of New York*, 187 Misc. 2d 1 (Sup. Ct. N.Y. Co. 2001).
207 Canadian Supreme Court – *Ross v. New Brunswick School District No. 15*, [1996] 1 S.C.R., paras. 44, 45 and 42-43.
208 Canada's Supreme Court – *Harelkin v. University of Regina*, [1979] 2 S.C.R. 561.
209 Supreme Court of the Philippines – *Tangonan v. Cruz Pano*, G.R. No. L-45157, 27 June 1985.
210 Australia's Human Rights and Equal Opportunity Commission – *Maria D'Souza v. Peter Geyer and Directorate of School Education*, No. H94/100, 1995-1996, and *T. v Department of Education of the State of Victoria*, No. H96/149, 1 July 1997.

[handwritten margin notes: this is work; right issue; Time; pressures; 2nd job; to do; reduces; time to prep; Not so much; Quality; issue; quality; issue still]

not the case. The government of Cambodia has pointed out that teachers are obliged to exercise a "secondary activity (e.g. as motorcycle taxi drivers or as farmers) in order to feed their families."[211] The Asian Development Bank has estimated teachers' salaries in Tajikistan at $5 per month,[212] which is much below the global poverty line of $1 per day, globally assessed as necessary for sheer survival. Similarly in Ukraine, the average income of teachers have fallen below "the officially established national subsistence minimum."[213]

A large part of the problem derives from commitments to *deliver education* as cheaply as possible. Because teaching is labour intensive and a large part of educational budget are teachers' salaries, the teachers are the first casualty of fiscal austerity. When teachers' status and wages were affected by structural adjustment programmes, the Freedom of Association Committee found that "a structural adjustment policy should not be detrimental to the principles of freedom of association and collective bargaining."[214] This finding has not been translated into practice in many, many countries. The ILO has also objected to the denial of the right to collective bargaining. Where the national law, in countries such as Germany, India or the Philippines[215] denied teachers the right to bargain collectively and the right to strike, the government should ensure that this protection is afforded.[216] Also, delays in the payment of teachers' salaries have constituted a problem in many countries, "fraught with serious social consequences."[217] These consequences have been exacerbated through the model for financing education, developed by the World Bank.

The World Bank's Fast Track Initiative (FTI)[218] has undermined governmental human rights obligations by a funding model that reinforces discretionary – and inadequate – budgetary allocations for education, at odds with international human rights law.[219] That framework was developed by extracting key education

---

[211]   Initial report of Cambodia under the Convention on the Rights of the Child, CRC/C/11/Add.16, 1998.

[212]   Dedolph, C. – Mongolia: Education for all, *ADB Review*, vol. 35, 2003, No.4: Education, available at www.adb.org.

[213]   Kasianov, G. – The impact of the ECHR on rights in and to education in Ukraine, in: De Groof, J. and Lauwers, G. (eds.) – *No Person Shall Be Denied the Right to Education: The Influence of the European Convention on Human Rights on the Right to Education and Rights in Education*, Studies in Human Rights in Education, Wolf Legal Publishers, Nijmegen, 2004, p. 599-601.

[214]   Freedom of Association Committee – 275th Report, 1990, Case No. 1537 (Niger), para. 103.

[215]   Freedom of Association Committee – 300th Report, 1995, Case No. 1514 (India); para. 21.

[216]   Freedom of Association Committee – 300th Report, 1995, Case No. 1514 (India); para. 21.

[217]   Report of the Committee on the Application of Standards, Part II, p. 112.

[218]   The FTI is described as "a global partnership between donor and developing countries" aimed at accelerated progress towards universal primary education by 2015. It encompasses "all major donors for education" and thereby amplifies World Bank's approach to education with respect to all poor countries with a "serious commitment" to achieve the education-related MDG goal, evidenced in their "sound national education plans." (The full description is available at www1.worldbank.org/education/efafti, 1 June 2005)

[219]   The absence of any reference to the international legal obligations of the states within the HIPC and/or FTI has prevented subsuming this process under the rule of law. The consequence is that commitments negotiated within HIPC and FTI can hinder rather than facilitate compliance with international human rights law. (Commission on Human Rights – Annual report of the Special Rapporteur on the right to education, Katarina Tomasevski, U.N. Doc. E/CN.4/2002/60, paras. 17-18) The disconnect between international legal requirements and HIPC and/or FTI strategies

policies pursued by those countries which were assessed by the World Bank as having been successful in meeting the minimum quantitative targets.[220] The background were calculations based on aggregates and averages. For example, "a teacher's salary in French-speaking Africa was 7.8 times the per capita income, whereas in English-speaking Africa it was 4.6 times more," [221] and teachers' salaries were set at 3.5 times per capita income. While this substituted governmental (or the World Bank's) fiat for collective bargaining, it also entailed considerable reductions in teachers' salaries in many countries.

A parallel strategy have been 'contract teachers' and Senegal can be taken as the case in point. A 1995 Education Volunteers Project aimed at recruiting and deploying 1,200 young people with a lower secondary education diploma, after a three-month pedagogical training, to teach for four years at half the salary level of qualified teachers. The CEART objected to 'the use of volunteers with minimal training.' The effects of the use of volunteers ('contract teachers') on the status of professional teachers were predictable.[222] The Conseil d'Etat of Senegal invalidated in 2000 the automatic exclusion of all physically disabled people from teaching. The case was initiated by the Senegalese National Association for Motor-Handicapped People (ANHMS) against the government.

is illustrated by the duration of primary education which is below the globally accepted minimum, or the denial of teachers' trade union freedoms as well as collective bargaining, as well as continued charges in primary education. (Commission on Human Rights – Annual report of the Special Rapporteur on the right to education, Katarina Tomasevski, U.N. Doc. E/CN.4/2003/9, paras. 12-13) For example, the EFA-FTI Status Report noted in November 2004 for Vietnam that "user fee charges remain a barrier to education in poor areas" and for Niger that teachers' salaries had been brought down as "contract teachers have a wage level that equals 3.9 times GNP per capita versus civil servant teachers whose average salary is more than 9 times GNP per capita." (Education for All (EFA) – Fast Track Initiative (FTI) – Status report prepared for the Education for All Fast Track Initiative Annual Meeting, November 10-12, 2004, FTI Secretariat. (www1.worldbank.org/education/efafti)

220 The background to the identification of FTI benchmarks was an analysis of the performance of the 155 developing countries, amongst which 36 were singled out as having accomplished the completion of primary education and 30 as likely to reach that goal by 2015. The focus was on those countries which were not likely to achieve universal primary education and thus needed international support, especially the 55 poorest. The analysis found that success in universalizing primary education depended more on education reform that increased funding. It identified eight key variables that ought to be altered so as to conform to the averages in the countries assessed as successful. These were (1) government revenues of 14-18% of GDP, (2) education expenditure of 20% of the recurrent government budget, (3) 50% of recurrent education expenditure for primary education, (4) average teachers' salaries of 3.5 GDP per capita, (5) pupil-teacher ratio 40:1, (6) 33% of recurrent education spending for non-salary costs, (7) the average repetition rate of 10% or lower, and (8) private enrolments of 10% of the total. (*Achieving Education for All by 2015: Simulation Results for 47 Low-Income Countries*, Africa Region and Education Department, The World Bank, Washington D.C., 24 April 2002, mimeographed) In the two following years the benchmark concerning private enrolments disappeared, the annual 850 to 1000 hours of instruction was added as was the construction cost of $10,000 or less per classroom, while the objective of attaining 100% intake rate for both girls and boys by 2010 and 100% completion rate for both sexes by 2015 was made explicit. *(Education for All (EFA) – Fast Track Initiative. Progress Report*, 26 March 2004, Doc. DC2004-0002/1, p. 3)

221 Mehrotra, S. – Improving cost-effectiveness and mobilizing resources for primary education in Sub-Saharan Africa, *Prospects*, vol. 28, No. 3, September 1998, p. 471.

222 Joint ILO/UNESCO Committee of Experts on the Application of the Recommendation concerning the Status of Teachers, Fourth Special Session, Paris, 15-18 September 1997, CEART/SP/1997/SP/13, Part D. Allegation received from the Single and Democratic Union of Senegal (SUDES), paras. 18-22.

The ANHMS asked the court to annul a decision of the Education Volunteers Employment Board on the exclusion of people with disabilities from employment as volunteer ('contract') teachers. That model had been developed so as to employ "volunteers", who may have been equally well educated and trained, but paid less than teachers with the full status. The Conseil d'Etat ruled in favour of the ANHMS. [223] South Africa's Constitutional Court also addressed the problem of 'contract teachers' and faulted a requirement for teachers to be citizens. The Court found that 'non-citizens are a minority in all countries and have little political muscle' and also rejected the Government's justification of the denial of teaching posts to non-citizens by providing employment to its own citizens, by giving preference to the provision of quality education.[224]

For teachers to have a collective voice in the creation of education strategy, they need to be represented. International human rights law provides for collective bargaining and trade union freedoms as the key safeguards. The ILO Freedom of Association Committee has affirmed, many times, that teachers have the right to strike,[225] including protest strikes, aimed at criticising a government's economic and social policies.'[226] Anti-union discrimination through labelling teachers' trade union work as "incitement to revolt and insubordination" constitutes a human rights violation.[227] The Human Rights Committee has also confirmed that "freedom to engage in political activity individually or through political parties, freedom to debate public affairs, to criticise the government and to publish material with political content" applies to university teachers, whether they are part of the public service or not.[228]

Language as barrier to learning

The language of education can be an insurmountable obstacle to children's learning. If the children do not understand the language, no learning can take place. A survey of education in the least developed countries in 1995 revealed that in Benin, Cape Verde, Togo and Zambia 100% of pupils were taught in a language different from the one they spoke at home; in Burkina Faso it was 94%, in Equatorial Guinea 98%, and in Tanzania 91%.[229] International ranks of language proficiency, which constantly show superior performance of learners in the North, reflect the fact that "the language of instruction is the same as the

---

[223] Case No. 12/2000, 29 June 2000, in Kane, I. – Direct application of the International Covenant on Economic, Social and Cultural Rights in France and francophone African countries, *INERIGHTS Bulletin*, vol. 13, 2000, pp. 53-55.)

[224] South Africa's Constitutional Court – *Larbi-Odam v. The Member of the Executive Council for Education (North-West Province)*, SA 745 (CC), 1998.

[225] Freedom of Association Committee – 272nd Report, 1990, Case No. 1503 (Peru), para. 117.

[226] Freedom of Association Committee – 304th Report, 1996, Case No. 1863 (Guinea), para. 358.

[227] Freedom of Association Committee – 295th Report, 1994, Case No. 1699 (Cameroon), para. 268.

[228] Human Rights Committee – *Adimayo M. Aduayom, Sofianou T. Diasso and Yawo S. Dobou v. Togo*, Communications No. 422/1990, 423/1990, and 424/1990, Views of 12 July 1996.

[229] Postlethwaite, N. – The conditions of primary schools in least-developed countries, *International Review of Education*, vol. 44, 1998, No. 4, p. 306.

language spoken at home by a dominant proportion of the pupils."[230] Table 8 illustrates the existing linguistic diversity and raises an obvious question: how are very poor countries with large number of languages supposed to cope to preserve them?

Table 8: Countries with the highest number of endemic languages

COUNTRY	NUMBER OF LANGUAGES
Papua New Guinea	847
Indonesia	655
Nigeria	376
India	309
Australia	261
Mexico	230
Cameroon	201
Brazil	185
Congo/Kinshasa	158
Philippines	153
United States	143
Vanuatu	105
Tanzania	101
Sudan	97
Malaysia	92
Ethiopia	90
China	77
Peru	75
Chad	74
Russia	71
Solomon Islands	69
Nepal	68
Colombia	55
Côte d'Ivoire	51
Canada	47

Source: Harman, D. and Malfi, L. – Are linguistic and biological diversity linked? *Conservation Biology in Practice*, vol. 3, 2002, No. 1, pp. 26-27.

The process of extending the right to education to colonized peoples, minority, indigenous and migrant children routinely entailed a requirement upon them to adapt to whatever formal schooling has been available. Adaptation required them

---

[230] Naumann, J. – Curriculum and languages: teaching in African languages and learning strategies, in: *Curriculum Development and Education for Living Together: Conceptual and Managerial Challenges in Africa, Final Report of the Seminar held in Nairobi, Kenya, 25-29 June 2001*, International Bureau of Education and Kenya National Commission for UNESCO, Geneva, 2003, p. 35.

to abandon their mother tongue: "'My people lost their freedom when schooling expanded throughout our communities', says Rafael Chanchari from the Shawi people of Peru. They were rebuked 'whenever they did not do what our teachers considered proper.' Now himself a teacher, Rafael looks back at how the education imposed on the people of the Peruvian Amazon alienated while generations from their cultural heritage."[231] They were placed in schools that provided instruction in an alien language and taught them history that denied their very existence. Exposure of such abuses came much later:

> Important studies have been realized during the last years to overcome the traditionalist Euro-centric and colonialist premises of language teaching and learning in education. Thus:
>
> - It is no longer common practice to punish pupils speaking African languages during breaks in the schoolyard.
> - It is more and more accepted that teachers and pupils use (vehicular) African languages to ask questions or to explain difficult issues (although the practice of 'awarding' a donkey's hat to pupils not sufficiently versed in using French is not yet extinct in Senegalese schools. [232]

This process has often been underpinned by inclusive educational goals ("all children to school"), but denied the right to be different. In practice, formal schooling has involved assimilation, and assimilation entailed uniformity. The model of education was built on the key characteristics of the earliest self-granted bearers of the right to education, favouring the male over female, the colonizer over the colonized. The language of the colonizer became the language of instruction and is, still, parental preference because they see it as offering their children a path towards formal employment and advancement. A guide for language policies in African schools thus outlined the two sides of the coin:

> When one goes out into the field to listen to the questions raised by pupils' parents, it is easy to discover which directions should be taken and which points should be developed to give the campaign the impact it requires. That is why a preliminary inquiry is necessary amongst the people to pick up the main criticisms of the education system as it stands. The analysis of those criticisms indicates the community's worries and hopes for change in schools. The most common comments heard in the villages are:
> a) Education is a problem for experts, we know nothing about syllabuses;
> b) Our children never succeed at school; most of them become lazy and unproductive;
> c) Schoolchildren all want to be 'whites', they have no respect for illiterates and their values;
> d) School encourages the flight by young people into town.
> In answer to these worries, the sensitization campaign in the villages could be based on the following ideas:

---

[231] Trapnell, L. – Identity crisis, *Developments*, Second Quarter 2003, p. 9.
[232] *Curriculum Development and Education for Living Together: Conceptual and Managerial Challenges in Africa. Final Report of the Seminar held in Nairobi, Kenya, 25-29 June 2001*, International Bureau for Education (IBE), The Kenya National Commission for UNESCO and the UNESCO Nairobi Office, IBE, Geneva, 2003, p. 37.

a) The use of national languages gives the school back to the village and the community;
b) The use of national languages will avoid children being behind, will decrease the failure rate caused by learning in a foreign language too early and will maintain the child in the work environment;
c) The use of national languages attributes the real value to the country's own culture and ancestral traditions;
d) The use of national languages is a brake on rootlessness and the flight from the countryside.[233]

Parental choice of language for their children, where it is recognized, has an impact on the preservation of indigenous and minority languages because, as Andrew Dalby has said, "success means belonging to the elite; to belong to the elite you must speak the official and international language." [234] Our vocabulary reflects the hierarchy of rights-holders and the rights-less. Former colonizers freely move around the world with the full range of self-granted rights as "expatriates" while the colonized are denied rights as "migrants". Similarly, speakers of international languages, especially English, provide expensive services for their mastery, internationally examined, graded and certified, while those speaking a "vernacular" are denied even a right to call their language by its proper name. Table 9 shows the most widely spoken languages two decades ago. While English remains the first (or second) language for roughly the same number of people, the numbers of people who are learning English are estimated at one billion. [235]

Table 9
Ten most widely spoken languages in 1975 and 2000

LANGUAGE	SPEAKERS IN MILLION	SPEAKERS IN MILLION
Chinese (Mandarin)	650	874
English	358	341
Russian	233	167
Spanish	213	358
Hindi	209	366
Arabic	125	175
Portuguese	124	176
Bengali	123	207
German	120	100
Japanese	110	125

Sources: For 1975: The principal languages of the world (based on Sidney Culbert's work), *1976 World Almanac*; for 2000: *Sharing a World of Difference: The Earth's Linguistic, Cultural and Biological Diversity*, UNESCO Publishing, 2003.

[233] Poth, J. – *Language Planning in a Plurilingual Educational Context (African Edition)*, Centre international de phonétique appliqué (CIPA), Mons, 1997, p. 36.
[234] Dalby, A. – *Language in Danger: The Loss of Linguistic Diversity and the Threat to Our Future*, Columbia University Press, 2003.
[235] The triumph of English: A world empire by other means, *The Economist*, 22 December 2001.

Inadequate human rights law

International human rights law affirms the right of each state to determine official languages as well as languages of instruction. As Table 10 shows, human rights treaties use negative formulations when defining language rights, opting for 'nobody shall be denied.' This is interpreted as not imposing any obligation upon the government except to tolerate the use of various languages by people in private: "A State may choose one or more official languages, but it may not exclude, outside the spheres of public life, the freedom to express oneself in a language of one's choice." [236] Such a formal acknowledgment that children do *not* have a right to be taught in a language they understand so that they can learn is gradually being replaced by less restrictive formulations. Nevertheless, international human rights law has not evolved much.

Table 10: Global human rights standards regarding language

UNESCO Convention against Discrimination in Education (1960)   It is essential to recognize the right of members of national minorities to carry out their own educational activities, including the maintenance of schools and, depending on the educational policy of each state, the use or the teaching of their own language, provided however: (i) That this right is not exercised in a manner which prevents the members of these minorities from understanding the culture and the language of the community as a whole and from participating in its activities, or which prejudices national sovereignty;   (ii) That attendance at such schools is optional.
International Covenant on Civil and Political Rights (1966)   In those States in which ethnic, religious or linguistic minorities exist, persons belonging to such minorities shall not be denied the right, in community with other members of their group, to enjoy their own culture, to profess and practice their own religion, or to use their own language.
ILO Indigenous and Tribal Peoples Convention (1989)   Measures shall be taken to ensure that members of the [indigenous and tribal] peoples have the opportunity to acquire education at all levels on at least an equal footing with the rest of the national community. Education programmes and services for the [indigenous and tribal] peoples shall be developed and implemented in co-operation with them ...   In addition, governments should recognize the right of these peoples to establish their own educational institutions and facilities, provided that such institutions meet minimum standards established by the competent authority in consultation with these peoples. Appropriate resources shall be provided for this purpose.   Children belonging to the [indigenous and tribal] peoples shall, whenever practicable, be taught to read and write in their own language or in the language most commonly used by the group to which they belong. When this is not practicable, the competent authorities shall undertake consultations with these peoples with a view to the adoption of measures to achieve this objective.   Adequate measures shall be taken to ensure that these peoples have the opportunity to attain fluency in the national language or in one of the official languages of the country.
Convention on the Rights of the Child (1989)   In those States in which ethnic, religious or linguistic minorities or persons of indigenous origin exist, a child belonging to such a minority or who is indigenous shall not be denied the right, in community with other members of his or her group, to enjoy his or her own culture, to profess and practise his or her own religion, or to use his or her own language.

---

[236] Human Rights Committee – *Davidson and McIntyre v. Canada*, Communications Nos. 359/1989, Views of the Committee, 31 March 1993, U.N. Doc. CCPR/C/47/D/359/1989/385/ 1989, para. 11.4.

The UNESCO Convention against Discrimination in Education, adopted in 1960 as shown in Table 10, includes the least human-rights-friendly definition, emphasizing that education in a language different from the official language of a country may not be permitted and, if it is, it is provided in separate schools created on the basis of parental demand, whose attendance cannot be obligatory. [237] That Convention is more than \forty years old and reflects the spirit of the time, when education was seen as a right of the state rather than an individual, least of all an indigenous, minority, or migrant right. One of the oldest and most famous judgments of the European Court of Human Rights on the language of education, from 1967, also reflects such a human-rights un-friendly vision of education. The European Court of Human Rights has affirmed the right of the State to determine official languages of the country which are thus the languages of instruction in public schools and denied that there was a right to education in a language of one's choice.[238] The negative formulation relating to the right to education, that "nobody shall be denied" rather than that everybody has the right to education, reflected the unwillingness of governments during the first decade after the Second World War to affirm the right to education. The Court upheld that narrow approach in 1967. An excerpt from its judgment follows:

The Belgian Linguistic Case [239]
The negative formulation indicates ... that the Contracting Parties do not recognise such a right to education as would require them to establish at their own expense, or to subsidise education of any particular type or at any particular level.
There neither way, nor is now, any question of requiring each State to establish [a general and official education system], but merely guaranteeing to persons subject to the jurisdiction of the Contracting Parties the right, in principles, to avail themselves of the means of instruction existing at a given time ...
[T]he Protocol consequently guarantees, in the first place, a right of access to educational institutions existing at a given time, but such access constitutes only a part of the right to education. For the 'right to education' to be effective, it is further necessary that, *inter alia*, the individual who is the beneficiary should have the possibility of drawing profit from the education received, that is to say, the right to obtain, in conformity with the rules in force in each State, and in one form or another, official recognition of the studies which he has completed ...
In particular, [the Convention] does not specify the language in which education must be conducted in order that the right to education should be respected.

---

[237] The Convention lays down the law thus: "When permitted in a State, the following situations shall not be deemed to constitute discrimination: (b) the establishment or maintenance, for religious or linguistic reasons, of separate educational systems or institutions offering an education which is in keeping with the wishes of the pupils' parents, if participation in such systems or attendance at such institutions is optional and if the education provided conforms to such standards as may be laid down or approved by the competent authorities..." (Convention against Discrimination in Education, adopted on 14 December 1960 by the UNESCO General Conference and in force as of 22 May 1962)

[238] European Court of Human Rights – *The Belgian Linguistic Case*, Judgment of 23 July 1968, Series A, vol. 6, p.31.

[239] European Court of Human Rights – *Case "relating to certain aspects of the laws on the use of languages in education in Belgium"*, judgment of 9 February 1967, Series A (Judgments and Decisions), 1966-1967, vol. 5, Strasbourg, 1967.

It must be concluded that if they had intended to create for everyone within their jurisdiction a specific right with respect to the language of instruction, [the Contracting Parties] would have done so in express terms ...

[The Convention] does not require of States that they should, in the sphere of education or teaching, respect parents' linguistic preferences, but only their religious and philosophical convictions. ... Moreover, the 'preparatory work' confirms that the object [of the Convention] was in no way to secure respect by the State of a right for parents to have education conducted in a language other than that of the country in question; ...

In the present case the Court notes that Article 14 [prohibiting discrimination], even when read in conjunction with Article 2 of the Protocol [on the right to education], does not have the effect of guaranteeing to a child or to his parent the right to obtain instruction in a language of his choice. The object of these two Articles, read in conjunction, is more limited: it is to ensure that the right to education shall be secured by each Contracting Party to everyone within its jurisdiction without discrimination on the ground, for instance, of language. This is the natural and ordinary meaning of Article 14 read in conjunction with Article 2. Furthermore, to interpret the two provisions as conferring on everyone within the jurisdiction of the State a right to obtain education in the language of his own choice would lead to absurd results, for it would be open to anyone to claim any language of instruction in any of the territories of the Contracting Parties.

The International Covenant on Civil and Political Rights, adopted in 1966 and in force as of 1976, specifies that members of minorities should not be denied the right to use their own language, the Convention on the Rights of the Child includes a similar provision for indigenous children and children belonging to minorities. This was, again, a reflection of the reluctance of governments, acting collectively to recognize minority rights as collective rights. Furthermore, learning other-than-official languages does not create claims upon governments to provide and/or finance such education. However, international prohibitions of discrimination include language, thus protecting educational institutions – both public and private – which preserve and enrich linguistic diversity. The exercise of parental choice can be a key to preserving and enhancing linguistic diversity. However, it is recognized only in law rather than in practice in many countries and, in addition, it can often only be exercised only if the parents bear the cost of their linguistic choice. The ILO Indigenous and Tribal Peoples Convention, adopted in 1989, includes far reaching safeguards for indigenous peoples and languages but it has been ratified by less than one-third of the countries in the world thus far. [240] Moreover, because the indigenous tend to be disproportionately poorer than non-indigenous, substantial and sustained public funding is needed if their rights affirmed in international law are to become real.

The Convention on the Rights of the Child, also adopted in 1989, highlights the importance of mother tongue during the first stages of education, reinforcing the objective of human rights whereby "the individual, guaranteed substantive equality of treatment, has the right to learn his or her own language in addition

---

[240] The Indigenous and Tribal Peoples Convention (No. 169) was adopted in 1989. Its text and information on ratifications is available at www.ilo.org.

to the official language."[241] While this objective would alter the very definition of education to the benefit of millions of children whose underperformance in school results from being forced to learn in an alien language, the law does not oblige governments to do much. Controversies span decision-making on the official language(s) of instruction for public schools, the teaching of as well as teaching in minority languages as well as the recognition thereof. In a series of cases, the Human Rights Committee has affirmed that no right to education in a minority language (or any other use of that language, for that matter) exists when a state has explicitly declined to undertake any international human rights obligations which entail the recognition of minorities and the corollary guarantees of their rights.[242] The Committee has been particularly accommodating of governments which deny, against all factual evidence to the contrary, that minorities exist on their territory.

France is a case in point. The Human Rights Committee had a series of communications regarding Breton language,[243] alleging violations of Article 27 of the International Covenant on Civil and Political Rights (ICCPR). Upon accession to the ICCPR, France declared that "Article 27 was not applicable" because, as it explained in its reports, "France is a country in which there are no minorities".[244] The Committee accepted this position and, in a case dealing with a Breton-speaking person's claimed right to interpretation to and from French, it concluded in 1990:

> The Committee finds that the French courts complied with [fair trial guarantees]. The author has not shown that he, or the witnesses called on his behalf, were unable to address the tribunal in simple but adequate French. In this context, the Committee notes that that the notion of fair trial does not imply that the accused be afforded the possibility to express himself in a language which he normally speaks with a maximum of ease. If the court is certain, as it follows from the decision of [the lower and higher criminal courts] that the accused is sufficiently proficient in the court's language, it is not required to ascertain whether it would be preferable for the accused to express himself in a language other than the court's language. French law does not, as such, give everyone the right to speak his own language in court. Those unable to speak or understand French are provided with the services of an interpreter. This service would have been available to the author had the facts required it; as they did not, he suffered no discrimination ... on the ground of his language.[245]

---

[241] Wilson, D. – *Minority Rights in Education*, available at www.right-to-education.org. (May 2005)

[242] Human Rights Committee – *Dominique Guesdon v. France*, Communication No. 219/1986, Views of 25 July 1990; *Yves Cadoret and Herve Le Bihan v. France*, Communications Nos. 221/1987 and 323/1988, Views of 11 April 1991; *Herve Barzhig v. France*, Communication No. 327/1988, Views of 11 April 1991.

[243] Human rights Committee – Communications No. 220/1987 *T.K. v. France* and No. 222/1987 *M.K. v. France* were declared inadmissible on 8 November 1989.

[244] U.N. Docs. CCPR/C/22/Add.2 and CCPR/C/46/Add.2.

[245] Human Rights Committee – Views concerning communication No. 219/1986, *Dominique Gueson v. France*, 26 July 1990.

In 1999, France signed the European Charter for Regional or Minority Languages,[246] and the reactions were heated. An excerpt illustrates the tone of public debate:

> The Socialist-led government's decision to adopt a mere 39 of the 98 clauses of the European Charter on Regional and Minority Languages has set off a wave of nationalist passion ... Jean-Marie Rouart, the youngest member of the French Academy, has lamented: "At the very moment that our language is being bastardized by Anglo-Saxon expressions, it is to be undermined from within by having to compete with local dialects." To give regional languages such "exorbitant rights" as those suggested in the Charter was to "begin a process which will sooner or later lead to separatist demands, violence and the dismantling of French identity. France must not be Balkanized.[247]

Invoking *balkanization* as a reminder than linguistic, ethnic and religious diversity can implode into warfare and genocide illustrates the key obstacle to affirming and cherishing linguistic diversity.

Why is language so controversial?

No government can have an obligation to ensure teaching and learning of all languages in the country as this would be simply impossible. There is disproportion between some 200 states in the world, mostly unilingual, and the diversity of languages, estimated at 6000. Education should be a principal means for preserving linguistic diversity but is often designed to enhance homogeneity (usually called 'nation-building') by making one and only language official. Whereas it is theoretically possible to provide court interpreters to translate the testimony of witnesses from a great variety of languages, the provision of a formal educational system is based on the premise that there are a substantial number of pupils speaking or writing the same language.[248]

Only few countries in the world have adopted multi-lingualism as their policy. Singapore, for example, "has four official languages i.e. Malay, Chinese, Tamil and English. Malay is the national language while English is the language of administration. A fundamental feature of Singapore's education system is the bilingual policy which ensures that each child learns both English and his mother tongue so as to maintain an awareness of his cultural heritage whilst

---

[246] The European Charter for Regional and Minority Languages was adopted by the Council of Europe on 5 November 1992 and by the end of 2004 has been ratified by 17 out of 46 member states. France is among the 12 states that that have signed but not yet ratified it. The Charter defined regional or minority languages as those "traditionally used within a given territory of a State by nationals of that State who form a group numerically smaller than the rest of the population; and different from the official language(s) of that State; it does not include either dialects of the official language(s) of the State or the languages of migrants."
[247] The French language: Our lingo, by jingo, *The Economist*, 3 July 1999.
[248] Tabory, M. – Language rights as human rights, *Israel Yearbook on Human Rights*, vol. 10, 1980, p. 214.

acquiring the skills to manage in a modern, industrialised economy."[249] Singapore's minister for education in 1986, Tony Tan Keng Yam, had this to say:

> Our policy of bilingualism, that each child should learn English and his mother tongue, I regard as a fundamental feature of our education system. Children must learn English so that they will have a window to the knowledge, technology and expertise of the modern world. They must know their mother tongues to enable them to know what makes us what we are.[250]

The Supreme Court of Canada has clarified that language "is part and parcel of the identity and culture", of cultural identity.[251] Detailed guarantees have been adopted with regard to education in English and French for these two linguistic communities. These language rights are based on political compromise.[252]

South Africa's Constitutional Court was in 1996 faced with its first case which probed into the politically explosive association between language (Afrikaans) and race. The Constitution 'creates a positive obligation on the state to accord to every person the right to have established, where practicable, schools based on a common culture, language or religion', leaving defining what is and is not 'practicable' for later. [253] Secondly, the obligation to respect the freedom to establish schools based on, *inter alia*, common language has created the opportunity for those able to afford it to set up their own schools. Since the financial endowment of different communities in South Africa has historically been racially stratified, allowing the testing of children for their linguistic competence in Afrikaans as a criterion of admission to school could perpetuate racial segregation in education. There is a long story behind this dilemma and it is worth summarizing.

The school children's uprising in Soweto on 16 June 1976 in protest against introducing Afrikaans as the language of instruction has been celebrated as of 1995 as the Youth Day. The brutal suppression of that demonstration, with the police unleashing dogs to attack protecting children, was one of the triggers for anti-apartheid movements but its origin – the language of instruction – is often forgotten. The background had been a change from English to Afrikaans in junior secondary schools in 1975 and the school children's resistance because, amongst many other factors, change from English to Afrikaans make learning more difficult and lowered the grades.[254]

---

[249] Initial report of Singapore under the Convention on the Rights of the Child, April 2002.

[250] Pakir, A. – Singapore, in: Wah Kam, H. & Wong, R.Y.L. (eds.) – *Language Policies and Language Education: The Impact in East Asian Countries in the Next Decade*, Times Academic Press, Singapore, 2000, p. 261.

[251] Canada's Supreme Court – *Mahe v. Alberta*, [1990] 1 S.C.R.

[252] Canada's Supreme Court – *Société des Acadiens du Nouveau-Brunswick Inc. v. Association of Parents for Fairness in Education*, [1986] 1 S.C.R. 549, p. 578.

[253] Constitutional Court of South Africa – *The Gauteng Provincial Legislature: Dispute concerning the constitutionality of certain provisions of the School Education Bill of 1995*, CCT 39/95, 4 April 1996, para. 5.

[254] Mxolisi Ndlovu, S. – *The Soweto Uprisings: Counter-Memories of June 1976*, Ravan Press, Randburg (South Africa), 1998.

Subsequent to the transition, detailed constitutional provisions on education have demonstrated South Africa's need to pursue two mutually opposed paths at the same time: to redress the effects of racial discrimination and to uphold parental freedom of choice. Ideally, all-inclusive education would have resulted to the same standards applied to all children, but that would have conflicted with the recognized parental freedom of choice. Its constitutional guarantee was limited only by the prohibition of exclusion on racial grounds. Nevertheless, the choice of language could – and did – operate as a proxy.

The Constitutional Court had to rule on the testing of children in Afrikaans as one of the conditions of access to school. The underlying question was whether the Court would challenge the guarantee of parental freedom of choice to educate their children – at their own expense – in a particular language, when that language was Afrikaans and the linguistic and racial boundary coincided. The Court has noted that the Constitution protects parental freedom to establish schools at their own expense "from invasion by the state", emphasising the negative heritage of Bantu education as the background:

> The constitutional entrenchment of that freedom is particularly important because of our special history initiated during the fifties, in terms of the system of Bantu education. From that period the state actively discouraged and effectively prohibited private educational institutions from establishing or continuing private schools and insisted that such schools had to be established and administered subject to the control of the state. The execution of those policies constituted an invasion on the right of individuals in association with one another to establish and continue, at their own expense, their own educational institutions based on their own values. Such invasions would now be constitutionally impermissible ...

The obligation to respect parental freedom to establish and operate schools based on, *inter alia*, a specific language of instruction favours those able to afford exercising this choice. Since the profile of wealth and poverty in South Africa remains racially stratified, allowing the testing of children for their linguistic competence in Afrikaans so as to enrol in Afrikaans-speaking schools could perpetuate racial segregation, defying the constitutional requirement whereby "the right to establish educational institutions based on common culture, language or religion cannot be exercised in a manner that discriminated against pupils on the grounds of race."[255]

In Namibia, Afrikaans speakers have challenged the government for denying their rights and won their case before the Human Rights Committee:

> The authors have also claimed that the lack of language legislation in Namibia has had a consequence that they have been denied the use of their mother tongue in administration, justice, education and public life. The Committee notes that the authors have shown that the State party has instructed the civil servants not to reply to the authors' written or oral communications with the authorities in the

---

[255] Constitutional Court of South Africa – *The Gouteng Provincial Legislature: Dispute concerning the constitutionality of certain provisions of the School Education Bill of 1995*, CCT 39/95, 4 April 1996, para. 5.

Afrikaans language, even when they are perfectly capable of doing so. These instructions barring the use of Afrikaans do not relate merely to the issuing of public documents but even to telephone conversations. In the absence of any response from the State party the Committee must give due weight to the allegations of the authors that the circular in question is intentionally targeted against the possibility to use Afrikaans when dealing with public authorities. Consequently, the Committee finds that the authors, as Afrikaans speakers, are victims of a violation of Article 26 of the Covenant. [256]

Formal guarantees of non-discrimination may exist but make no difference where they are based on an asserted right of speakers of whichever language to use it in their contacts with public authorities without the corresponding obligation of the state to enable them to do so. Miklos Kontra has provided an example, quoting the 1999 legislation on languages of national minorities. That law ostensibly allowed members of minorities to use their languages in contacts with government authorities but stated that government officials are not required to know any of them.[257] This example illustrates the paradox to which the passive governmental obligation not to interfere leads, when language rights are treated as if they were civil and political rights only, demanding that the state respect individual freedoms. The underlying dichotomy has been highlighted by Fernand de Varennes, with his definition of "the principle of non-discrimination [to mean] that there should be no unreasonable differentiation or limitation – assuming, in the first place, the existence of a legitimate public interest on the basis of which the State may interfere at all" to then state that "State's refusal to provide public services in [a minority] language would appear unreasonable and therefore discriminatory since it denies them a benefit or advantage that is available to others, namely the benefit of public service in their own language."[258]

What safeguards need to be in place has been aptly summarized by Raj Mehta, who merged pronouncements of the Supreme Court of India regarding minority languages so as to highlight the scope of human rights protection:

- Every minority community has the right not only to establish its own educational institutions, but also to impart instruction to the children of its own community in its own language. Minorities are, however, not entitled to have educational institutions exclusively for their own benefit.
- Even though Hindi is the national language of India and [the Constitution] provides a special directive upon the state to promote the spread of Hindi, nevertheless, the objective cannot be achieved by any means which contravenes cultural and educational rights of minorities.
- In making primary education compulsory, the state cannot compel that such education must take place only in the schools owned, aided or recognized by

---

[256] Human Rights Committee – *Diergaardt et al. v. Namibia*, Communication No. 760/1997, Views of the Committee, 25 July 2000, U.N. Doc. A/55/40, vol. II, p. 140, para. 10.10.

[257] Kontra, M. – Some reflections on the nature of language and its regulation, *International Journal on Minority and Group Rights*, vol. 6, 1999, No. 3, pp. 283-284.

[258] De Varennes, F. – Equality and non-discrimination: Fundamental principles of minority language rights, *International Journal on Minority and Group Rights*, vol. 6, 1999, No. 3, pp. 312-313.

the state so as to defeat the guarantee that a person belonging to a linguistic minority has the right to attend institutions run by the community.

- Even though there is no constitutional right to receive state aid, if the state does in fact grant aid to educational institutions, it cannot impose such conditions upon the right to receive such aid as would, virtually, deprive the members of religious or linguistic communities of their rights. ... This means that surrender of fundamental rights cannot be exacted as the price of aid by the state for its would completely destroy the right of the community to administer the institution.

- Similarly, in matters of extending recognition to any institution, the state cannot impose any condition contrary to the provisions relating to fundamental rights of such minority institutions.

- Minority institutions are however subject to regulation by the educational authorities of the state to prevent maladministration and to ensure proper standard of education.

- A minority community may reserve up to fifty per cent of the places for the members of its community in an educational institution administered by it even if the institution is getting aid from the state. [259]

Methods of teaching: Outlawing corporal punishment as a benchmark

From the rights of the child perspective, the obligation to make primary school acceptable goes far beyond parental freedom of choice or the language of instruction, and poses a great deal of challenge. Restrictions upon school discipline are a good example because they have considerably increased in the past decade to protect the child against humiliation or degradation. They were, and are likely to remain, subject to litigation.

Instruction that combines forcing children to memorize with a threat of physical punishment for their failure to memorize and accurately regurgitate are obviously incompatible with core objectives and purposes of education. Instruction is not education but training. It is disliked by teachers and children alike. The process of outlawing corporal punishment is a useful benchmark for moving the methods from instruction to education. Table 11 lists countries which have legally prohibited corporal punishment in school, demonstrating how rapid this process of change has been in all regions of the world.

---

[259] Raj Mehta, V. – Linguistic rights in India, in: UNESCO – *Cultural Rights and Wrongs: A Collection of Essays in Commemoration of the 50th Anniversary of the Universal Declaration of Human Rights*, UNESCO Publishing & Institute of Art and Law, 1998, pp. 127-128.

Table 11: National legal prohibitions of corporal punishment in school

Albania, Andorra, Armenia, Austria, Azerbaijan, Bahrain, Belarus, Belgium, Bosnia and Herzegovina, Bulgaria, Burkina Faso, Cameroon, China, Colombia, Congo, Costa Rica, Croatia, Cyprus, Czech Republic, Denmark, Dominican Republic, Egypt, El Salvador, Eritrea, Estonia, Ethiopia, Fiji, Finland, France, Georgia, Germany, Greece, Guinea-Bissau, Honduras, Hong Kong, Hungary, Iceland, Indonesia, Iran, Iraq, Ireland, Israel, Italy, Japan, Kazakhstan, Kenya, Korea, Latvia, Liechtenstein, Lithuania, Luxembourg, Macedonia, Malawi, Maldives, Malta, Mauritius, Moldova, Monaco, Mongolia, Namibia, Netherlands, New Zealand, Norway, Oman, Philippines, Poland, Portugal, Qatar, Russia, Samoa, San Marino, Serbia, Slovakia, Slovenia, South Africa, Spain, Sri Lanka, Suriname, Sweden, Switzerland, Taiwan, Thailand, Trinidad and Tobago, Turkey, Uganda, Ukraine, United Kingdom, Uzbekistan, Zambia, Zimbabwe

Source: www.endcorporalpunishment.org (October 2005).

Although it is known that "children's violent behaviour often has its origin in adult violence to children,"[260] this type of knowledge is suppressed because, as Catherine Bonnet has argued, it reveals the shameful behaviour of adults.[261] The Uganda Human Rights Commission has addressed a case of physical punishment of a schoolboy by his teachers, apparently triggered by the boy's attempt to enter the staffroom upon a request by another teacher to fetch something. The facts remained unclear because the teachers' violence against the schoolboy was never recorded. The Commission settled the case by ordering financial compensation for the boy.[262] The Supreme Court of Sri Lanka decided in April 1998 on the constitutionality of a law that aimed to outlaw and suppress *inter alia* verbal abuse (called ragging, bullying and/or harassment) within educational institutions. The victimization of students, especially newcomers, through verbal abuse (words which are obscene, abusive, derogatory, humiliating, degrading or contemptuous) intended to humiliate and degrade them should be outlawed, the Court has affirmed, being 'necessary to ensure the peace of mind which new students, in particular, need in order to benefit from their stay in educational institutions.' The Court has maintained that 'ragging has far too long been cruel, inhuman and degrading. Our society has been unable to deal with the root causes of ragging, and the anxieties, fears and frustrations of youth on which ragging has fed and flourished.'[263]

An attempt by parents whose religious doctrine deemed physical punishment of children to be legitimate and necessary to challenge Sweden's 1979 policy against corporal punishment of children forced the European Commission on Human Rights to revisit the issue that had already been the object of considerable litigation. The parents complained against the encroachment upon

---

[260] International Child Development Centre – Children and Violence, *Innocenti Digest No. 2*, Florence, September 1997, p. 15.

[261] Bonnet, C. – *L'Enfant Cassé*, Albin Michel, Paris, 1999.

[262] Human Rights Commission of Uganda – *Mpondi Emmanuel v. Nganwa High School*, Complaint No. 210 of 1998, Decree of 2 July 1999.

[263] Supreme Court of the Democratic Socialist Republic of Sri Lanka – Petitions Nos. 6/98 and 7/98 concerning An Act to Eliminate Ragging and Other Forms of Violence, and Cruel, Inhuman and Degrading Treatment, from Educational Institutions, 7 April 1998.

their rights, but did not persuade the Commission to rule against Sweden.[264] A similar case was litigated in South Africa two decades later, with a similar result.

The Constitutional Court of South Africa has examined the interplay between different, sometimes conflicting, demands upon education – to reconcile collective and individual rights, the rights of parents and the rights of children, the government's commitment to the parental right to educate their children in accordance with their religious beliefs, to translating the right to freedom from violence from a constitutional guarantee into a rule of conduct for schools. Its judgment summarized the rationale for banning corporal punishment:

> The central question in this matter is: when Parliament enacted a law to prohibit corporal punishment in schools, did it violate the rights of parents of children in independent schools who, in line with their religious convictions, had consented to its use?
>
> In support of its contention that parents have a divinely imposed responsibility for the training and upbringing of their children, the appellant ... contends that corporal punishment is a vital aspect of Christian religion and that it is applied in the light of its biblical context using biblical guidelines which impose a responsibility on parents for the training of their children. It has further claimed that according to the Christian faith, parents continue to comply with their biblical responsibility by delegating their authority to punish their children to their teachers.
>
> In an affidavit submitted on behalf of the respondent, the Director-General of the Department of Education contends that corporal punishment in schools is contrary to the Bill of Rights. ... According to the affidavit, corporal punishment is inherently violent, and involves a degrading assault upon the physical, emotional and psychological integrity of the person to whom it is administered. South Africans have suffered, and continue to suffer a surfeit of violence.
>
> It is clear from the above that a multiplicity of intersecting constitutional values and interests are involved in the present matter – some overlapping, some competing. The parents have a general interest in living their lives in a community setting according to their religious beliefs, and a more specific interest in directing the education of their children. The child, who is at the centre of the inquiry, is probably a believer, and a member of a family and a participant in a religious community that seeks to enjoy such freedom. Yet that same child is also an individual person who may find himself 'at the other end of the stick' and as such be entitled to [constitutional protection]. Then, the broad community has an interest in reducing violence wherever possible and protecting children from harm. The overlap and tension between the different clusters of rights reflect themselves in contradictory assessments of how the central constitutional value of dignity is implicated. On the one hand, the dignity of the parents may be negatively affected when the state tells them how to bring up and discipline their children and limits the manner in which they can express their religious beliefs. The child who has grown up in the particular faith may regard the punishment, although hurtful, as designed to strengthen his character. On the other hand, the child is being subjected to what an outsider might regard as the indignity of suffering a painful and humiliating hiding deliberately inflicted on him in an institutional setting. Indeed, it would be unusual if the child did not have

---

[264] European Commission on Human Rights – *Seven individuals v. Sweden*, Application No. 8811/79, decision of 13 May 1982 on the admissibility of the application, *Decisions and Reports*, vol. 29, p. III-112.

ambivalent emotions.

The respondent has established that the prohibition of corporal punishment is part and parcel of a national programme to transform the education system to bring it into line with the letter and spirit of the Constitution. The creation of uniform norms and standards for all schools, whether public or independent, is crucial for educational development. A coherent and principled system of discipline is integral to such development.

The state is further under a constitutional duty to take steps to help diminish the amount of public and private violence in society generally and to protect all people and especially children from maltreatment, abuse or degradation. More specifically, by ratifying the United Nations Convention on the Rights of the Child, it undertook to take all appropriate measures to protect the child from violence.

Courts throughout the world have shown special solicitude for protecting children from what they have regarded as the potentially injurious consequences of their parents' religious practices. It is now widely accepted that in every matter concerning the child, the child's best interests must be of paramount importance. Section 12 of the Constitution now adds to the rights protected by the interim Constitution the following provisions: ... Everyone has the right ... to be free from all forms of violence ... It should be noted that these rights to be violence-free are additional to an not substitutes for the right not to be punished in a cruel, inhuman or degrading way. Under section 7(2) the state is obliged to 'respect, protect and fulfil' these rights. It must accordingly take appropriate steps to reduce violence in public and private life. Coupled with its special duty towards children, this obligation represents a powerful requirement on the state to act.

As part of its pedagogical mission, the Department [of Education] sought to introduce new principles of learning in terms of which problems were solved through reason rather than force. In order to put the child at the centre of the school and to protect the learner from physical and emotional abuse, the legislature prescribed a blanket ban on corporal punishment. ... The ban was part of a comprehensive process of eliminating state-sanctioned use of physical force as method of punishment. The outlawing of physical punishment in the school accordingly represented more than a pragmatic attempt to deal with disciplinary problems in a new way. It had a principled and symbolic function, manifestly intended to promote respect for the dignity and physical and emotional integrity of all children. [265]

The lead by the Constitutional Court of South Africa towards making education violence-free closes a gap in the human rights rationale against violence in education. The traditional focus in human rights on the protection against abuse of power by the government relies on self-policing by governments themselves, individually and collectively. The existing international standards represent a patchwork while domestic approaches vary a great deal. Some governments recognize their obligation to guarantee individual security and/or safety, others accept only some limits upon resort to violence by the agents of the state. Violence by non-state actors is addressed as a variety of different and unrelated phenomena – racial (or racist) violence, or violence against women, or communal violence, with child abuse occasionally raised to prominence to then disappear again from the public agenda. What governments should – or should

---

[265] Constitutional Court of South Africa – *Christian Education South Africa v. Minister of Education*, Case CCT 4/00, judgment of 18 August 2000, full text available at http://www.concourt.gov.za.

not – do to prevent victimization, including by 'normalization' of violence at home, in school, in the media, or through computer games, is fiercely debated. What children and young people observe (as different from what they are told) is combating violence with violence, for which the ~~proverbial~~ examples are death penalty for homicide or corporal punishment lest school children become violent.

Violence has appeared on the human rights agenda in its different manifestations, ranging from arbitrary executions and death penalty to football hooliganism and child abuse. Calls to recognize a right to violence-free life illustrate desires to extend human rights further. Thus the Declaration on Violence against Women included, in an early draft, a 'right to violence-free private and family life,'[266] which does not appear in its final text. Such a right was, however, written into the Inter-American Convention on Violence against Women, which declares that 'every women has the right to life free of violence.'[267] In 1993, the General Assembly of the United Nations, responding to information on widespread killings of street children, recognized that all children have the right to 'freedom from violence and harassment.' [268] Attention of the United Nations subsequently shifted to violence *by* not only *against* children.

The mass media are often accused of glorifying violence, sometimes also of nudging people, particularly children, to imitate the violence portrayed on TV screens or computer games. A hypothesis that violent behaviour results from exposure to violence has been subjected to empirical verification many times, especially for children, yielding mutually contradictory outcomes. A middle-of-the road view holds that 'exposure to images of brutality could turn an already disturbed child towards violence. At the very least, such images may give a child a picture of how it might vent its rage,'[269] and thus may lead to copycat violence.

Controversies regarding teaching about wars, conflicts and associated abuses occur daily, worldwide. School textbooks have been found to have included descriptions of 'Serbian aggressors' as 'merciless barbarians who ran amok' in Croatia.[270] In Serbia, the same historical period was described as 'enforced expulsion of the Serbian population,' reminiscent of the 'genocide fifty years earlier.'[271]

---

[266] Division for the Advancement of Women – Background material on international action relevant to a draft declaration on violence against women, 28 August 1992, p. 6.

[267] Organización de los Estados Americanos – Convención interamericana para prevenir, sancionar y erradicar la violencia contra la mujer (Convención de Belem do Para), adopted on 6 June 1994, Article 3, Doc. OEA/Ser.P AG/doc.3115/94 rev.2, 9 June 1994.

[268] United Nations – Plight of street children, General Assembly resolution 48/136 of 20 December 1993, preamble.

[269] We must protect young minds, *The Independent*, 26 November 1993.

[270] Pingel, F. – *The European Home: Representations of 20th Century Europe in History Textbooks*, Council of Europe, Strasbourg, September 2000, p. 87.

[271] Gachesha, N. et al. – *Istorija za III razred gimnazine prirodno-matematickog smera i IV razred gimnazine opsteg i drustveno-jezickog smera* (History for 3rd grade of secondary school of natural science-mathematics orientation and 4th grade of secondary school of general and social science-linguistics orientation), Secretariat for Textbooks and Teaching Tools, Belgrade, Eighth Edition,

In some countries, children are protected from excessive exposure to violence. The Constitutional Court of Germany has explained the need to prevent children from access to harmful material by focusing on 'all printed matter, films, or pictures that glorify violence or crime, provoke racial hatred, glorify war, constitute [moral] harm and thus may lead to serious or even irreversible injury.'[272] This has led to heightened criteria for scrutiny for children than for adults. It is useful to recall that the German Criminal Code prohibits the production or dissemination of material that describes 'cruel or inhuman acts of violence against human beings in a manner expressing glorification or intentional minimization of such acts of violence or demonstrating the cruel or inhuman acts in a manner injuring human dignity.'[273] This example is an exception to the widespread marketing of violent films and games to children.

Violence is not only films and games for too many children but a part of life. Children committing atrocities have attracted much international attention and many research projects have been devoted to identifying the cause of violence, based on an assumption that 'violence is a preventable disease'. [274] Seeking a cure, a simple remedy, often follows such a diagnosis. This follows from the implicit assumption that violence can be explained, its causation described, types of perpetrators profiled, and subsequently violence can be eliminated. Education is seen as a key, especially for children. However, 'where violence is a means not of expressing identity, but of creating it,' [275] there does not seem to be a ready-made answer.

2000, p. 274 and 178.

[272] Judgment in the Nudist Magazine case of 23 March 1971, reproduced from: Kommers, D.P. – *The Constitutional Jurisprudence of the Federal Republic of Germany*, 1989, p. 423-424.

[273] Section 131 of the Criminal Code, reproduced from: Harfst, G. and Schmidt, O.A. – *German Criminal Law*, 1989.

[274] Will, G.F. – Violence is a 'preventable disease,' *International Herald Tribune*, 28-29 November 1992.

[275] Woollacott, M. – Terrorism and the warfare of the weak, *Guardian Weekly*, 7 November 1993.

4

Adaptability

Definitions of education can be very broad or extremely narrow. The most widespread one is also the narrowest. It defines education as a sector, as a part of governmental structure. Don Adams has proposed a broader definition of education, saying that "development of nations is fundamentally an education process in which people learn to create new institutions, utilize new technologies, cope with their environment, and alter their patterns of behaviour."[276] Another wide-ranging definition of education, by Rabbi Jonathan Sacks, says that it is "the handing on of the accumulated wisdom to the next generation."[277]

Formal schooling constitutes only a minuscule part of education. The prevailing administrative notion of schooling describes an age-based educational pyramid wherein statistical majorities are allocated to the lowest rungs on the ladder and minorities progress upwards. This is called *education* but may be *instruction*. Its human rights impact can be negative, as was aptly described in the 2004 Arab Human Development Report. Rather than adapted to affirm and enhance human rights, the process is slanted in the opposite direction:

> Starting with the child's upbringing within the family, passing through educational institutions, the world of work, and societal formation, and ending with politics, each link in the chain takes its portion of freedom from the individual and delivers her or him to the next which, in turn, steals a further share.[278]

Equating education with formal schooling was exacerbated through the entry of the World Bank in global education and the underlying influence of the US government. The vocabulary changed. The *right* to education became *access to* education, the *process* of learning was transformed into a *product* measures by endless tests, the *process* of teaching became *service delivery*, and education was reduced to the *monetary returns to schooling*. An image of education as a service that can be delivered is contrasted by defining education as a process:

> [T]he education of children is the whole process whereby, in any society, adults endeavour to transmit their beliefs, culture and other values to their young, whereas teaching or instruction refers in particular to the transmission of

---

[276] Adams, D. – *Education and National Development: Priorities, Policies and Planning*, Asian Development Bank and Comparative Education Research Centre, The University of Hong Kong, Education in Developing Asia, volume 1, Manila/Hong Kong, 2002, p. 1.

[277] Sacks, J. – Finding our way back to the family, *The Independent*, 6 March 1995.

[278] UNDP – *Arab Human Development Report 2004: Towards Freedom in the Arab World*, United Nations Development Programme, Arab Fund for Economic and Social Development, and Arab Gulf Programme for United Nations Development Organizations, UNDP, Regional Bureau for Arab States (RBAS), New York, 2005, p. 17.

knowledge and to intellectual development.[279]

Getting human rights back in necessitates affirming and defending the right *to* education, human rights protection *in* education, and promotion of human rights *through* education. The vocabulary of access to education hides the difference between the sale and purchase of educational services which challenges the very *right* to education. The focus on outputs, in the forms of learning accomplishments may hide human rights violations *through* education. The mastery of a language as a monitored output often hides an assimilationist design of education and the obliteration of indigenous and minority languages. The skills exhibited by learners in multiple-choice tests say nothing about an authoritarian schooling or corporal punishment that force children to perform well. Well-funded and well-performing education systems can perpetuate xenophobia, but this cannot be seen because the "essential political task of socialization at school"[280] is not monitored.

Advocating a broad definition of education, adaptable to its beneficiaries, requires a look back at the road travelled thus far. The extension of the right to education to previously un-schooled categories can be described by highlighting four typical stages. The first stage involved recognizing education as a right. When the right to education was recognized, non-citizens were often explicitly excluded. Children without identity documents are still implicitly excluded where such documents are required for enrolment. In many countries, non-citizens do not have a legally recognized right to education. In making education an universal, that is, human right, we have not yet taken this first step. The hope that acceptance of universal human rights obligations would gradually underpin it has not materialized. Indeed, we may be moving away from it.

Once there is a recognition of education as a human right, the second stage involves segregation, whereby girls, indigenous people, children with disabilities, or members of minorities, are given access to education but confined to separate, routinely inferior schools. The third stage consists of moving from segregation over assimilation towards integration. Categories newly admitted to mainstream schools have to adapt, abandoning their mother tongue or religion, or their usual residence if they are enrolled in boarding schools. Girls are admitted to schools whose curricula were designed for boys. Indigenous and minority children are placed in schools that provide instruction in an alien language and, often, teach them history that denies their very existence. This process may be underpinned by inclusionary goals but, in practice, assimilation entails imposition of uniformity. Education as a sector is a massive, permanent process which uniformity makes easier, faster and cheaper. The import of human rights has challenged this uniformity and formal descriptions of education from assimilation to integration. This step entails an acknowledgment of diversity but only as a departure from the 'norm'. The entrants have to adjust

---

[279] European Court of Human Rights – *Campbell and Cosans v. United Kingdom*, Judgment of 25 February 1982, Series A.48, p. 14.
[280] Melber, H. – Educational reform – unto what end? , in: Tötemeyer, G., Kandetu, V. and Werner, W. (eds.) – *Namibia in Perspective*, The Council of Churches in Namibia, Windhoek, 1987, p. 128.

to the 'norm' which favours male over female, or speakers of the dominant national language over those speaking a vernacular. The fourth stage necessitates adaptation to diversity, and this Chapter outlines key challenges. The requirement upon children to adapt themselves to whatever education is made available to them is replaced by adapting education to the best interests of each child. This is, of course, a key feature of individualized education which caring parents ensure for their children if they can afford the cost. Converting this into a birth right of each person which public education should accommodate appears utopian. And yet, it is necessary to outline the contours of road to be travelled in arguing that education should be but is not adaptable.

The different stages in affirming and putting into practice the right to education can be recognized in different parts of education systems in all countries in the world. No country has, as yet, achieved full compliance with all international human rights obligations in education. Thus, international human rights bodies are always critical when assessing each country's compliance, pointing out shortcomings and suggesting improvements. The most important facet of human rights is that ensuring their recognition and protection is a permanent process. ⇒ non-regression.

A basic feature of every education system is that it selects the few who make it to the pinnacle of the education pyramid and excludes the many who start at the bottom but do make it all the way up. Most children enter primary school but a fraction reaches the university. Prerequisites for moving upwards are apparently objective and justified, and are rarely challenged as a violation of the equal right to education. And yet, the very design of education denies an equal opportunity to reach the pinnacle to the majority of those who start school. Failures are necessary because each step upwards education pyramid accommodates fewer people. To avoid becoming a failure, small people whom we call children have to adapt to what is required of them to move up.

This feature of education clashes with the egalitarian postulate embodied in the equal right to education and highlighted in the best interests of each child. There is an abundance of descriptions of what education *could* look like if it were to adapt to each child. Increasingly, education policies stipulate that education *should* be child-centred. This would imply transforming children from objects of education into subjects of rights, bearers of an equal right *to* education and equal rights *in* education. Furthermore, this necessitates balancing the rights of children against those of their parents.

The law has historically deemed children to be the property of their parents. This is reflected in the rights and freedoms of parents regarding education of their children, which are enforceable in many countries as well as internationally. The notion of the rights of the child is formally unacceptable to the United States of America, which remains – alongside Somalia – the only country that is not party to the Convention on the Rights of the Child. The United Kingdom has formally subscribed to this Convention but not to the substantive changes that it requires. Its law has specified "the *parents'* charter ... *parental* choice of school ... *parent* governors ... the *parental* right of withdrawal from religious education ... the *parent's* right to withdraw his or her children from sex education."[281] In a rare court case, a child, sixteen years old, was given a right to challenge the parental choice of school. Judge Dalcq in Bruxelles acknowledged that the best interest of the child should prevail. The case involved a girl whose divorced parents had disagreed on the choice of school. As a consequence, she ended up not going to school for a time.[282] This cases epitomizes how much of a challenge human rights have created. Adapting education to the child, asking the child and accommodating her wishes, remains an exception rather than the rule.

Court cases which have affirmed a voice for children in their own education are challenging the historical heritage of rights-less school children. US courts have affirmed the right to challenge an officially prescribed dogma for university students and teenagers but not for younger children.[283] The Constitutional Court of Colombia has gone much further. It has defined "reciprocal respect of the subjects of the educational process with the same possibility for free expression under the sole condition of not jeopardizing the rights of others or the just order" [284] as the pillar of a different, rights-based vision of education.

That vision necessitates exposing and opposing abuses of education, which are particularly widespread in the denial of diversity. In 1978, UNESCO forged the concept of a right to be different[285] and this notion was taken forward by Albie Sachs in 2000. Delivering a judgment in the name of South Africa's Constitutional Court, he has affirmed "the right of people to be who they are without being forced to subordinate themselves to the cultural and religious norms of others."[286] The requirement upon education to adapt to the best interests of each child has reversed the previous requirement upon children to adapt themselves to whatever schooling was made available to them. Adaptation necessitates affirming the right of each child to be regarded as different while children are, in practice, reduced to the few denominators that are statistically monitored and inform education policy. These are often only sex and age, rarely disability, only sometimes the child's mother tongue, religion, minority, migrant or indigenous status, race or provenance. Although we know that no real person conforms to any statistical average, the sheer size of the educational endeavour entails planning on the basis of averages. Diversity is reduced, often obliterated. Children are reduced to the minimum denominator, the individual is forced "to sink or swim within the mainstream".[287] Children who do not adapt are doomed to sink, they become failures.

---

[281] Bainham, A. – Sex education: A family lawyer's perspective, in: Harris, N. (ed.) – *Children, Sex Education and the Law*, National Children's Bureau, London, 1996, p. 30.

[282] Tribunal de Bruxelles – *A.M. (16 ans) v. K.N., O.M. et l'asbl Institut d'enseignement secondaire général La Retraite du SacréCœur*, 98/1510/c, 3 février 1999.

[283] US Supreme Court – *Tinker v. Des Moines Independent Community School District*, 393 U.S. 503, 1969.

[284] Constitutional Court of Colombia – Judgment T-259 of 27 May 1998.

[285] UNESCO – Declaration on race and racial prejudice, adopted by the General Conference of UNESCO on 27 November 1978, Article 1 (2).

[286] Constitutional Court of South Africa – *Christian Education South Africa v. Minister of Education*, Case CCT 4/00, judgment of 18 August 2000, para. 24.

[287] Supreme Court of Canada – *Eaton v. Brant County Board of Education*, [1997] 1 S.C.R., 241, para. 67.

Educational failures *versus* the best interests of each child

The import of human rights in education can be seen most clearly from the frequency of references to *failures* as an inevitable output of education. Selection of those who will move up the education pyramid converts the rest into failures. The requirement upon education to adapt to each child clashes against its in-built propensity to designate some, even many learners as failures, sometimes very early in their educational experience.

A good illustration is the education model in Northern Ireland. As prospects of peace have (probably) improved with the historic event in 2005, whereby for "the first time in their 200-year history Irish republicans have agreed to give up their weapons,"[288] a time may come to look into a design of post-conflict education. Looking at role of education in generating and sustaining conflict is necessary because education is never neutral. Its design reflects the values it embodies, such as inclusion or exclusion, equal or unequal opportunities, secular or religious education. The way that education in Northern Ireland was designed reflected its priority for segregation over inclusion and for unequal over equal opportunities:

> Secondary education is proverbially the weakest link in the process that is today expected to extend to lifelong education, and Northern Ireland exemplifies this. The ongoing process of reforming post-primary education has generated immense debate and widely diverging proposals.
> Since compulsory education ends at the age of 16, one might think logical a division at the post-compulsory rather than post-primary stage. Being compulsory, education triggers the coercive powers of the State and thereby heightened human rights safeguards, especially entitlements regarding the quality and contents of education. Northern Ireland has, however, preserved segregation at the age of 11, following what is known as the 11+ transfer test, previously used throughout the United Kingdom. The transfer test takes two hours and covers only English, mathematics, and science. The two-thirds of the children who do not perform well enough to qualify for a grammar school tend to perceive themselves as educational failures, relegated to inferior schools: "the smart people go to really good schools and the not so smart people go to the not so smart schools" The ongoing debate has tended towards a narrow focus; some have argued against selection, others have initiated campaigns to preserve the grammar school. Two English models, grammar and comprehensive school, have become a frequent point of reference. For example, Sinn Féin is opposed to "the selective, elitist 'ethos' of the grammar school," while the Ulster Unionist Party opposes changes that might "compromise Northern Ireland's enviable record of examination success."
> Much as elsewhere, a considerable investment would be necessary to equalize educational opportunities for all children. Such investment requires a clearly articulated definition of equality, the corresponding determination of means necessary for achieving it, and specification of accountability. The political agenda of negotiating power-sharing has influenced the human rights discourse, prioritizing equality *between* "the two communities" over equality *of* all individuals. The Equality Scheme for the Department of Education has defined its objective as

---

[288] Chrisafis, A. – IRA destroys entire arsenal, *Guardian Weekly*, 20 September – 6 October 2005.

enhancing "equality of opportunity between groups in terms of outcomes." Equality of outcomes has been critiqued by the European Court of Justice ...

UNICEF's Innocenti Report Card on Educational Disadvantage in Rich Nations has found that "a family's social, cultural and economic status tends to act as a rifle-barrel setting an educational trajectory from which it is difficult for a child to escape." Nevertheless, the frequent resort to the term "underachievement" in measuring learning outcomes implies that "underachievers" could and should have performed better. And yet, obstacles they face may not have been even acknowledged. Obstacles such as disability or poverty ought to be overcome before learners are assessed by a yardstick developed for those who do not face them. The Committee on the Rights of the Child has noted "the sharp differences in [education] outcomes for children according to their socio-economic background." Nevertheless, elimination of poverty as an obstacle to children's enjoyment of their right to education is not part of the human rights agenda but is addressed through New Targeting Social Need (NTSN). Therein, equality is also defined in inter-group terms, as removing "socio-economic differentials between groups in Northern Ireland." A policy aimed at redressing poverty should be, by definition, generously funded, but this is not the case. Poverty is widespread.[289]

A frequent critique of the sector of education, "that the school finds itself in the business of producing failures,"[290] demonstrates that the problem is both known and widespread. The priority for excellence enhances institutionalized competition between children and their schools and their countries for the highest possible rating in learning accomplishments. Children who learn slowly, or at a different pace, or who do not like to compete do not fit. Adaptation of education to each child and youth would necessitate an anti-competitive logic, adjusting teaching to the pace and the way in which each child learns. Instead, evaluations of learning performance force teachers and schools into discarding children who cannot – or do not want to[291] – compete; they become failures.

The OECD has furnished the simplest and clearest definition of failures as "those pupils whose academic performance is significantly below the average for their age group."[292] Why is their performance significantly below the average? The reasons can be many. In the worst case scenario, the reasons are not identified. If there is a search for reasons and they are identified, improving that child's academic performance will necessitate time and attention, patience and persistence. The main barrier is cost. Additional resources to help raise the pupil's academic performance are rarely available within public education. Exceptions have been created in the form of entitlements for those with special needs so that they would not sink with the mainstream. However, it is the

---

[289] Commission on Human Rights – Report submitted by Katarina Tomasevski, Special Rapporteur on the right to education: Mission to the United Kingdom (Northern Ireland), 24 November – 1 December 2002, U.N. Doc. E/CN.4/2003/9/Add. 2.

[290] Leach, F. E. and Little, A. W. – *Education, Culture and Economics: Dilemmas for Development*, Falmer Press, New York, 1999, p. 119.

[291] Regardless of the rhetoric of the rights of the child that may be referred to in education policies and laws, a right of a school child to refuse learning to compete does not exist. Children who want to opt out can do so only if their parents have the will and the means to transfer them to another educational institution, provided that such an institution exists and is within reach.

[292] OECD – *Overcoming Failure at School*, Paris, 1998, p. 11.

mainstream that defines the grounds rule, which is opposite to the postulate of human rights law: those who cannot or will not swim with the mainstream and doomed to sink. Two interlinked factors exacerbate the likelihood of changing the ground rules so as to accommodate diversity: "'special needs' students are not only expensive, but deflate test scored on those all important league tables." [293]

Statistical averages *versus* diversity of educational intake

International human rights law demands identification of all obstacles that a child may face in access to school and in learning once at school. Education statistics that portray school children through their age and sex alone ought to be amplified by recording and monitoring all relevant factors. These are alluded to in terms such as vulnerable or marginalized categories, but does not go further to discern who the children are and why they are vulnerable or marginalized. The obstacles that impede children's education remain undocumented, hence education policies can ignore them. Many lies outside the sector of education. Even for those factors that are recorded, such as age, the adaptation of education to the diverse abilities and disabilities of children is impeded by the rule of statistical averages.

Age

Children may be refused access to school because they are above or below a legally determined age. Those assessed as too young stand a chance of going to school later. Those too old may be precluded from school, and lose their right to education, even if they are merely 9 or 10 years old. UNESCO has suggested that "the existence of large numbers of over-aged pupils must not prevent access to school for those of official school age and thereby delay the achievement of UPE [Universal Primary Education] goals."[294] Dismissing over-aged children from school according to an administratively defined age collides with the very notion of the best interests of each child. Also, this increases the number of illiterate adults.

South Africa's Constitutional Court was faced with discrimination against children aged six because they were precluded from primary school for which the starting age was set at seven:

> The contention was that the discrimination was unfair and against the best interests of the child because the requirement allowed for no exemptions for children who did not reach seven during the year, even if they were manifestly ready for school. The initial focus on exemptions resulted in affidavits dealing extensively with the validity of school-readiness tests in a multi-cultural society,

---

[293] Apple, M. W. – Creating profits by creating failures: standards, markets, and inequality in education, *International Journal of Inclusive Education*, vol. 5, 2001, No. 2/3, p. 108.

[294] *The 2001 Monitoring Report on Education for All,* UNESCO Publishing, Paris, 2001.

the main disagreement between the respective experts being whether reliable and objective tests could at present be employed in South Africa. [295]

The Court elegantly avoided the impact of the school-starting age of 7 on the children some of who will and others will not be "manifestly ready for school". There may well be "reliable and objective tests" whose results apply across the internal boundaries of a multi-cultural society, but the first issue that any ministry of education would raise would be the prohibitive cost of administrating such tests. Thus, administrative rules define the mainstream and the averages upon which they are based go unchallenged.

Classes are based on age groups, which is hard for children who differ sharply from the average. This *average* sums up the design of education. Human rights law posits that everybody has the right to education but education tends to be defined as an age-specific right. It may constitute an entitlement only for children aged 6-11. Herd boys in Lesotho are a case in point:

> The employment of herd boys, an inherited and enduring tradition, is widespread in Lesotho but no one knows their exact numbers. Spending weeks at a time alone with their herds, the boys travel long distances away from their villages. This time away from home results in missed opportunity for education, poor socialization and inadequate nutrition. In the past, there was no age limit for enrolment in primary school. Herd boys typically began work at a young age and continued into their early teens, at which point some would enrol in school. As a result, the herd boys were much older than their classmates, and these age differences in the classroom created social tensions. In an attempt to address these tensions, the GOL [Government of Lesotho] implemented a policy of non-registration of overage children. As a result, when herd boys complete their duties in their early teens, the possibility of enrolling in school is closed off and they are excluded from formal education. [296]

The varying ages in education laws define entitlements to education or exclusion from it. Since leaving school too early is a key predictor of social exclusion, [297] the age at which children enter and leave school is important. International human rights law provides useful guidance by linking the school-leaving age with the minimum age for employment. [298] Because poor families depend on the work of each member of the family for their survival, enabling children to go to school often necessitates elimination of all financial barriers, not only direct but also opportunity costs of education. Subsidies to poor families so as to free children to attend school have been particularly successful in Latin America.[299]

---

[295] Constitutional Court of South Africa – *Minister of Education v. Doreen Harris*, Case CCT 13/01, 5 October 2001.

[296] The World Bank – Project appraisal document on a proposed credit to the Kingdom of Lesotho for a second education sector development project, 25 March 1999, Report No. 18388-LSO, p. 7

[297] Commission of the European Communities – *Joint Report on Social Exclusion*, December 2003.

[298] Further details about the 80-year old global linkage between free and compulsory education and the elimination of child labour can be found in Tomasevski, K. – *Education Denied: Costs and Remedies*, Zed Books, London, 2003, pp. 24-27.

[299] Morley, S. and Coady, D. – *From Social Assistance to Social Development: Targeted Education Subsidies in Developing Countries*, Center for Global Development and International Food Policy Research Institute, Washington D.C., August 2003.

This highlights the proverbial cost-consciousness of all contemporary public education policies. This closes off further debate through the very choice of the term *cost*. Were the chosen term *investment in education,* a debate would become easier.

Disability

Providing education for children defined as *expensive-to-educate* is immensely difficult at a time when the cost of education is a major consideration. The resources – space, time, teaching staff, teaching and learning aids – are in short supply, while budgetary stringency and increased competitiveness are making things worse worse. Reduced governmental allocations for public institutions have further diminished prospects for the equal right to education for all those who are dependant on public funding, especially when additional funding is necessary to equalize their educational opportunities.

Learners with visual, hearing, physical or mental impairments tend to be segregated in special schools or denied schooling altogether. A court case in Ireland focused on the assertion that no child is un-educable:

> The mother of a seven-year old boy sought in Ireland in 1992 judicial review to challenge an assessment of her son as 'ineducable' and secure free primary education for him. Her claim was that every child had a right to education and so the child's mental and physical disability should not be used to deny the child the right to education. In the quadripartite classification of mental handicap (mild, moderate, severe and profound), her son had been classified as profoundly handicapped and then assessed as 'ineducable ... by reason of being profoundly mentally and physically disabled ... and all that can be done for him is to make his life more tolerable is to attempt to train him in the basics of bodily function and movement.'

> A broad definition of education, adopted in a previous case by the Chief Justice, served as guidance in that education had to be seen as 'the teaching and training a child to make the best possible use of his inherent and potential capacities, physical, mental and moral' wherein 'teaching children to minimise the risk of dental caries by brushing their teeth constitutes education by inducing them to use their own resources. That guidance has been supported by the process of gradual inclusion of all children in education, starting with those with mild handicap towards those with profound handicap. The court has noted that making education compulsory for all children, regardless of the severity of their disabilities, in the United States, England, Scotland, Wales and Denmark makes it seem 'inconceivable that this enormous commitment of resources would have been undertaken without convincing evidence that it was worthwhile to do so.'
> The court has found that

> ... there is a constitutional obligation imposed on the State by ... the Constitution to provide for free basic elementary education of all children and that this involves giving each child such advice, instruction and teaching as will enable him or her to make the best possible use of his or her inherent and potential capacities, physical, mental and moral, however limited these capacities may be. ...
> This process will work differently for each child, according to the child's natural

gifts, or lack thereof. In the case of the child who is deaf, dumb, blind, or otherwise physically or mentally handicapped, a completely different programme of education has to be adopted and a completely different rate of progress has to be taken for granted, than would be regarded as appropriate for a child suffering from no such handicap.

Admittedly, it is only in the last few decades that research into the problems of the severely and profoundly physically and mentally handicapped has led to positive findings that education in a formal setting, involving schools and teachers, educational equipment of many kinds, and integration as far as possible in the conventional school environment, can be of real benefit to children thus handicapped. But once that has been established – and my conclusion is that is has been established on a world-wide basis for many years past – then it appears to me that it gives rise to a constitutional obligation on the part of the State to respond to such findings by providing for free primary education for this group of children in as full and positive a manner as it has done for all other children in the community.

... The ordinary national school curriculum has always had a significant 'non-academic' content under the headings of physical education, health and fitness, music and singing, social and environmental education and such-like. All that occurs in the special schools for the handicapped is that the emphasis of the educational process is laid on this limited group of subjects, to the exclusion of subjects which would make too great a demand on the intellectual powers of the mentally handicapped. ... The actual content of the curriculum ... is directed towards the promotion of the child's physical, intellectual, emotional, social, moral and aesthetic development to the maximum extent that it is possible to do so having regard to the degree of handicap from which the child is suffering. [300]

The very notion of equal rights requires comparison between the children who are singled out as different and "all other children in the community", as the court has put it. Which criteria should be used for identifying differences and demanding their accommodation within education in a "full and positive manner"? Answering this question triggers the process of adaptation because varied criteria will define different categories of children as different. The Supreme Court of Canada has argued that a making schools formally open to all members of society does not amount to equal access. Rather, the Court has found that differential treatment and/or accommodation of differences constitutes the necessary step towards securing equal access to education.[301]

The requirement upon schools to adapt to learners with special needs has been subjected to a great deal of litigation. The principle of non-discrimination has been interpreted narrowly, as a comparison between learners with and without disabilities in order to detect and correct less favourable treatment of learners with disabilities. A positive obligation to treat learners with disabilities favourably has not been affirmed, mostly because of anticipated costs. [302]

The European Commission on Human Rights has held that the right to education "does not require the admission of a severely handicapped child to an

---

[300] O'Donoghue v. Minister for Health, judgment of the High Court of 27 May 1993, [1992 No. 75 J.R.] The Irish Reports, 1996, pp. 20-72.
[301] Supreme Court of Canada – Adler v. Ontario, [1996] 3 S.C.R., paras. 73 and 75.
[302] Tomasevski, K. – Education Denied: Costs and Remedies, Zed Books, London, 2003, pp. 151-156.

ordinary school because of the expenses of additional teaching staff or to the detriment of other pupils" when education can be provided in a special school. [303] The US Supreme Court has held that disabled children should be provided with education which enables them to benefit educationally and meets general educational standards; for children within compulsory school age-age, such education should be free.[304]

Courts in the Netherlands have gone one step further and held that a reduction of public funding, which impeded an increase in the number of teachers regardless of increasing numbers of special-needs students, constituted a human rights violation. [305] The European Committee of Social Rights has followed this line and faulted France for having "failed to achieve sufficient progress in advancing the provision of education for persons with autism." The Committee has examined a range of benchmarks whereby the implementation of the right to education for people with autism can be assessed. The key benchmarks, whether the definition of autism was as broad as it should be and whether official statistics were available to monitor progress, were missing. The Committee then emphasized the essence of governmental human rights obligations. As long as governmental provision and/or funding is inadequate, families have to bear all the burden which undermines the very notion of the *right to* education:

> When the achievement of one of the rights in question is exceptionally complex and particularly expensive to resolve, a State Party must take measures that allows it to achieve the objectives of the Charter within a reasonable time, with measurable progress and to an extent consistent with the maximum use of available resources. States Parties must be particularly mindful of the impact their choices will have for groups with heightened vulnerabilities as well as for other persons affected including, especially, the families on whom falls the heaviest burden in the event of institutional shortcomings. [306]

Culture

Question related to the distribution of burdens become even more controversial where the obstacles which children face in exercising an equal right to education are social rather than individual. The notion of social exclusion brings into the equation *what* the children are categorized as (migrants or minorities) alongside *who* the children are. Selected features of collective identity, such as religion or language, define children as members of a group rather than only individuals. This is best subsumed under *culture*. Indeed, the OECD team which reviewed French education policy pointed out the phenomenon of exclusion through

---

[303] European Commission on Human Rights – *Martin Klerks v. the Netherlands*, Application No. 25212/94, Decision on admissibility of 4 July 1995, *Decisions & Reports*, vol. 82, 1994, p. 129.

[304] US Supreme Court – *Hendrick Hudson District Board of Education v. Rowley*, 458 U.S. 176, Judgment of 28 June 1982.

[305] Raad van State – *Kemper v. City of Leiden*, Judgment of 10 May 1989; Tribunal of 's Gravenhage – *City of Leiden v. the Netherlands*, Judgment of 26 July 1989.

[306] European Committee of Social Rights – *Autism-Europe v. France*, Complaint No. 13/2002, Decision on the merits, 4 November 2003, para. 53.

underachievement, whereby "failure at school degenerates rapidly into a social failure" but schooling as "effective acculturation" makes avoiding failure particularly difficult for those who are required to undergo most adaptation.[307] Conflicts triggered by the uni-dimensional adaptation imposed upon migrants and minorities have focused on headscarves, and this is addressed below. But they are much broader and deeper.

The tendency of human rights discourse to focus on the individual and the state disregards multiple individual and collective identities which any definition of culture necessitates. The World Commission on Culture and Development has affirmed that cultural rights are collective, namely "the right of a group of people to follow or adopt a way of life of their choice."[308] Education is the key to transmitting that way of life to the next generation. When it is seen as effective acculturation, it is often rejected, sometimes violently.

UNRISD has acknowledged that "culture is one of the most contested issues of all" and defined as 'culturalist groups' those undertaking action against dominant cultures.[309] Such action faces two obstacles: the nation-state and globalization. Correspondence between a nation and a state exist only in cons- titutions of some countries. Contradictions between such an uni-cultural entity and the multiple racial, ethnic, religious, linguistic ·communities within each nation-state are obvious. Demands that each community's claim to its own culture be accommodated generate endless controversy. Girls are often the first victims of acquiescence to collective rights because their rights might be denied by those speaking for a culturalist group, and this deepens and broadens the underlying controversy.

Religion

Education involves much more that transmission of knowledge and skills. The values which education espouses might be openly endorsed or cloaked behind its apparent neutrality but they are part and parcel of any education. The orientation of education might be secular or religious, the methods used might favour teaching children what to think or else how to think. The power which is exercise by the authorities which decide on the contents and methods of education should be subjected to human rights safeguards lest this power be abused.

Global human rights instruments were adopted during earlier decades, with an assumption that all countries would be governed by secular rather than religious law. The implicit assumption was that freedom of religion would constitute one out of the many human rights exercised in the private sphere. That assumption

---

[307] OECD – *Reviews of National Policies for Education: France*, OECD, Paris, 1996, p. 175.
[308] UNESCO – *Our Creative Diversity. Report of the World Commission on Culture and Development*, UNESCO Publishing, Paris, 1995, p. 25.
[309] UNRISD – *States of Disarray: The Social Effects of Globalization. An UNRISD Report for the World Summit for Social Development*, Geneva, March 1995, p. 96 and 102.

was not factually substantiated during the earlier decades and this is even less so today.

Design of education varies between a country-wide, uniform network of public schools and an affirmation of the freedom of communities to establish and operate schools. Some constitutions affirm that education can be provided by religious communities, others regulate religious education in public schools, yet others define public education as exclusively secular while allowing private religious schools.

In few countries education is only secular, the People's Republic of China is one example.[310] In some, it is only religious, for example, in Iran.[311] In Indonesia, the 1999 Law on Human Rights stipulated that "every child has the right to access to education and schooling as befits his interests talents and intellectual capacity." The pre-existing dual system of public and private, free and for-fee, religious and secular schools was thereby affirmed in national human rights law, guaranteeing freedom of fund-raising for "private schooling and education."[312] Some constitutions explicitly affirm that education can be provided by religious communities. For example, the 1957 Constitution of Malaysia and the 1963 Constitution of Singapore specify that "every religious group has the right to establish and maintain institutions for the education of children in its own religion, and there shall be no discrimination on the ground only of religion in any law relating to such institutions or in the administration of such law."[313] Such approaches safeguard particular features of collective identity within individual countries, such as religion, but raise important questions from the viewpoint separate, parallel education systems.

Religion in education

Public education which is designated as secular raises important questions regarding the presence or absence of religion. The Human Rights Committee

---

[310] During my mission to China in September 2003, I found that religious education remained prohibited both in public and in private education. Commission on Human Rights – The right to education. Report submitted by the Special Rapporteur, Katarina Tomasevski: Mission to the People's Republic of China, 10-19 September 2003, U.N. Doc. E/CN.4/45/Add.1, para. 6.

[311] Golnar Mehran has thus described the effect of this policy on girls and women: "On the one hand, one witnesses a significant increase in female enrollment and completion rates at every educational level, a reduced gender gap in primary and secondary schooling, and an increase in the rate of university acceptance and enrollment among women. On the other hand, postrevolutionary educational policy in characterized by the banning of coeducation, the compulsory veiling of female students beginning at age 6, explicit gender stereotyping in school textbooks, and guiding female students toward feminine specializations deemed appropriate for women." Mehran, G. – The paradox of tradition and modernity in female education in the Islamic Republic of Iran, *Comparative Education Review*, vol. 47, 2003, No. 3, p. 270.

[312] The House of Representatives of the Republic of Indonesia – Legislation Number 39 of 1999 Concerning Human Rights, Jakarta, 23 September 1999, *State Gazette of the Republic of Indonesia* No. 165 of 1999.

[313] Tomasevski, K. – *Manual on Rights-based Education. Global Human Rights Requirements Made Simple*, UNESCO, Bangkok, 2004, p. 52.

had a series of 'Nordic cases' which revolved around the accommodation of religious and secular parental preferences in public education.[314] In one of them, the Committee examined a complaint against "compulsory instruction for atheists in the history of religion and ethics" to find that such instruction, if "given in a neutral and objective way and [if it] respects the convictions of parents and guardians who do not believe in any religion" does not constitute a human rights violation. [315] The boundary between such education carried out in conformity with human rights law or in its violation is thin indeed. The need to accommodate the diversity of learners and, in particular, choices made by the parents, is unlikely ever to stop generating similar cases.

Respect of parental religious convictions in education has emerged with particular frequency with regard to Jehovah's Witnesses, world-wide. The European Court of Human Rights analysed a complaint concerning a girl who was suspended from school because she had refused to participate in a parade, which she regarded as a commemoration of war. The Court took note of the parents' pacifist convictions but found no human rights violation in her suspension from school. [316] Disappointingly, not only that the Court failed to identify what was deemed a human rights violation in other regions, it did not even mention the pacifist beliefs of the girls, treating her as an object of schooling rather than a subject of rights and freedoms.

Similar cases concerning Jehovah's Witnesses have been litigated in Zambia, in India, and before the Inter-American Commission on Human Rights against Argentina, In Zambia, the case was triggered by the requirement of singing the national anthem and saluting the flag as a condition for attending governmental schools. Refusal to do so led to the expulsion of the pupil concerned. Domestic courts outlawed that requirement as contrary to freedom of conscience or religion,[317] but the government justified (and continued) that imposition saying that "these were conditions if a student wished to attend a government or aided school." [318] Elizabeth Evatt, then a member of the Human Rights Committee, noted while the Committee was examining Zambia's report that "freedom of

---

[314] De Zayas, A. and Møller, J. – Optional Protocol cases concerning the Nordic States before the United Nations Human Rights Committee, *Nordic Journal of International Law*, vol. 55, 1986, No. 4, pp. 384-400.

[315] Human Rights Committee – *Erkki Hartikainen v. Finland*, Communication 40/1978, Views of 9 April 1981.

[316] European Court of Human Rights – *Efstratiou v. Greece* and *Valsamis v. Greece*, Judgments of 18 December 1996.

[317] The case, *Kachasu v. Attorney General* (1967), was widely reported as a precedent for a judicial affirmation that education laws could be inconsistent with human rights obligations. Felia Kachasu, a girl attending the fourth grade of public primary school at the time, was first suspended and then expelled from school because she refused to sign the national anthem and salute the flag. As a child, he was legally precluded from vindicating her rights and the case was filed by her father. The key argument was that, as Jehovah's Witness, it was contrary to her religious beliefs to worship political authorities. The High Court found against her but, on appeal, the Court of Appeals overturned that ruling. Its principal argument was that freedom of religion was a fundamental right and took precedence over ordinary legislation. Thus, the education law was declared to be null and void in the part in which it compelled pupils to act against their faith and the girl should be allowed to resume her education.

[318] U.N. Doc. CCPR/C/63/Add.3 (1995), para. 80.

religion became meaningless if the price of exercising that freedom was exclusion from education."[319] The Supreme Court of India confirmed the ethos of accommodation in a similar case. It concerned the expulsion of school children who, upholding their beliefs as Jehovah's Witnesses, refused to sing the national anthem justifying this by their conscientious objection and stood in respectful silence while other children sang it. The Supreme Court found their expulsion to have a been a human rights violation, ending its judgment with this observation:

Our tradition teaches tolerance;
Our philosophy preaches tolerance;
Our Constitution practices tolerance;
Let us not dilute it. [320]

The case against Argentina was triggered by a decree which followed the military coup in 1976, whereby Jehovah's Witnesses were declared to be a sect "endorsing principles opposed to basic principles of the State and its laws". In its aftermath, 300 children were expelled from school and prohibited from re-enrolling. The Inter-American Commission on Human Rights found in 1978 that Argentina had violated a range of human rights, including the right to education.[321]

Canada's Supreme Court has rejected a claim by a parent to "educate his children as he pleases," based on "his authority over his children and his duty to attend to their education" which comes from God, as he put it. Although Canadian law allows parents to exempt their children from attending school if they are 'under efficient instruction at home or elsewhere,' the applicant had refused to apply for an approval of his home education claiming that this would violate his religious freedom. The Supreme Court has found that "accommodation of defendant's religious beliefs would entail a complete exemption from state regulation" and thus "severely impede the achievement of important state goals."[322]

How these goals are defined varies in time and place. Exemptions from compulsory education have been granted by the US Supreme Court to Amish children in order not to jeopardize the Amish way of life. Compulsory education longer than eight years was seen as

an impermissible exposure of [Amish] children to a "worldly" influence in conflict with their beliefs. The high school tends to emphasize intellectual and scientific accomplishments, self-distinction, competitiveness, worldly success, and social life with other students. Amish society emphasizes informal learning-through-doing; a life of "goodness" rather than a life of intellect; wisdom rather than technical knowledge; community welfare rather than competition; and separation

[319] U.N. Doc. CCPR/C/SR.1489 (1996), para. 42.
[320] Supreme Court of India – *Bijoe Emmanuel v. State of Kerala*, AIR 1987 SC 748.
[321] Case no. 2137 [Argentina], *Annual Report of the Inter-American Commission on Human Rights*, 18 November 1978, p. 43.
[322] Supreme Court of Canada – *R. v. Jones*, [1986] 2 S.C.R, 284.

from, rather than integration with contemporary worldly society.

The length of compulsory education was reduced by two years so as to avoid de-culturating the children.[323]

The Supreme Court of Colombia examined in 1998 a complaint by two boys, both minors, who had been prevented from continuing their education by attending evening classes on the grounds of their sexual orientation. The Court faulted the school for having failed to exhibit the values of tolerance and respect of diversity, adding that a public school could not preclude entry to learners by asserting that "homosexuality is sinful." Thereby, the school violated the boys' right to education, their freedom from discrimination and the right to full development of their personality.[324] The complaint of discriminatory exclusion of a teacher who 'had been engaged in a protracted confrontation with the authorities over his teaching and his employment,' has led the Human Rights Committee to determine that his rights had been violated by constant harassment which made his continuation in public service teaching impossible. The background to the case was that teacher's denial of the certificate by the ecclesiastic authorities[325] necessary for him to continue teaching religion. The Committee has agreed that the teacher could be removed from teaching religion because of his advocacy of liberation theology but not prevented from continuing in public service teaching.[326]

Unfinished history

Disagreements relating to the values promoted through education highlight two levels at which they are supposed to be settled. Education policy is an articulation of societal values upon which government acts. They vary in time and place and are never shared by all members of society. The power of parliament to define the rights and duties, freedoms and responsibilities creates space for affirming and respecting minority and individual rights. This power can be abused and is questioned where the rights of individuals (and, increasingly the rights of indigenous peoples and minorities) have been denied or violated. While there is no right bestowed upon individual parents to choose a specific religious or secular slant in public education, they have the right to challenge public education which, in their view denies equal rights of their children.

A part of what we commonly define as *culture* is grounded in our pre-human-rights historical heritage. The Supreme Court of Canada was faced with a

[323]   US Supreme Court – *Wisconsin v. Yoder*, 406 U.S. 205 (1972), 15 May 1972.
[324]   Supreme Court of Colombia – *Pablo Enrique Torres Gutierrez and José Prieto Restrepo v. Instituto Ginebra La Salle*, T-147493, Judgment of 24 March 1998.
[325]   The Government of Colombia has explained that applicants for the post of a teacher of religion must possess the certificate of suitability, which is issued by the Catholic church which also supplies the curricula and verifies whether religious education is provided in accordance with the precepts of the Catholic church.
[326]   Human Rights Committee – *William Eduardo Delgado Paez v. Colombia*, Communication No. 195/1985, Views of 12 July 1990.

complaint against a denial of public funding to some private religious schools. It affirmed that the purpose of public is inclusiveness, provision of education for all members of the community, together. The exercise of parental freedom to educate their children in accordance with their religious beliefs in separate schools (or at home) prevents their children from taking advantage of public schools and creates costs for the parents; such exercise of parental freedom does not entail an entitlement to public funding, however.[327] Canada's constitutional arrangements have, however, entrenched unequal public subsidies for specific communities. [328] A complaint against unequal funding for religious education in Canada was examined by the Human Rights Committee in 1999. The complaint alleged discrimination and violation of minority rights because Roman Catholic schools were public, and thus publicly funded. Schools established by other religious denominations were not publicly funded and were precluded from incorporation in the public school system. That has been enshrined in Canada's Constitution and originated from a political compromise dating from 1867. The Human Rights Committee decided thus:

> [T]he Covenant does not oblige States parties to fund schools which are established on a religious basis. However, if a State party chooses to provide public funding to religious schools, it should make this funding available without discrimination.[329]

The government of Canada replied to the Committee in February 2000 that the decision would not be translated into practice because education was not a federal but a state prerogative (the state in this case was Ontario) and the federal state in question would not alter that policy.[330] In a less politically visible case, the Supreme Court of Canada has addressed discriminatory effects of the teaching schedule derived from Christianity, which is thus discriminatory against teachers belonging to other religions:

> Teachers who belong to most of the Christian religions do not have to take any days off for religious purposes, since the Christian holy days of Christmas and Good Friday are specifically provided for in the calendar. Yet, members of the Jewish religion must take a day off work in order to celebrate Yom Kippur. It thus inevitably follows that the effect of the calendar is different for Jewish teachers. They, as a result of their religious beliefs, must take a day off work while the majority of their colleagues have their religious holy days recognized as holidays from work. In the absence of some accommodation by their employer the Jewish

---

327 Supreme Court of Canada – *Adler v. Ontario*, Judgment of 21 November 1996, [1996] 3 S.C.R. 609, (1996) 140 DLR (4th) 385.

328 The Supreme Court of Canada has affirmed that educational rights 'granted specifically to the Protestants in Quebec and the Roman Catholics in Ontario make it impossible to treat all Canadians equally. The country was founded upon the recognition of special or unequal educational rights for specific religious groups in Ontario and Quebec.' *Reference re Bill 30, An Act to Amend the Education Act (Ont.)*, [1987] 1 S.C.R., 1148, p. 1199-1200.

329 Human Rights Committee – *Arieh Hollis Waldman v. Canada*, Communication No. 694/1996, Views of 3 November 1999.

330 UNDP – *Human Rights and Human Development: Human Development Report 2000*, UNDP/Oxford University Press, New York, 2000, p. 93.

teachers must lose a day's pay to observe their holy day.[331]

Similarly in France, the law reform triggered in 2004 by the Stasi Commission,[332] which became known as 'the battle of headscarves', included a correction of the obvious inconsistency between the professed secularism of education and the fact that school holidays recognized Christian while not non-Christian religious holy days.[333]

Adaptation of education to different religions would be difficult enough to attain without further difficulties stemming from those religions which have become institutionalized in education as different from those perceived as 'imported' through migration, not only in Canada or France. Within the European Union, religious education is obligatory in Greece while not part of the curriculum in France, Finland recognizes 40 minority religions and Spain only 2.[334] Discrimination between religions stems from the privileged status of one institutionalized religion in Denmark, Finland, Greece, Italy, Portugal, Spain, Sweden and the United Kingdom at the expense of other recognized religions and, even more so, those religions that are regarded as sects. [335] This illustrates how little similarity there is even within a region which has transformed much of the previously national into European law.

Seeking a proper balance between freedom *of* religion and freedom *from* religion in Germany generated an endless stream of court cases and much public controversy. The first part revolved around Christianity[336] and, although controversial, was in hindsight relatively easy. The German Federal Constitutional Court found that the affixation of a crucifix in non-denominational primary schools in Bavaria breached the constitutional protection of freedom of religion. The Court noted the duty of religious neutrality, pointing out that "through the cross symbol deep, lasting effect was being exercised on the mental development of easily influenceable school-age children." It emphasized that the possibility of

---

[331] Supreme Court of Canada – *Commission scolaire régionale de Chambly v. Bergevin*, [1994], 2 S.C.R., 525, p. 9.

[332] The Stasi Commission, Commission de reflexion sur l'application du principe de laïcité dans la Republique, submitted its report on 11 December 2003. It is available, together with accompanying documents at www.assemblee-nat.fr/dossiers/laicite.

[333] M. Stasi prone l'interdiction des signes religieux et politiques à l'école, *Le Monde*, 13 décembre 2004.

[334] Ministerio de Educacón, Cultura y Deporte – La enseñanza de la religion en la Unión Europea y la Conferencia internacional consultive sobre la educación escolar el relación con la libertad de religion, de convicciones, la tolerancia y la no discriminación, *Boletín CIDE de temas educativos*, Centro de investigación y documentación educative, Madrid, diciembre de 2001, número 8.

[335] European Parliament – Report on the human rights situation in the European Union, Rapporteur: Joke Swiebel, Committee on Citizens' Freedoms and Rights, Justice and Home Affairs, Doc. A5-0451/2002, available at www2.europarl.eu.int, PE311.039/DEF (July 2003).

[336] The historical and cultural role of Christianity is affirmed in German constitutional practice as well as in its education policy and most schools are inter-denominational. The principle of governmental policy is neutrality which, for example, inhibits making a school prayer obligatory but permits keeping its optional. The governance of education is decentralized with the competences of the federal states by far overwhelming those of the federal authorities. This notion of neutrality is thus differently interpreted and applied in individual federal states. Muehlfoff, I. – Freedom of religion in public schools in Germany and in the United States, *Georgia Journal of International and Comparative Law*, vol. 28, 2000, pp. 405-457.

sending children to private schools was not 'an escape' from the exposure of the children to learning 'under the cross'. The fees charged in private schools made them inaccessible for many due to their inability to afford the cost. The Court then concluded:

> The Federal Constitutional Court has drawn the conclusion that the legislature is not utterly barred from introducing Christian references in designing the public elementary schools, even if those with parental power who cannot avoid these schools in their children's education may not desire any religious upbringing. There is a requirement, however, that this be associated with only the indispensable minimum of elements of compulsion. ... [The cross] cannot be divested of its specific reference to the beliefs of Christianity and reduced to a general token of the Western cultural tradition. It symbolizes the essential core of the conviction of the Christian faith, which has undoubtedly shaped the Western world in particular in many ways but is certainly not shared by all members of society, and is indeed rejected by many. ... Positive religious freedom is due to all parents and pupils equally, not just the Christian ones. The conflict arising cannot be resolved according to the majority principle, for the fundamental right to religious freedom specifically is aimed in a special degree at protecting minorities. Insofar as the school, in harmony with the Constitution, allows room for [activating religious convictions in State institutions], as with religious instruction, school prayers and other religious manifestations, these must be marked by the principle of being voluntary and allow the other-minded acceptable, non-discriminatory possibilities of avoiding them. [337]

This judgment was probably as much criticised as the decision of the Human Rights Committee regarding public funding for Catholic schools in Ontario. Similarly, it triggered a rejection by the authorities to which it was addressed. Such problems have been exacerbated when "non-Christian religions approached the Christian hemisphere."[338]

European conundrum: School girls with headscarves

Many cases have been generated by the need for schools in Western European countries to adapt to the wearing of headscarves. In some countries headscarves have been prohibited and the European Court of Human Rights has endorsed such a prohibition. In others, they have been permitted. In either case, there are here to stay. Europe, embodied in the Council or Europe or the European Union, has demonstrated its inability to articulate a common human rights position. The permissiveness of the European Court of Human Rights has allowed individual countries to prohibit headscarves. The German Constitutional Court has gone one step further and permitted individual federal states to prohibit headscarves for teachers. [339] The resulting European mosaic does not bode well

---

[337] Federal Constitutional Court of Germany – Order of the First Senate of 16 May 1995, 1 BvR 1087/91.

[338] Graulich, K. – Religion in education: A German point of view, *International Journal for Education Law and Policy*, Special Conference Edition, issue 1-2. 2004, p. 206.

[339] BVerfG, 2 BvR 1436/02, 24 September 2003, available in German at www.bverfg.de.

for the protection of human rights in education, especially those revolving around Islam.

Both the prohibitive and the permissive side in the many 'battles of headscarves' have built their respective cases on human rights arguments. However, the issue was transferred from human rights law into a highly visible political battlefield and then violence overwhelmed the underlying questions. One would have wanted an ombudsman-type institution to silence the assorted public figures, compete through inflammatory statements and displays of militancy, saying: "not in front of the children!" The core of the problem was forgotten: school girls are children targeted by two conflicting duties: to wear a headscarf if the parents insist on it or she perceives it as her religious duty, and to go to school because the law of the country insists on its. That a child cannot comply with both duties is obvious. That no child should have incompatible duties forced upon her would have been obvious if the issue was not taken out of human rights and education early and, perhaps, irrevocably.

By the end of 2004, prohibitive legislation took root in continental Europe, with five German federal states banning headscarves at school as well as France.[340] Following the adoption of a law banning headscarves in France, two French journalists were taken hostage in Iraq ostensibly to coerce the authorities to rescind it.[341] Theo van Gogh, a Dutch filmmaker, was shot and a letter was affixed to his dead body by plunging a knife into his chest, attributing that gruesome homicide to 'Submission', a film which some deemed to have been legitimate exercise of freedom of artistic expression and others abuse of that freedom targeting Islam and Muslims.[342] How school children have perceived such conduct of adults we may learn if they are asked. At worst, they would have internalized a message contrary to anything that their formal education might have taught them about human rights, namely that extreme views and gruesome violence raise one's visibility while thoughtful and tolerant platforms do not. They, especially the girls with headscarves, found themselves in a crossfire.

In the Netherlands, the accommodation of girls with headscarves was posited by the Equal Treatment Commission in the late 1990s. Muslim girls had refused to attend physical exercise, although it constituted a part of the compulsory curriculum. The Equal Treatment Commission of the Netherlands found that the refusal of a school to allow Muslim girls to wear long-sleeved T-shirts, long trousers and headcaps constituted discrimination. Having examined a complaint with regard to loose headscarves during physical exercise, the Commission did not find a human rights violations because the rationale for the prohibition was

---

[340] Vallières, V. – EU's ethnic integration thrown into sharp relief by violence, *European Voice*, 25 November – 1 December 2004.

[341] Two French journalists, Christian Chesnot and Georges Malbrunot, had been taken hostage in August 2004 by an armed organization in Iraq, the Islamic Army, and released in December 2004 through an apparently successful French diplomatic initiative. (Hopquin, B. – Christian Chesnot et Georges Malbrunot sont rentrés en France, *Le Monde*, 23 December 2004). Because they were forced by their captors to plead for the abrogation of the law banning headscarves lest they would be executed, public sympathy and solidarity diminished critique of the law.

[342] Anthony, A. – A knife in the Dutch heart, *Guardian Weekly*, 17-23 December 2004.

the safety of learners during exercise. In another case, the efforts of a school to accommodate a Muslim girl by offering her to wear clothing adapted to her religious convictions and a separate dressing room have been found to constitute sufficient accommodation.[343] In yet another case, the Commission found discrimination against a young women who, as part of her practical training at teachers' college which requires teaching at a primary school, wished to teach at her former primary school but was refused when she answered the question as to whether she was wearing a headscarf in the positive.[344]

In France, the courts have had, at various points in time, both annulled and upheld the expulsion of girls from school because they wore headscarves.[345] The first act of an intensely public drama took place in 1989, when two girls were expelled from school by their school's director for having refused to take off their scarves. The Conseil d'Etat pronounced itself first in 1989, in the form of advice to the government, and stated that "the wearing of religious symbols is not in itself incompatible with the secularism of public schools." This had apparently permitted headscarves and was followed by additional rulings. In 1992, the Council nullified a school-based prohibition of headscarves. It drew the line between a required tolerance of the display of religious symbols and proselytizing, which is prohibited in the French secular public school system, thus:

> In educational institutions, the display of symbols whereby learners manifest that they pertain to a particular religion is not by itself incompatible with secularism as long as this constitutes the exercise of freedom of expression and the manifestation of religious beliefs; such freedom does not, however, permit the learners to display symbols of their religion which, due to the very nature of such symbols, or to the particular circumstances in which they are displayed, individually or collectively, or to their ostentatious or demonstrative character, constitute an exercise of pressure, provocation, proselytizing or propaganda.[346]

The key word was "ostentatious" (*ostentatoire*) and it has remained the boundary between the tolerable and the intolerable.[347] Until the 2004 law, the interpretation was left to individual schools, occasionally facilitated (or made more difficult) by ministerial or administrative guidance. The question became a

---

[343] Equal Treatment Commission of the Netherlands – Rulings 1998-79 of 6 July 1998. 1997-149 of 24 December 1997, and 1999-106 of 23 December 1999.

[344] Equal Treatment Commission of the Netherlands – Ruling 1999-103 of 22 December 1999.

[345] A permissible or light headscarf reveals the hairline, neck and ears, while the impermissible headscarf is one that is called 'Islamic' or known by its name in Arabic as *hijab*. That one and the same headscarf can be adjusted to appear permissible or impermissible has not escaped the attention of the critics of the series of judicial, ministerial and administrative rulings. Of course, ingenious children delighted at having a prohibition which tedious adults have imposed upon them played these subtle definitional differences to extract from them as much defiance and ridicule as possible.

[346] Conseil d'Etat – *Kherouaa, Kachour, Balo & Kizic* (2 November 1992), *Milles N. and Z. Yilmaz* (14 March 1994), *M. et Mme Aoukili* (10 March 1995) available at www.conseil-etat.fr/ce-data/juris/jurisprudance.

[347] The speech by president Jacques Chirac, on 17 December 2004, used that term to express his conviction that "religious symbols which ostentatiously demonstrate one's affiliation should be banned". (Le discourse de Jacques Chirac sur la laïcité, *Le Monde*, 18 December 2004.

highly visible political issue in the 1990s and even more so after the turn of the millennium. Religion is statistically invisible in France because no questions related to religious affiliation can be asked in the census. The legal guarantee of secularity, which became a hundred years old in 2005, was supposed to keep religion in the private sphere, and especially out of public education. The 2004 law banned ostentatious religious symbols and when it was applied, at the beginning of school year 2004-2005, 36 school girls were expelled for wearing headscarves and 4 Sikh boys for wearing turbans. [348] Without doubt, this is not the end of the controversy.

In Switzerland, the balance needed between a display of religious symbols, which should be tolerated, and a display of religious symbols which should be outlawed has included the requirement upon public education to respect the religious convictions of every individual child and its parents. In a case involving a Muslim teacher wearing a headscarf, the Swiss federal court opted for a restrictive approach, fearing disputes amongst children belonging to different religions and their parents. Moreover, because teachers are a role model for learners, the court has affirmed their need to be religiously neutral. [349]

The European Commission of Human Rights held that the learner's choice of particular education (at issue was the girl's enrolment in a secular university) entailed the acceptance of the rules applied in that educational establishment. The Commission did not find that the prohibition of wearing a headscarf constituted a human rights violation. [350] This was confirmed by the European Court of Human Rights in its judgment concerning the prohibition of headscarves for teachers in Switzerland, in the above mentioned case. The Court has had this to say:

> The Court accepts that it is very difficult to assess the impact that a powerful external symbol such as the wearing of a headscarf may have on the freedom of conscience and religion of very young children. The applicant's pupils were aged between four and eight, an age at which children wonder about many things and are also more easily influenced than older pupils. In those circumstances, it cannot be denied outright that the wearing of a headscarf might have some kind of proselytising effect, seeing that it appears to be imposed on women by a precept which is laid down in the Koran and which, as the Federal Court noted, is hard to square with the principle of gender equality. It therefore appears difficult to reconcile the wearing of an Islamic headscarf with the message of tolerance, respect for others and, above all, equality and non-discrimination that all teachers in a democratic society must convey to their pupils.[351]

---

348 Bronner, L. – Trente élèves exclus pour cause de posrt de signes religieux ostensibles, *Le Monde*, 27 November 2004.

349 *X v. Etat du Canton de Genève*, Arrêt du Tribunal Fédéral, 123 I 296, 12 November 1997.

350 European Commission on Human Rights – *Karaduman v. Turkey*, Application No. 16278/90, Decision of 3 May 1993, *Decisions & Reports*, vol. 74, 1993, p. 93.

351 European Court of Human Rights – *Dahlab v. Switzerland*, Judgment of 15 February 2001, p. 13, available at http://hudoc.echr.coe.int.

5

Beyond law: Monitoring and indicators

The field of human rights is overpopulated with lawyers who look at education by examining the law and analysing the jurisprudence. Previous chapters have summarized a range of cases which have challenged education on human rights grounds and sometimes changed it. Most cases deal with the plight of an individual. Systemic problems often lurk behind an individual face and an individual fate but human rights law, at best, sets the minimal criteria to protect explicitly recognized rights and freedoms. Education functions according to its own underlying logic, which is rarely informed by human rights law. This underlying logic derives from successful educational models, which are used as the yardstick for assessing performance world-wide. The current focus is on outputs rather than inputs, and learning accomplishments rather than financial incentives needed to level the playing field are prioritized. Increased autonomy is bestowed upon educational institutions so as to enable them to enhance performance, and they are held accountable for ensuring the best attainable performance. A country's rank in internationally tested learning accomplishments has become the key driver of change. This obliterates attention to all those who are excluded from education and leads to the exclusion of those who cannot compete. This underlying logic is inspired by the free-market.

Economics and politics being connatural, the human-rights lens also has to focus on the impact of short electoral cycles on education. By my own count, there were 37 major policy initiatives in 1997-2001 in the United Kingdom following the memorable triple sound-bite, 'education, education, education', whereby the prime-minister-to-be had announced the three priorities for his government.[352] Similarly, Luc Bronner has asked 'why ministers for education?', having listed the endless major initiatives by consecutive French ministers of education in the past decade.[353] The OECD has diagnosed that "education is becoming increasingly politicised, particularly in times of economic stringency and sharpened ideological differences" and noted, for Greece, an average of two ministers of education in 1981-1996 which led to a confusing array of reforms on the statute book.[354]

The economics and politics of education as its driving forces necessitate careful strategizing of the role which human rights law can – and should – have as a source of values which inform education. Older human rights treaties, inspired

---

[352] Commission on Human Rights – Report by Katarina Tomaševski, Special Rapporteur on the right to education, on her mission to the United Kingdom, 18 – 22 October 1999, U.N. Doc. E/CN.4/2000/6/6/Add. 2 of 16 November 1999.
[353] Bronner, L. – A quoi servent les ministres de l'éducacion?, Le Monde, 25 June 2005.
[354] OECD – *Reviews of National Policies for Education: Greece*, Paris, 1997, p. 138.

by governmental obligation to provide free education to all, are favoured in the human rights literature although the practice of states has changed. Points of convergence are found in the global commitment to ensure free primary education for all children, which is inspired by the spirit of human rights law if not informed by its wording. The frequent mention of 'equity' in education reflects an instinctive opposition to the unfairness of educational systems which transmit privilege and deprivation from one generation to another or, today, condition entry in education by the purchasing power alone. Thus, there is convergence at the interface between education and human rights. It provides foundations for macro-analyses of education using human rights as the yardstick.

Confluent public policies

The overlap between education and human rights is seen most clearly in their shared objectives even if different vocabularies are used. Points of convergence are found in international commitments to rights-based education. The EFA (Education for All) Global Monitoring Report 2003/4 [355] integrated human rights so as to emphasize their importance in attaining education for *all*. That human rights were integrated in monitoring but had been omitted from the design of global education strategy is illustrative of the resistance to the use of human rights as guidance. Nevertheless, their inclusion in monitoring is an important step because a future strategy is likely to be informed by assessments of the previous one, and these will include human rights. Moreover, because gender parity in education has been elevated to a globally shared objective in education, points of convergence are easy to discern. Although the promise of gender parity by 2005 has been betrayed, the fact that progress and retrogression is monitored is, again, an important step towards integration of human rights. The priority for all-encompassing and free education for all children is, after the 15-year gap described earlier, shared between global strategies and international human rights law. This all facilitates integration of human rights throughout education policy and practice at all levels, from global to local, emphasizing "the centrality of human rights in all activities."[356] Conceptual bridges between human rights and education, between the economics of education and the economics of human rights, are derived from the shared global goals of education for all, poverty eradication as well as gender equality.

Education is not only an end in itself but also a means for attaining all other globally agreed goals. International human rights law constitutes ready-made framework for assessing progress in attaining these goals because it reaches far beyond enrolments and learning outcomes to the aims, purposes and methods of education aimed at enjoyment all human rights by all.

---

[355] Gender and Education for All: The Leap to Equality. EFA Global Monitoring Report 2003/4, available at www.unesco.org/education/efa_report.

[356] General Assembly – Road map towards the implementation of the United Nations Millennium Declaration: Report of the Secretary-General, U.N. Doc. A/56/326, para. 201.

Nevertheless, obstacles are many. The term *right to* education is openly rejected, such as in a OECD's review of Italy's education policy in 1998. It was noted that Italy "has instituted a "right" to education to 18 years for all those who can profit from it."[357] Although the word "right" was placed between inverted commas so as to denote how alien it was, that same evaluation clarified an important part of its rationale by summarizing the purpose of compulsory education:

> Compulsory education still has a strong symbolic value. It corresponds to a commitment from the state which guarantees all children the possibility of education for a certain number of years. Raising the school leaving age irreversibly consolidates the progress that has been made in getting children to attend school. Even though most young people stay at school beyond leaving age, compulsory education is at least a guarantee that the least well-off will receive an education.
> Wider objectives have been attached to compulsory schooling, such as the construction of a national identity and, more recently, the promotion of greater equality of opportunity (both of which may imply attending a school common to all).
> The reform proposal also provides for a right to education until the age of 18. This idea has already been taken up in a number of OECD countries, especially in northern Europe. The connection between this right to education and the notion of compulsory schooling remains to be defined.[358]

It is precisely "this connection between the right to education and compulsory schooling" that lies at the core of governmental human rights obligations. This seems to be poorly known outside the human rights circles, hence the need for crossing disciplinary boundaries. Fears of misinterpretations of the right to education are likely to diminish with increased exposure of educationists to human rights law.

An examination of educational statistics through the human rights lens points to the road to be travelled. This highlights the need for human rights lawyers to understand how statistics is created and what it means. It is as customary as it is erroneous for education statistics to be misrepresented as if it referred to the right to education, but this is perhaps a consequence of the widespread lack of knowledge about quantitative data which is proverbial amongst human rights lawyers. Profound conceptual issues are involved. Where education is sold and purchased against a price, it constitutes a service regulated by commercial rather than human rights law. Access to education then reflects the individuals' purchasing power. The rights of those who cannot afford the cost of education are denied in the very vocabulary: they do not have *access* to education and remain beyond educational statistics. If education is imposed upon the young generation so as to force them to adopt an alien language or ideology, it represents a denial of human rights. Children may be at school and so education statistics look good. But if they are forced to alter their identity or, worse, if 'education' conforms to the definition of genocide, quantitative data on education will hide the denial of human rights at the very core of educational

---

[357] OECD – *Reviews of National Policies for Education: Italy*, Paris, 1998, p. 104.
[358] OECD – *Reviews of National Policies for Education: Italy*, Paris, 1998, p. 36.

practice. Therefore, all facets of education have to be assessed by the pertinent human rights criteria so as to discern whether education conforms to international human rights law and, if not, what needs to be done to ensure such conformity.

Statistics operate in averages while human rights law posits everybody's equal right to education, and this necessitates creating data which do not exist as yet. National or local averages camouflage gender, racial, ethnic or linguistic fault-lines and, thus, impede any effective prohibition of discrimination because it is simply impossible to monitor whether it is being translated into practice. This is highlighted in Figure 14 below. Inequalities defy internationally prohibited discrimination.

Furthermore, the principle of indivisibility of human rights requires assessing the impact of education on *all* rights and freedoms. The consequence of treating education as a means for poverty reduction is the need to assess its impact on the ability of school-leavers to sustain themselves by finding or creating employment. The phenomenon of graduate unemployment, noted in Figure 12 below, is a good illustration of the need to rescue education from being merely a self-contained sector. It is an indictment of education to see statistics which show that the likelihood of unemployment increases with the level of education. Therefore, the quantity, quality and orientation of education ought to be evaluated against its relevance for graduates' subsequent lives. Also, the current global focus on primary education may undermine poverty reduction if its lasts merely 3 or 5 years and school-leavers are children much too young to be allowed to work. Where primary education is designed merely as a preparatory stage for further schooling, it will not be geared towards useful skills for all the children who cannot progress further.

Education as the main institutional form for the socialization of children makes the values it transmits to new generations crucial for its impact on society. The role of education in combating social exclusion and preventing conflicts is much too important to be left out of human rights monitoring. Because segregated education creates fragmented societies, difficult questions of reconciling the freedom of parents and communities to educate *their* children with the need for education to facilitate all-inclusive societies have to be faced. Answers may not be guided by the empirical evidence of the human rights impact of segregated or inclusive education, but the absence of such evidence makes it impossible to argue that education policy should be rights-based as well as evidence-based.

Human rights indicators

It is a truism that statistics reveal a lot but hide exactly what we want to know. This is particularly true for education statistics. A good illustration is Burundi's education plan developed in 2004, which uses as the basis for planning an estimated population size of 6.482.662. On that basis, the government reports 2.075.793 primary-school children to the year 2015, needing 27.677 classrooms and 36.417 teachers.[359] After years of armed and political conflicts, such precise figures are not based on counting the people because this has not been done. Rather, they are produced by mathematical modelling. The source of educational statistics is included in a technical appendix, in very small print, or not at all. The figures are cited and quoted and become seen as a true portrayal of the people they are supposed to relate to. It is rarely stressed that Lebanon has not had a census since 1932[360] or that the last census in Congo was held in 1984.[361]

Furthermore, even in the wealthiest countries in the world, not all school-age children enjoy their right to education. Enrolment statistics reveal a missing percentage, [362] but do not tell us who and where these children are, or why they are not in school. In poor countries and communities, too many children never enrol, but not even their numbers are known to the closest million. Estimates range between 100 and 140 million.[363] Pointing to poverty as the main cause for so many out-of-school children is insufficient by the human rights criteria. One important reason is that, regardless of the human rights obligation to accord them priority in resource allocation, military expenditure takes precedence over education in too many countries. The imbalance between military expenditure and investment in education highlights differences between poverty- and policy-based exclusion, evident in the priority for military expenditure in the Middle East and for education in Latin America. The first regional survey by the UNESCO Institute for Statistics (UIS) in 2002 reproduced government data on public expenditure on education in 15 Middle Eastern countries. Only five reported their budgetary allocations for education (Bahrain, Jordan, Lebanon, Morocco, and Syria). [364] This reinforced the findings of previous studies for UNICEF, which noted excessive military expenditure by North African and Middle Eastern countries, at 12.6% of GDP more than double than the world

---

[359] Burundi: Plan d'action national d'éducation pour tous (EPT), Ministè de l'Éducation Nationale, 20 September 2004, available at http://portal.unesco.org/education.

[360] Lebanon: Nerve-jangling change is coming, The Economist, 11 June 2005.

[361] Africa's unmended heart: Special report on Congo, The Economist, 11 June 2005.

[362] The enrolment rate for children aged 5-14 in the OECD countries is 98%, which shows that 2% of children are missing from the very enrolment, while a larger proportion misses out on attendance and completion. These "missing" children tend to be migrants, minorities, or children with disabilities, those that are increasingly defined as victims of social exclusion. Education at a Glance: OECD Indicators, Paris, 2001, p. 134.

[363] The slow progress in the past decade is reflected in disparate estimates of the number of out-of-school children as well as the numbers of children behind them. In 1996, the EFA (Education for All) estimated number for out-of-school children aged 6-11 was 110 million and UNICEF's estimate was 140 million. (International Working Group on Education – Selected Issues in Development Assistance to Education: Meeting of the International Working Group on Education (IWGE), Nice, France, 6-8 November 1996, International Institute for Educational Planning, Paris, 1997, p. 35 and 37) In 2003, the EFA estimate of the number of out-of-school children was lowered to 104 million (from 115 million in 1999) because the size of the school-going child population had been reduced in some large countries, such as China and India, by moving upwards the age for starting school from 6 to 7 years. (Gender and Education for All: The Leap to Equality, EFA Global Monitoring Report 2003/4, UNESCO, Paris, 2003, p. 49) UNICEF's estimate was that 121 million children were out of school in 2003, based on supplementary information on whether school-age children were attending school from household surveys. (The State of the World's Children 2004, UNICEF, New York, 2003, p. 7)

[364] UIS/UNESCO – Arab States: Regional Report, UNESCO Institute for Statistics, Montreal, 2002, available at www.unesco.org/uis.

average.[365] Differently in Latin America, in quite a few countries educational investment by far exceeds military expenditure, such as in Argentina, Belize, Bolivia, Brazil, or Costa Rica.[366]

Moreover, the effects of poverty on education vary. Some poor countries compensate their insufficient resources by making a huge effort to secure education for all, some wealthy countries do nothing of the kind. Within most countries, poverty affects girls differently from boys. Girls or children with disabilities are rarely prioritized when educational resources are scarce. Minority and indigenous children tend to be disproportionately victimized. Human rights indicators can and should be designed to monitor and evaluate the extent to which education policies and practices conform to international legal obligations of governments. *i.e. cove content + principles cHKs*

The proverbial sense of precision attached to numbers makes whatever is measured important. Whatever is not translated into figures remains unimportant, perceived as inexact nor incomparable. Hence, making human rights measurable elevates their visibility in designing education strategies, both global and national. *i.e it's always changing improving it's an ideal*

The aim of monitoring is to discern changes that can be related to specific laws, *but n* policies or interventions. The rationale is simple: there is no 'perfect' state of *that '* human rights that can be attained once and for all. The purpose of monitoring is *never* to discern the effort and changes that can be attributed to it. The utility of *fulfill* indicators is determined by the existence of a response mechanism, in order to ensure that corrective action is undertaken if indicators point to retrogression rather than progressive realization of human rights. The term 'progressive' suggests that indicators ought to reflect the centrality of improvement in the enjoyment of human rights. The obvious method is to supplement cross-national comparisons by assessing the situation in the country against its recent past, cross-temporally.

Human rights are founded on the rule of law and, thus, indicators need to capture the willingness and ability of governments to translate legal norms into real-life practices. Progress towards fulfilling core human rights obligations necessitates assessing the experiences of different countries within a common framework. This framework consists of the core contents of the right to education which is reflected in the corresponding government human rights obligations, which was explained in this book and is summarized in Figure 12. The conceptual framework which highlights what should be monitored follows governmental human rights obligations structured into a 4-A scheme: making education available, accessible, acceptable and adaptable. This integrates all human rights dimensions within a comprehensive monitoring scheme, specifying the ends to be attained and the necessary means. Monitoring enables

---

[365] Rihani, M. – *Strategies for Female Education in the Middle East and North Africa*, UNICEF Middle East and North Africa Regional Office, Amman (Jordan), 1993, p. 11.

[366] *SIPRI Yearbook 2003*, Stockholm International Peace Research Institute, available at www.sipri.org.

determination whether the means employed are leading to the desired ends and to the necessary corrective action if this turns out not to be the case.

Figure 12: 4-A monitoring scheme

	KEY ISSUES	HUMAN RIGHTS REQUIREMENTS
AVAILABILITY	1. The nature and scope of the commitment to the right to education 2. Legal and fiscal commitments 3. Guarantees for freedom *of* and *in* education	1. Effective guarantees comprising full scope of education as a human right 2. Concordance between budgetary allocations and educational rights 3. Access to justice for denials of freedom *of* and *in* education
ACCESSIBILITY	4. Obstacles for completion of compulsory education 5. Inequalities corresponding to prohibited grounds of discrimination 6. Underperformance of categories historically deprived of education	4. Effective remedies against educational exclusion 5. Disaggregation of education statistics by all prohibited grounds of discrimination 6. Differentiated treatment informed by equal rights for all *(as appropriate)*
ACCEPTABILITY	7. State responsibility to regulate and supervise all educational institutions 8. Rights and freedoms of the teaching profession 9. Rights-based learning	7. Enforcement of human rights requirements throughout education 8. Teachers' access to justice for violations of their rights 9. Access to remedy for equal rights of learners
ADAPTABILITY	10. Uniformity of education in denial of human diversity 11. Irrelevance of education for economic self-sustainability illustrated by graduate unemployment	10. Education tailored to the enjoyment of all human rights by all 11. Youth unemployment or fertility rates by the level of education

A merger between quantitative and qualitative data is needed to capture governmental commitments and efforts, obstacles, progress or retrogression. In accordance with the human rights obligations of governments, the focus is on two key variables: their willingness and their capacity to implement them. The difference between them is crucial for assessments of governmental performance, which require differentiating between governmental unwillingness (that is, the lack of commitment) and their insufficient capacity to comply with their human rights obligations. Also, the effort to implement human rights obligations, or the lack thereof, does not automatically translate into an improvement in the enjoyment of human rights. [367] It is therefore crucially

---

[367] Tomaševski, K. – Measuring compliance with human rights obligations, in: Rehof, L. A. and Gulmann, C. (eds.) – *Human Rights in Domestic Law and Development Assistance Policies of the Nordic Countries. Proceedings of the Fourth Nordic Seminar on Human Rights*, Martinus Nijhoff

important to differentiate between commitment and capacity as well as to analyse both in parallel.

Assessing commitment to the right to education

Different models are applied in the practice of states so as to harmonize international with national human rights law. In many countries, international human rights treaties do not apply domestically, while the extent to which national constitutions and laws, policies and practices have been harmonized with international human rights obligations varies a great deal. Gaps between international requirements and national practices are many, worldwide. Universal human rights standards lay down the global minimum, leaving to each state the choice of methods for attaining and sustaining it. Progress depends on the strength of commitment in each country, within and outside government. While international assistance helps, the history of human rights shows that national commitment and protection are decisive.

Similarities in national approaches are reflected in constitutional provisions. The practice of states reflects the thrust of international human rights law since the vast majority of countries in the world constitutionally guarantee the right to education.[368] Constitutions, however, lay down only the general framework of individual rights and corresponding government obligations in education. Education governance is divided between central and regional and/or local administration, and regulated by national and sub-national legislation. Moreover, foreign and development cooperation policies play a significant role, as does trade in education services. Differences in national laws and policies on education are thus many between countries, and their effects vary within countries. However, human rights obligations pertain to the state, and it is the central government that should ensure their implementation throughout the country.

Formal guarantees of education as a human right vary a great deal. Ratifications of international human rights treaties are often deemed to indicate the human rights commitment of a government. [369] However, differences between states

---

Publishers, 1989, pp. 109-127.

[368] A review of all written constitutions in 2000 revealed that the right to education was guaranteed in 142 countries while 44 has no constitutional guarantee. Commission on Human Rights – Annual report of the Special Rapporteur on the right to education, Katarina Tomasevski, U.N. Doc. E/CN.4/2001/52, paras. 66-67.

[369] Formal adherence to international human rights treaties is easy to record and tabulate, and the data are widely available from a variety of sources. The list of ratifications of all treaties that deal with education, including reservations thereto, is available at www.right-to-education.org. Such a list enables an immediate identification of those governments that have not accepted particular treaties, or parts thereof, which indicates their lack of commitment. It does not, however, reveal anything about the real (as different from formal) commitment for those states that are party to the treaties and have not reserved the right not to apply education-related provisions. The constitutions and laws as well as education policies and practices reveal an enormous variety regarding the existence or absence of effective guarantees of the right to education.

bound by identical international human rights obligations are huge. Some have constitutionally mandated allocations for education, other have not yet defined the implications of the right to education for fiscal allocations. Individual entitlements to free public education for all school-aged children exist in many countries. Some have, in addition, specified practical measures for overcoming exclusion and discrimination or established public institutions bestowed with powers to monitor human rights performance and recommend, or even enforce, correctives that may be needed. Thus, children deprived of education can seek and obtain redress before a national human rights commission or a children's ombudsman.

Differently in the United States, economic and social rights are not recognized and, furthermore, the Supreme Court has declared taxation as well as economic and social policy to lie beyond its purview. It has held that raising and disbursing tax constitutes a legislative function beyond the remit of courts. The core of the case was the financing of education at the district level out of property tax, which has created a great deal of difference between the levels of funding between rich and poor districts. The Court has refrained from questioning funding "depending on the relative wealth of the political subdivisions in which citizens live" to affirm "freedom to devote more money to the education of one's children." The argument continued in the opposite direction from where human rights would have led, with the Court favouring local autonomy at the expense of placing "the financial responsibility in the hands of the State." 370 However, the US Supreme Court has faulted denial of access to education "directed against children ... on the basis of a legal characteristic over which children have little control," highlight its cost: "It is difficult to understand precisely what the State hopes to achieve by promoting the creation and perpetuation of a subclass of illiterates within our boundaries, surely adding to the problems and costs of unemployment, welfare and crime. It is thus clear that whatever savings might be achieved by denying these children an education, they are wholly insubstantial in light of the costs involved to these children, the State and the Nation." 371

The European Union (EU) has been a pioneer in setting the boundaries between the right to free and access to for-fee education. Having developed from the common market, it crosses the boundaries between public and commercial law in defining fundamental rights. Its definition of the right to education in the Charter of Fundamental Rights, included in the constitutional treaty, does not define education as an individual entitlement but rather lays down "the possibility" of receiving education. This "clarifies that free compulsory education has to be possible, not that all compulsory education has to be free." 372 The background is the EU's need to refrain from interfering with the provision of free and compulsory education, which remains the sovereign prerogative of each

---

370   US Supreme Court – *San Antonio School District v. Rodriguez*, 411 U.S. 1 (1973), 21 March 1973.
371   US Supreme Court – *Plyer v. Doe*, 457 U.S. 202, 15 June 1982.
372   Winkler, R. – The right to education according to Article 14 of the Charter of Fundamental Rights of the European Union, *International Journal of Education Law and Practice*, Issue 1-2, December 2004, Special Conference Edition, p. 99.

member, while focusing on the legal infrastructure for trade in education services. The European Court of Justice has differentiated between education as a paid service from education as an individual entitlement by the criterion of payment, specifying that fee-for-service "is absent in the case of courses provided under the national education system." [373] Within the European Union, the right to free education has been preserved for children and young people in the compulsory education age, but post-compulsory education – both public and private – is increasingly subjected to required payments.

These different definitions of education as a right demonstrate how important it is to precisely determine what the commitment is before proceeding to examine whether performance matches it.

Accountability requires an explicit standard against which performance is measured, and creation of a mechanism for assuring that the standard is met. To measure the performance of governments, one needs to define what they are required to do, compare this with what they are willing and able to do. Credibility of this process depends on internationally accepted human rights standards, especially by the governments concerned, hence the importance of the commitment.

As mentioned above, formal commitments to human rights are routinely equated with the ratification of human rights treaties. However, a government may ratify human rights treaties and subsequently ignore them. There is not much evidence that those government which have ratified specific treaties perform better than those that did not, nor that better performance follows from the ratification of a treaty. There is no inducement for compliance nor sanction for non-compliance, which makes human rights work as difficult as it is. Therefore, one needs to move beyond the formal ratifications of human rights treaties to determine real commitments. [374]

While in international law the lack of commitment does not excuse the government from implementing its obligations, it certainly undermines its performance. In reviewing factors which determine eradication of poverty, the World Bank has concluded that "the larger policy environment was perhaps the single most important factor in the success or failure" of anti-poverty projects

---

373 *Belgian State v. Humbel* [1988] ECR 5365, para. 15.
374 The lack of commitment to the right to education occurs where the key institutional actor bound by human rights obligations, the state, fails to support its goals (most importantly, free and compulsory education for all school age children), the priority for the right to education in fiscal allocations (which translates legal and political into fiscal commitment), and the agreed means for the progressive realization of the right to education (such as making post-compulsory education free as circumstances permit). In order to assess commitment, it is necessary to identify those institutional actors within the state who have the power to influence educational policy and practice. Such influences can facilitate or impede the realization of the right to education. Formal legal guarantees, adopted by parliament, can be deprived of influence if they do not serve as blueprint for budgetary allocations and their beneficiaries do not have legal standing to claim and obtain effective enforcement.

and stressed the importance of analysing "government policies as a whole".[375] The same reasoning applies to education.

Different models, continental European, Anglo-American and Soviet, [376] profoundly influenced international and domestic guarantees of the right to education. The Soviet model envisaged government- provided all education as a free public service, but denying freedom of choice. The prevalence of compulsory education in the practice of states constitutes only one component of the right to education. If primary education is compulsory, provided against the payment of a fee, in a uniform state-run school system from which parents do not have freedom to opt out, education is not *free* in any meaning of this word. Therefore, the required universal coverage of primary education was comple- mented by parental freedom of choice. As explained earlier, governmental human rights obligations are dual. On the one hand, they ought to enable all children to benefit from primary education, making primary education compulsory, and ensuring that it is free of charge. On the other hand, they should respect parental freedom of choice. Respect for parental freedom to have their children educated in conformity with their religious, moral or philosophical convictions has been affirmed in the Universal Declaration of Human Rights and thereafter in all general human rights treaties. However, pre-school education was not defined as government responsibility, and for good reasons. The tension between parental and government prerogatives regarding children's education was – and remains – a constant bone of contention. Their early slant towards the affirmation of the right of the government to impose and enforce uniform schooling in the name of the right to education was a product of cold-war political compromises. The right to education was, however, categorized as a civil and political right as well as economic and social right so as to ensure safeguards for freedom alongside entitlements.

There variations in the definition of the right to education are present in national constitutions. They lay down the general framework of rights and the corres- ponding obligations in education. The competence in regulating education is divided between central and regional and/or local government, and regulated by national and sub-national legislation. However, human rights obligations pertain to the state, and it is the central government that should ensure their implement- tation throughout the country and is responsible for human rights violations. This makes education an object of regulation at all levels, from local to global. The aim underpinning education as a universal human right was to also universalize the corresponding governmental obligations. This has not materialized, perhaps never will. Furthermore, the process of decentralization has lowered financial responsibility for education from the national to the local level. This process prioritizes analysis of the capacity to translate the right to education into practice both on the country level, as is usual, but also with regard to differences within countries. This type of analysis is, regretfully overdue in human rights research

---

375 World Bank – *World Development Report 1990*, Oxford University Press, pp. 131 and 134.
376 Tomasevski, K. – *Education Denied: Costs and Remedies*, Zed Books, London, 2003, pp. 44-50 and 64-66.

Appraising the capacity to implement human rights obligations

There is close correlation between the poverty of families, communities and countries and the lack of education for their children. The identification of financial obstacles is the crucial first step towards their elimination. This is mandated by universal human rights standards whereby primary education should be free and compulsory. The law cannot oblige either parents or governments to ensure education for all if it is beyond their means. Hence, international human rights law mandates progressive realization of the right to education.

Insufficient resources impede the implementation of all human rights obligations. All human rights necessitate developed infrastructure and continuous investment for their effective protection. Obstacles such as the lack of infrastructure or resources cannot always be eliminated by the political will of a government. The lack of enjoyment of human rights does not result from violations only. A government may be incapable of guaranteeing the right to education. The reservations of Barbados, Madagascar, and Zambia to the International Covenant on Economic, Social and Cultural Rights related to the inability of the government to ensure fully accessible primary education free of charge. Barbados reserved "the right to postpone the application of article 13 (2) (a) of the Covenant [primary education shall be compulsory and available free to all] since, while the Barbados Government fully accepts the principles embodied in the same articles and undertakes to take the necessary steps to apply them in their entirety, the problems of implementation are such that full application of the principles in question cannot be guaranteed at this stage." The reservation of Congo said nothing about the capacity to ensure compulsory education free of charge, but asserted the principle of state monopoly in denial of allowing parents the liberty to choose for their children schools other than those established by the public authorities: "In our country, such provisions are inconsistent with the principle of nationalization of education and with the monopoly granted to the State in that area."[377] The different slant of these reservations points to self-assessed capacity or incapacity by the governments themselves relating to their human rights obligations in education.

Ideally, as shown in Figure 12, governmental human rights obligations should be matched by its fiscal commitments. Ensuring conformity between the diversity of the intake and the corresponding inputs into the process of teaching and learning is an objective that remains an unrealized ideal for most children in the world, however. Education proverbially receives less funding than would be necessary to ensure quality education for all children. The main reason is that educational allocations are in most countries discretionary. Constitutionally guaranteed budgetary allocations translate the commitment from legal into fiscal. Taiwan takes the pride of place as one of the oldest constitutionally guaranteed budgetary allocations for education, in place as of 1947. The original

---

[377] Reservations, declarations and objections relating to the International Covenant on Economic, Social and Cultural Rights, U.N. Doc. E/C.12/1988/1 of 10 November 1987.

Article 164 of the Constitution, which came into force on 25 December 1947, required at least 15% of the total national budget to be allocated to education, at least 25% of the total provincial budgets, and at least 35% of the total municipal budgets. It was amended in 1997, preserving the priority for education, science and culture in the budget by eliminating a specific percentage. [378] This model transforms the fiscal corollary of legally guaranteed education from discretionary into obligatory. As is well known, budgetary allocations otherwise force education authorities to distribute insufficient funds amongst a variety of nationally or locally defined priorities, while the funds are insufficient for meeting any of them. Therefore, the correspondence between children's entitlement to quality education and the government's obligations in the form of constitutionally guaranteed educational allocations is an important step in advancing rights-based education.

Tables 13 and 14 rank countries by their fiscal commitment to education. Tables 13 uses as the yardstick the investment in education as percentage of GDP, and Table 14 the percentage allocated to education within governmental budget. Both apply a relative rather than as absolute figure in order to highlight government's effort. It can be huge, as Table 14 shows with the pride of place for Yemen in its effort to overcome decades of neglect and ensure primary education for all. Yemen is also ranked highest in Table 13, together with Lesotho (which has boosted its investment in education so as to make it free). In the case of Yemen, 45% of the investment budget has been financed by external creditors and donors. [379] Lesotho introduced free primary education in 1999. Just a few years earlier the government had been concerned that "primary education is not compulsory and it is not free"[380] and focused on ensuring seven years of education for all children.

The government of Lesotho reported in 1998 that free primary education would be implemented as soon as resources became available [381] and primary education was made free for children who started school in 1999-2000. As a result, the intake in primary school increased to 183% of the estimated number of school-aged children, demonstrating how many over-aged children had been out of school because of its cost.[382] The enormous effort needed in poor countries with large and young populations to ensure education for all demonstrates how important it is to assess their capacity and, almost always, to supplement their insufficient capacity through international cooperation.

---

[378] The text of the amendments and accompanying description are available on the e-government website http://english.www.gov.tw.

[379] *Republic of Yemen: Education Sector Assistance Strategy*, The World Bank, MNSHD Discussion Paper Series No. 3, November 1999, pp. 5 and 12.

[380] The Development of education 1996-1998. National report of Lesotho for presentation at the forty-fifth session of the International Conference on Education by the Ministry of Education.

[381] U.N. Doc. CRC/C/11/Add.20, 1998, para. 198.

[382] EFA Global Monitoring Report 2003/4, p. 45.

Table 13: Education as percentage of GDP in 2001/2002

Above 8%	Cuba, Denmark, Lesotho, Vanuatu, Yemen
7 – 8%	Israel, Malaysia, Sweden
6 – 7%	Barbados, Belize, Bolivia, Iceland, Jamaica, Kenya, Mongolia, New Zealand, Norway, Tunisia
5 – 6%	Austria, Bhutan, Cameroon, Canada, Cyprus, Finland, France, Hungary, Iran, Latvia, Mexico, Morocco, Poland, Portugal, Swaziland, Thailand, USA
4 – 5%	Australia, Brazil, Chile, Colombia, Costa Rica, Côte d'Ivoire, Czech Republic, Ethiopia, Germany, India, Ireland, Italy, Jordan, Moldova, Oman, Panama, Paraguay, Slovakia, Spain, Syria, Togo, Ukraine
3 – 4%	Armenia, Azerbaijan, Benin, Burundi, Congo, Gabon, Greece, Japan, Korea, Kyrgyzstan, Laos, Madagascar, Nepal, Philippines, Russia, Senegal, Sierra Leone, Turkey
2 – 3%	Angola, Bangladesh, Botswana, Cambodia, Dominican Republic, El Salvador, Eritrea, Gambia, Georgia, Lebanon, Madagascar, Niger, Papua New Guinea, Rwanda, Tajikistan, Uruguay
1 – 2%	Burma, Ecuador, Guatemala, Guinea, Indonesia, Pakistan, Sri Lanka
Below 1%	Equatorial Guinea

Table 14: Education as percentage of government budget in 2001/2002

30 – 40%	Yemen,
20 – 30%	Azerbaijan, Belize, Botswana, Burundi, Cameroon, Costa Rica, Côte d'Ivoire, Guinea, Iran, Kenya, Malaysia, Thailand, Togo
10 – 20%	Australia, Bangladesh, Barbados, Bhutan, Bolivia, Brazil, Cambodia, Chile, Colombia, Congo, Cuba, Denmark, Dominican Republic, El Salvador, Ethiopia, Finland, France, Gambia, Georgia, Guatemala, Hungary, India, Ireland, Jamaica, Japan, Korea, Kyrgyzstan, Laos, Lebanon, Lesotho, Madagascar, Nepal, Nicaragua, Norway, Philippines, Poland, Portugal, Russia, Syria, Tunisia, Ukraine, Uruguay, USA
Below 10%	Brunei Darussalam, Czech Republic, Ecuador, Equatorial Guinea, Germany, Indonesia, Panama, Pakistan, Paraguay

Source: *UIS Global Education Digest 2004,* Table 10, pp. 122-131.

Tables 13 and 14 show that the yardstick used does not divide countries into rich and poor, or post-industrializing and developing. A strong commitment to education in Cuba or Malaysia results in a high rank. For countries such as the United States or Germany, low investment in education by the federal government reflects the principal financial responsibility for education of the individual states. As mentioned above, the need to study the pattern and impact of the localization in public finance has become as overdue as it is important.

Both tables highlight the ease with which diverse practices of states can be analysed in a summarized fashion. With all imperfections which the figures in them reveal, their message is twofold. Such quantifications reveal the general practice of states and, thus, highlight the thrust of this practice as one of the principal sources of international law. Thus, the acceptance of education as a governmental responsibility is evident in the practice of the vast majority of states. Differences in the relative priority for education are exemplified by Equatorial Guinea, ranked at the bottom of both tables. As an oil exporting country, it would theoretically have a capacity adequate to guarantee the right to education for its small population. However, the commitment to human rights, in education or in any other area, is lacking. Although the 1991 Constitution guarantees "the right to general basic education which shall be compulsory, free and guaranteed", half of school age children were not attending school in 1996. In 2001, the last year when the Special Rapporteur of the United Nations Commission on Human Rights on Equatorial Guinea visited the country, the budgetary expenditure for education further decreased and, thus, also the coverage of education.[383]

This example highlights the import of human rights in analysing the ill fate of education in Equatorial Guinea. While insufficient capacity can be supplemented through international cooperation, there is little, if anything, that can be done where the commitment to human rights is lacking.

---

[383] U.N. Docs. E/CN.4/1996/67, 1996, paras. 66-67 and E/CN.4/2001/38, 2001, para. 84.

Summing up:

The need to ask questions

Education is often defined as the glue that holds societies together. As always happens in human rights, this optimistic vision comes against findings that education can do more harm than good, that education can be a part of the solution to many problems we are grappling with, but also a part of the problems we are trying to tackle. Hence the need for education to be rights-based, to fully protect the right *to* education and human rights *in* education and enhance human rights *through* education.

How is this best done? This book does not include a range of recipes because this is the worst way of getting anything done. They would add to the top-heavy pressures upon education, which include endless policies and guidelines, instructions and best practices. Rather, the best way to move forward in human rights is to ask questions. The biggest problems are created through silence, the failure to acknowledge a problem, which then festers.

Judged by the rhetoric, human rights appear to be broadly, if not universally accepted. If this image reflected reality, human rights work would be redundant. The need for human rights stems precisely from widespread resistance to changes which human rights require. This resistance is reflected in the roadblocks which have to be overcome and the pitfalls which have to be avoided to integrate human rights in education.

Obstacles include rejection of the assertion that people have rights. Centuries of the treatment of children as the property of their parents, worldwide, make this understandable. It is a challenge to recognize it openly and honestly so as to counter it effectively. Where formal human rights commitments have been made, parental statements that children "are uncontrollable because they know that they have rights" [384] are driven underground. Kevin O'Brien and Lianjiang Li have found that the denial of access to information about legal rights in rural China works on the assumption that "as soon as ordinary people learn anything about the law then they become impossible to govern."[385]

Unchallenged and unchanged, resistance to human rights impedes change. Children may be taught *about* human rights, but not educated as people *with* rights. In practice, then, human rights may amount to no more than a recital of abstract terms culled from international human rights instruments. These are

---

[384] Khumalo, G. – Corporal punishment lives on, *Natal Witness*, Pietermaritzburg (South Africa), 20 March 2003.
[385] Diamant, N.J., Lubman, S.B. and O'Brien, K.J. (eds.) – *Engaging the Law in China*, Stanford University Press, Stanford, 2005, p. 176.

poorly translated, or not at all, from American English, which has become the language of globalization, including in human rights.

Abstract human rights norms come dangerously close to a secular religion, a set of universal truths that pretends to be self-evident. This might be so in an ideal world, but not in ours. The distance from the lives of learners and their teachers is enormous, most cannot understand terms such as "empowerment" or "mainstreaming" (or "gender", for that matter), or differences between "equality" and "equity". The results of such a learning process are negligible, if not altogether absent. Worse, the results often confirm what bishop Eamon Walsh has said about the abyss between words and deeds: "The way we treat people forms the kind of people they become."[386]

To bridge the gap between formal human rights commitments and the real-life environment in which teaching and learning take place, a learning process of its own is necessary. More than anything, it requires courage, the courage to acknowledge that human rights are denied and violated everywhere, that human rights necessitate protection against abuse of power that has not yet been attained, anywhere, hence we need to learn how to recognize and oppose abuses so as to be able to prevent them in our own environment.

When asked about human rights, children inevitably say "show, don't tell" but they are very, very rarely asked. If we were to honestly and openly answer their questions, we would have to acknowledge that a great deal of change is needed to create space for human rights in education. The key changes that are needed can be summarized in five necessary questions.

Does education promote or deny equal rights?

Education can be a means to retain and eliminate inequality. As it can serve two mutually contradictory purposes, two opposite results may ensue. Literature on discrimination abounds with assertions that prejudice breeds discrimination, yet the reverse is also true. Discrimination as a medium of indoctrination breeds prejudice; it is meant to do so. Children learn through observation and imitation. They are likely to start perpetuating discriminatory practices much before they learn the word *discrimination*. By the time their curriculum includes the term *discrimination*, they are likely to have internalized the underlying prejudice. Prejudice is formed in late childhood and adolescence and sustained from one generation to another through social usage. When it favours individual and group self-interest, it is easy to rationalize. Discriminatory practices can be countered by changing the rules of behaviour, their underlying rationale usually remains unexplored. It is customary to label this underlying rationale as irrational and believe that its cause is ignorance, which be eliminated through education. However, this rationale often includes preservation of an assumed superiority.

---

[386] *Newsletter for Irish Prisoners Overseas*, Issue No. 28, Dublin, January 1999, p. 4.

In this area, our knowledge is inversely correlated with the importance of the object of study. We know a great deal about the wording of education policies and laws since these are available, in a codified form, and translated into English. We know less about the process of teaching and least of all about learning. Whether these two parallel processes, teaching and learning, translate human rights objectives for education into reality depends on the congruence between these objectives and the operative guidance for teaching and learning as well as the concordance – or discord – between in-school and out-of-school learning.

On the highest level of abstraction, national education policies include the language of human rights, peace, tolerance, sustainable development, social inclusion, gender equality, environmental protection and much else. A look at the 'products' of national education systems reveals an abyss between such objectives and learning outcomes. A good example is the European Union. On the one hand, "all European education systems aim to be inclusive."[387] On the other hand, Eurobarometer surveys in the past two decades have shown an increase in the proportion of Europeans self-declared as 'quite racist' or 'very racist.'[388] The fact that this proportion has increased in the past two decades and reached one-third of Europeans highlights the necessity to ask why the abyss between the commitment to inclusiveness in national and European policies and self-assessments by the 'products' of national education systems. Translation of abstract commitments to human rights, tolerance and to cherishing diversity apparently fails to effectively guide education in the desired direction. Various steps in translating general principles into operative guidance for teaching and learning alter the meaning of commitments to human rights or tolerance.

Although often introduced as the functional equivalent of human rights education, citizenship education undermines human rights as properties of *all* members of humanity and substitutes only "those who have the rights of citizens."[389] Moreover, citizenship education sometimes focuses on response-bilities[390] rather than rights. Citizenship is not an all-inclusive concept because it implies excluding non-citizens. Ultimately, citizenship education may underpin xenophobia. Gender equality may exist in the forms of a general commitment but virtually all school teachers may be underpaid and overworked women, who may fail to get the ear of policy-makers in education, who may all be men.

At the intersection between school and society, conflicting messages saw confusion. Formal schooling is only one message carrier since education is, in

387   European Commission – European Report on Quality of School Education, Brussels, May 2000, p. 6.
388   European Monitoring Centre on Racism and Xenophobia – *Attitudes Towards Minority Groups in the European Union. A Special Analysis of the Eurobarometer 2000 Survey*, Vienna, March 2001.
389   Qualifications and Curriculum Authority – *Education for Citizenship and the Teaching of Democracy in Schools. Final Report of the Advisory Group on Citizenship*, London. 22 September 1998, p. 9.
390   Citizenship education in England comprises "social and moral responsibility, community involvement and political literacy." *Citizenship education and human rights education: an overview of recent developments in the UK*, British Council, Manchester, 2003, p. 8.

the broadest sense of this term, the sum-total of what children learn from their parents and peers, on the playground and in the street, from the mass media as well as from the hugely developed advertising and entertainment industry, much of which is specifically targeted at children and young people. Teachers become "mediators between the students and varied sources of information."[391] It is teachers who translate abstractly defined aims of education into messages which children can recognize and internalize. With the advent of human rights education, it is teachers who are required to help children learn about human rights. And yet, *their* rights are often denied or violated.[392]

Translating abstract human rights principles and norms into a language which young children can understand is by definition difficult. Children learn through observation, and the best practices in conveying the human rights message to them rely on educating them as people with rights. The underlying logic is not to treat human rights education as an add-on, but rather to integrate human rights throughout teaching and learning. This is an immense challenge, everywhere, as it requires analysis and assessment of entire education through the human rights lens. An appropriate beginning step is to introduce a right for teachers and learners to challenge the contents or methods which they deem to be incompatible with human rights.

Do the means of education defy its professed ends?

Education statistics highlight those quantitative and qualitative dimensions of education that have been prioritized, globally and nationally. These vary in time and place. Differences between and within countries reveal an insufficient number of schools without essential safety and environmental health safeguards as well as untrained and, often, poorly paid teachers and, on the other hand, schools that produces outcomes ranked high within internationally administered tests of learning accomplishments. The quality of education for the most disadvantaged is a useful indicator of the compatibility of the whole education system with the equal right to education for all.

Commonly used definitions of quality reflect the key purpose of education, namely learners' achievement, and use an input-process-outcome framework. Indicators highlight those quantitative and qualitative dimensions of education that have been prioritized to enhance the process of learning. These vary in time and place. Differences between and within countries reveal, on the one hand, an insufficient number of schools without essential safety and environmental health safeguards as well as untrained and, often, unpaid teachers and, on the

---

[391] Savova, J. – *Education and Teachers in Central and Eastern European Countries, 1991-1995*, International Bureau of Education (IBE/UNESCO), Geneva, 1996, p. 21.

[392] Particularly high casualties amongst teachers and institutionalized denial of their rights has been noted in Ethiopia, while in Colombia there are still three teachers killed every month. Commission on Human Rights – Report of the Special Rapporteur on the right to education, Katarina Tomasevski, U.N. Doc. E/CN.4/2003/9, para. 37, and Report on mission to Colombia, U.N. Doc. E/CN.4/2004/45/Add.2/Corr.1, paras. 39-42.

other hand, schooling that produces outcomes ranked high within internationally administered tests of learning accomplishments. Governmental obligation to define and ensure the quality of education requires an assessment of the existing conditions against postulated goals of education, a definition of standards that should be in place everywhere, and an identification of institutions and procedures whereby these standards will be implemented, monitored, and enforced.

Human rights emphasize learners and the impact of the educational process. Human rights law requires adding to the framework for educational assessment intake and impact, thus the framework becomes intake-input-process-outcome-impact. The key principle of the Convention on the Rights of the Child whereby education has to be designed and implemented with the best interests of each child in mind necessitates the identification of those factors that ought to be eliminated as they impede the child's learning. The exit of learners from education into society also demands scrutiny by human rights criteria. Where learning outcomes are satisfactory but graduates are doomed to unemployment, the needs for cross-sectoral linkages become apparent.

Human rights law broadens the usual focus on quantitative data to encompass *all* rights of *all* key actors in education. As UNESCO has put it, "the inclusion of human rights in education is a key element of a quality education." [393] This entails an altered design of education strategies, which should accommodate minimal universal human rights standards. These necessitate creating quantitative and qualitative data which do not, as yet, exist because the process of integrating human rights throughout the process of education is new. This process is outlined in Figure 15, in the form of a monitoring scheme for the human rights dimensions of education through a series of pertinent questions.

---

[393] UNESCO Executive Board – Elements for an overall UNESCO strategy on human rights, Doc. 165 EX/10 (2002), para. 31.

Figure 15: Monitoring education using human rights as the yardstick

KEY AREAS	TYPICAL HUMAN RIGHTS QUESTIONS	SOURCES OF DATA
INTAKE	Children without birth registration certificates: How many? Who are they? Why? What remedies exist? School age children not enrolled in school: How many? Where they are? Why? Administrative obstacles for enrolment (certificates of birth or citizenship): What remedies exist for children without them? Which data about school children is missing (mother tongue, religion, origin, race, abilities and disabilities, etc.) Does national census and school census include all internationally prohibited grounds of discrimination?	Birth registration Census of school-age children National census Educational statistics
INPUTS	Correspondence between fiscal allocations and legal obligations The gap between public funding for education and its real cost (school fees, enrolment fees, tuition fees, financial contributions) The profile of teachers (feminization, race, language, religion, etc.) Curricula and textbooks, and teaching methods	Budgetary allocations for education (national, regional, and local level) Real cost of schooling and its financial sustainability Available statistics on teachers Procedures defined by national law for the approval of textbooks and other learning materials
PROCESS	How are basic aims and purposes of education defined (e.g. fostering economic competitiveness, or educating subjects of human rights)? What is the scope of access to an effective remedy for the rights and freedoms of educators and learners? How are acceptable forms of school discipline defined?	Regulations for teaching which guide the conduct of teachers The existing national and international case law Prohibition of corporal punishment
OUTCOMES	How have the learning outcomes been defined (e.g. "accurately memorized rote-learning")?	Inequalities in the learners' performance (e.g. results of tests in mathematics)
IMPACT	What is the linkage between the right to education and the right to work? What is the linkage between the right to education and the right to marry and found a family?	Youth unemployment by the level of education Fertility rates by the level of education

Are educational messages self-contradictory?

Where diversity and tolerance are explicitly addressed in educational curricula, the messages may be self-contradictory. School textbooks should be "accurate, neutral and fair" [394] as the Japanese Supreme Court has put it. And yet, the congruence between the contents of education and human rights may be questionable even in textbooks that bear 'human rights' in their title. Cherishing "the esteem of the glorious Turkish history" and honouring "the great Turks whose services have made the great Turkish nation" forms part of the curriculum in Turkey. [395] A textbook for human rights education in Turkey ends its first chapter by suggesting homework. Pupils should go to the nearest military barracks to study the army's enthusiasm and love for the country. [396] A textbooks for civics in India goes one step further and mis-describes rights, emphasizing that the individual "must have sense of loyalty and love for the state. In return the government of the state gives him some social and political rights – such as the right to vote." [397]

It is as difficult as it is necessary to expose school children to abuses of power that have led to the development of human rights protections. Textbooks on human rights education are often criticised as a 'cosy curriculum'. Coupled with politically correct language, they often amount to a conceptual distortion of reality. They describe all the rights that all people should have in an ideal world that none of the learners (nor any of their teachers) live in. This becomes a constraint than inhibits learning rather than a resource that facilitates it. However, individuals as well as countries tend to remember the pain they have suffered, not the pain they have inflicted on others, making perceived victimhood one-sided. History textbooks epitomize what David Tyack calls 'the pedagogy of patriotism.'[398] They rarely describe abuses committed by one's own government against populations of other countries or the people in one's own country, although history abounds with such examples.

Colliding interpretations of the same event are common in real life but are routinely expunged from history textbooks. The one and only, objectively and/or scientifically true version of history is as impossible as it is widespread in school textbooks. In practice, that one and only version of history is only possible if alternative interpretations are censored. As is typical in human rights, mobilization against censorship and self-censorship of history textbooks was triggered by abuses of history. It was found that, in 1914, historians had "placed

---

394 Supreme Court of Japan – *Ienaga v. Japan*, (O) No. 1428 of 1986, Judgment of 16 March 1993, para. 2.
395 Kazamias, A. M. – *Education and the Quest for Modernity in Turkey*, University of Chicago Press, 1966, p. 148.
396 Yamanlar, E. – *Vatandaslik ve insan haklari egitimi* (Education in Citizenship and Human Rights), Ders Kitaplari Anonim Sirketi, Istanbul, 2000, p. 62.
397 Sharma, A.C. – *Learning Civics*, vol. 1, Pitmar Publishing Company, New Delhi, Fifth Revised Edition, 1997, p. 58.
398 Mondale, S. and Patton, S.B. (eds.) – *School: The Story of American Public Education*, Beacon Press, Boston, 2001, p. 5.

their scholarship at the service of the war effort" [399] and, indeed, "all political systems have used history for their own ends." [400] Controversies regarding descriptions of wars, conflicts and associated abuses occur daily, worldwide. Croatian textbooks were found in the 1990s to have included descriptions of 'Serbian aggressors' as "merciless barbarians who ran amok". [401] In Serbia, the same events were, at the same time, described as "enforced expulsion of the Serbian population" from Croatia, reminiscent of the "genocide fifty years earlier." [402] Converting the image of history from a body of knowledge to be memorized and accurately repeated to investigation of the past based on evidence from different viewpoints would make all the difference to learning.

Conflicting demands upon education affect the distortion of general commitments to human rights, diversity and tolerance by prioritizing competition and income-earning skills. It would be difficult to image children learning to compete and cooperate at the same time. As they compete against each other for better test results and/or higher grades, as do their schools and their countries, the notion of cooperation remains abstract as children learn by example, not exhortation. Although it is difficult to find many teachers who enjoy teaching-to-test, and most learners intensely dislike it, measuring learning outcomes is growing in scope and importance.

What is education *for*?

In an ideal world, education would adapt to each child. In our imperfect world, the right of each child to be regarded as different remains a distant dream. Because education encompasses huge numbers of learners and teachers, the emphasis is on numbers and, thus, statistical averages. Diversity as a value then clashes against the assimilationist slant of most education systems through the teaching of one language, one version of history and geography, and one vision of the future. Much as national education policies may demand the adaptation of education to diverse society, in practice it is those who do not conform to the dominant model that have to adapt. Immigrants, minorities and indigenous people have to shed large parts of their identity – the language, name, dress code – to conform to the mainstream model.

[399] Keynote address by Georg Iggers, in *The Misuses of History. Learning and Teaching about the History of Europe in the 20th Century, Oslo (Norway), 28-30 June 1999*, Council of Europe Publishing, Strasbourg, July 2000, p. 13.

[400] Council of Europe – Recommendation No. 1283 on history and the teaching of history in Europe, Parliamentary Assembly, 22 January 1996.

[401] Pingel, F. – *The European Home: Representations of 20th Century Europe in History Textbooks*, Council of Europe, Strasbourg, September 2000, p. 87.

[402] Gachesha, N. et al. – *Istorija za III razred gimnazije prirodno-matematickog smera i IV razred gimnazije opsteg i drustveno-jezickog smera* (History for 3rd grade of secondary school of natural science-mathematics orientation and 4th grade of secondary school of general and social science-linguistics orientation), Secretariat for Textbooks and Teaching Tools, Belgrade, Eighth Edition, 2000, p. 274 and 178.

(margin handwriting: "get → them look at")

The objective towards which education should be moulded is often defined as tolerance. Setting the limits of the intolerable is the first necessary step towards creating space for teaching and learning tolerance. Tolerance implies acceptance, albeit passive, of 'the other,' and 'the other' is constantly created and re-created. Shared humanity yields to the emphasis of differences in provenance, lifestyle, or status. The internationally prohibited division of humanity by race, sex, or colour has been expunged from educational curricula. An emphasis on provenance, however, defines 'the other' as immigrants and race is routinely the principal denominator. Marc Ferro has suggested to "begin by drawing up a list of taboos and look at them through the eyes of other people." [403]

Schools reflect the surrounding setting and tend to reinforce prejudicial portrayals of victims of discrimination. Education is embedded in the existing values but also helps create new values and attitudes. Its goal may be defined as an affirmation of everybody's right to be different, or merely as tolerance of departures from 'the norm.' As long as the goal remains defined as tolerance, it endorses an implicit 'norm' and, thus, assimilationist strategies. Hence, human rights law mandates the deliberate employment of education to eliminate discrimination, which requires a permanent process so that education can be adjusted to changes in society and foster its further change. In 1947, the first United Nations report on discrimination emphasized that "the whole field of action to prevent discrimination requires a vast programme of education." Law cannot be effective, and may be counterproductive, unless it enjoys support by those whom it addresses. Hence, the emphasis on education to engender such support. Looking back to 1947, it is worthwhile to recall that outcomes can be both positive and negative:

> Forcing a prejudiced person to read or hear exhortations on tolerance may only increase his prejudice. Overenthusiastic appraisals of the contributions of a minority may create a reaction of distaste for members of that minority; and programmes improperly presented, even with the best intentions, may create an awareness of group difference that did not previously exist. [404]

Teaching about peace-making or human rights violations without discussing concrete solutions and providing tools for action can do more harm than good. Learners can feel overwhelmed and helpless. Teaching about the prevention of violence in society may be undermined through inculcating obedience at school, where "punishment for children who misbehaved, however harsh, had to be accepted without question or complaint." [405]

---

[403] Keynote address by Marc Ferro at the symposium *Towards a Pluralist and Tolerant Approach to Teaching History: A Range of Sources and Didactics*, 10-12 December 1998, Brussels (Belgium), Council of Europe Publishing, Strasbourg, November 1999, p. 125.

[404] Sub-Commission on the Prevention of Discrimination and the Protection of Minorities – Report on the prevention of discrimination (Prepared by the Secretary-General), U.N. Doc. E/CN.4/Sub.2/40 of 7 June 1949, paras. 17 (c) and 177.

[405] Dagenais, R. and Mackay, C. – *Christians and the Holy Spirit. Pupil's Book, Primary 7*, Uganda Joint Christian Council, Kampala, 1976, p. 32.

At the intersection between school and society, conflicting messages may saw confusion. Formal schooling is only one message carrier since education is, in the broadest sense of this term, the sum-total of what children learn from their parents and peers, from the mass media as well as from the hugely developed advertizing and entertainment industry, much of which is specifically targeted at children. Studies into violence have revealed that 'youth who observe adults accepting violence as a solution to problems are apt to emulate that violence.' [406] Catherine Bonnet has argued that violence against children was a taboo until the 1960s because it reveals the shameful behaviour of adults.[407] Children victimized by violence are likely to become violent adults, but this early link in the causation of violence is seldom explored. School-based programmes for the prevention of violence, where they exist, tend to be an optional add-on to the compulsory curriculum.

In most countries, domestic law protects individuals against being publicly insulted but prohibitions of group defamation are rare. Maligning 'foreigners' can be deemed an expression of patriotism and is often a vote-winner. This has often been emphasized by the ECRI (European Commission against Racism and Intolerance) which has, in the case of Denmark, pointed out that negative stereotypes and prejudices "are promoted by public opinion leaders, including political elites from across the political spectrum."[408] Their inevitable influence on children and young people undermines human rights messages. In addition, David Coulby has pointed out that schools and universities "are being involved in the encouragement of xenophobia as a mode of state-building."[409] Eliminating obstacles to rights-based teaching and learning is therefore necessary, from the local to the global level, throughout the world.

[406] Crawford, D.K. and Bodine, R.J. – Conflict resolution education: Preparing youth for the future, *Juvenile Justice*, vol. 8, No. 1, June 2001, p. 21.

[407] Bonnet, C. – *L'Enfant Cassé*, Albin Michel, Paris, 1999.

[408] European Commission against Racism and Intolerance – Second Report on Denmark adopted on 16 June 2000, Doc. CRI (2001) 4 of 3 April 2001, para. 28.

[409] Coulby, D. – Education in times of transition: Eastern Europe with particular reference to the Baltic states, in Coulby, D. et al. (eds.) – *Education in Times of Transition. World Yearbook of Education 2000*, Kogan Page, London, 2000, p. 17.